Evolution
and Individual Behavior

Other books by Christopher Badcock

Evolution and Individual Behavior

*An Introduction to
Human Sociobiology*

Christopher Badcock

Basil Blackwell

Copyright © Christopher Badcock 1991

First published 1991

Basil Blackwell Ltd
108 Cowley Road, Oxford, OX4 1JF, UK

Basil Blackwell Inc.
3 Cambridge Center
Cambridge, Massachusetts 02142, USA

British Library Cataloguing in Publication Data
A CIP catalogue record for this book is available from the British Library.

Library of Congress Cataloging in Publication Data
Badcock, C. R.
Evolution and individual behavior: an introduction to human sociobiology / Christopher Badcock.
p. cm.
ISBN 0–631–17428–1—ISBN 0–631–17429–X (pbk.)
1. Genetic psychology. 2. Behavior evolution. 3. Sociobiology.
4. Cooperativeness. 5. Human evolution. I. Title.
BF701.B23 1991   155.7–dc20   90–48244
CIP

Typeset in Bembo in 11 on 13pt
by Hope Services (Abingdon) Ltd
Printed in Great Britain by
Billing & Sons Ltd, Worcester

To readers of all ages
still young enough to learn

Contents

Preface　　ix

INTRODUCTION: DARWIN'S DIFFICULTIES　　1
Historical set-backs　　1
Genetic puzzles　　5
Fallacies of fitness　　13
The problem of altruism　　23

1　THE EVOLUTION OF COOPERATION　　32
Prisoner's Dilemma　　32
Computing cooperation　　40
The rewards of reciprocity　　48
The solution to the problem of altruism　　57

2　THREE KINDS OF COOPERATION　　61
Kin altruism　　61
"Kin selection" confusions　　72
Reciprocal altruism　　79
Induced altruism　　87

3　EVOLUTION, COOPERATION, AND
HUMAN NATURE　　94
The issue of free will　　94
The question of consciousness　　99
Altruism and identification　　108
The biology of morality　　117

4 MALE BEHAVIOR AND MISBEHAVIOR 123
The fundamental factor 123
Four forms of the family 129
Sex and violence 137
Cryptic conflict 149

5 SEX AND FEMALE INTERESTS 157
Abortion, fat, and fertility 157
Sex and female choice 167
Secrets of the sexual cycle 176
Mysteries of menstruation 181

6 FAMILY, SEX, CONFLICT, AND
COOPERATION 188
Parent–child conflict 188
Conflicts that kill 197
Problems of paternity 207
The infant strikes back 215

7 FREUDIAN FINDINGS 222
Parental investment and oedipal behavior 222
Penis envy and parental preference 229
The prime role of the father 238
Oedipal effects in adult life 243

CONCLUSION: THE NATURE OF CULTURE 252
Culture as a problem of scale 252
Three cultures of cooperation 257
Culture, conflict, and parental investment 264
The gene–culture interface 271

Notes 281
Glossary of Technical Terms 289
Suggestions for Further Reading 294
Index 297

Preface

This book is intended to be a basic introduction to recent evolutionary thinking as applied to human beings. Its style and content are based on my experience of teaching this material to undergraduates who cannot be assumed to have any grounding in biology or evolution. Consequently, it assumes no prior knowledge of the subject. On the contrary, if prospective readers had never heard the word "evolution" or the name of Darwin, much of the first chapter would have been unnecessary, designed as it is to correct common misapprehensions about Darwin's key theory of evolution by natural selection. Throughout, I have tried to keep the style simple and direct and have avoided jargon wherever possible. Unavoidable technical terms are italicized, defined when first introduced, and summarized in the glossary at the end of the book. I have avoided elaborate reference citation in the interests of clarity but have provided key references where necessary as end-notes. Suggestions for further reading are supplied as an appendix.

My principal aim in all this is clarity and comprehensibility first and foremost, and although this book is primarily intended for those without very much existing knowledge of the field, I hope that it will also reward study by those who do have more extensive acquaintance with it. Basic concepts such as natural selection, "fitness," and the question of the level at which selection operates are not always as clearly understood as they might be, and ideas based upon them, such as altruism, inclusive fitness, reciprocity, and parental investment, also frequently give rise to misunderstandings which I have done my best to help readers of this book avoid. Unlike most other introductions to the topic, I have founded my exposition of modern social theory on Robert Axelrod's epoch-making book on the evolution of cooperation and then gone on to show how his fundamental findings relate to W. D. Hamilton's and Robert Trivers's slightly earlier formulations of the evolutionary theory of altruism. Although this does not follow the historical sequence in which these momentous discoveries were made, experience has taught me that this is the best and simplest way to introduce them, both to those completely unfamiliar with modern social theory and to those who may not have realized the extent to which Hamilton's and Trivers's formulations were founded on wholly individualistic concepts of selection and social action. My discussion of altruism and identification represents my present view of the matter and to some extent supersedes the earlier and more restricted formulation which I gave in previous works, when I still thought of identification primarily as relating to kin altruism (whereas I now believe it to be equally fundamental to reciprocity as well). Again, my discussion of "identification with the defector" is new and reflects the same basic insight.

In treating the whole sensitive subject of sex I have tried to reveal the essential objectivity and evenhandedness of modern evolutionary theory by discussing it in two chapters, one devoted to male, and one to female behavior. The concept of "cryptic sexuality" may be new to many readers (especially as a theory of homosexuality in men), as may the recent findings regarding testis size as an indicator of male sexual behavior. As far as issues relating to women are concerned, I have tried to show how the fundamental concept of the modern evolutionary theory of sex, parental investment, is particularly pertinent to females in general and to women in particular, underlying as it does numerous critical factors such as female choice, fatness and fertility, cryptic estrus, and menstrual synchrony. In the chapter devoted to parent–child conflict I have included material relating to preferential parental investment with regard to offspring sex in human beings and have shown how parent–offspring conflict theory explains much of what Malinowski found in the Trobriand Islands, believing it to contradict, rather than vindicate, biology. Finally in that chapter, I have included a brief account of my own insight (partly shared with Randolph Nesse) into oral behavior as a means of manipulating maternal fertility.

Of course, recent evolutionary biology has also given rise to controversy, and I have not avoided it here. However, rather than argue the many differing cases concerned and repeat the confusion, errors, and misunderstandings on which so much of the controversy is based, I have instead concentrated on presenting as clearly and concisely as possible the fundamental propositions and have left it to the reader to pursue the question of their ultimate value and applicability. Nevertheless, a number of commonly en-countered worries, such as those relating to the issues of free will, morality, human nature, and the question of conscious-ness are briefly discussed in a manner which will, I hope, help readers to see what insights evolutionary ideas can bring to them.

Scientific theories can be likened to computer software and, like it, appear in numerous – and sometimes confusing – versions. Looked at in these terms, the evolutionary theory expounded in this book might be termed "Darwin version 3.3." Of course, the neatly reiterative sound of this gives its purely metaphoric meaning away, but, qualifications aside, it does serve to represent in simple terms an admittedly complex situation. For present purposes, let us regard Darwin's original outline of this theory, published in 1859, as "Darwin version 1." In the course of his own lifetime he produced a number of new editions and additions to this. We might regard Darwin version 2 as the kind of evolutionary theory associated with his name by others both during his lifetime and until fairly recently. As we shall see in my introduction, much of what passed for Darwinism in this version was rather dubiously Darwinian in a strict sense and was certainly distinguishable from Darwin's own version of his theory by its tendency to think in terms of so-called group selection: a view of natural selection which saw it as working on groups, or populations, without necessary regard to the individuals who make them up. Finally, we might refer to the recent resurgence of authentic, individual-istic Darwinism associated with what is often termed "neo-Darwinism" or "synthetic Darwinism" as version number 3 in our classification. This in turn breaks down into three sub-versions.

The synthesis referred to in the second of these terms is the unification of Darwinian evolution and Mendelian genetics carried out by a number of workers earlier this century and largely complete by the time of World War II. As we shall see in a moment, genetic difficulties were a major stumbling block for Darwin, and their resolution was a major break-through for evolutionary theory. This initial synthesis we might label "Darwin version 3.1." If so, version 3.2 must represent the next major advance monumentally summarized in E. O. Wilson's book *Sociobiology: The New Synthesis*. This also introduced "sociobiology" as a term predominantly associated with this version of Darwinism and gave rise to some controversy. Although Wilson was responsible for the term and for the presentation of a vast collection of material, what distinguished what I am calling version 3.2 from the earlier one was principally the work of W. D. Hamilton, R. Trivers, D. Lack, and others. Unfortunately, Wilson's own formulation of evolutionary theory, both in that book and in others, was not entirely free of some of the "bugs" which had compromised version 2 throughout. In particular, latent traces of group selection remained which made his formulation of evolutionary intellectual software distinctly dubious in places, and nowhere more so than in the so-called co-evolutionary theory of gene–culture evolution which he elaborated with the help of C. J. Lumsden. The group-selectionist treatment of culture which this theory was based upon has led to an almost complete omission of any discussion of it here since I would see it as belonging to version 3.2. However, the question of culture considered from a more individualistic and dynamic viewpoint is briefly discussed in my conclusion.

The version of Darwin presented here – 3.3 in my imaginary numbering system – could be seen in terms of my software analogy as a thoroughly debugged revision of what I have called version 3.2. Its principal manual would not be Wilson's monumental work of 1975, but Robert Trivers's much more recent and more manageable publication of 1985, *Social Evolution*. Such works as this are easily distinguished from those associated with Wilson's formulation by their explicit repudiation of group selection; but the differences are not all negative. Important additions and developments include a much more dynamic and individualistic approach represented by discussions of parental investment, parent–offspring conflict, deception and self-deception, and cryptic sexuality – all discussed in detail here.

One of the most surprising departures represented by this version is the realization that many of the findings of Freud seem to relate to important predictions and theoretical insights of evolutionary theory reformulated in this essentially dynamic and individualistic way. This too will be a major theme of some parts of the present study and, as suggested in my penultimate chapter, may comprise one of the most promising departures where human evolutionary theory is concerned. Finally, I conclude by suggesting one possible way in which an evolutionary reformulation of the Freudian model of the mind might provide a unifying principle for behavioral science as a whole.

This book is modeled on the successful formula of my earlier book *Essential Freud*, and I plan a second edition of that book which will be designed closely to complement this one, but concentrating on Freud and ending with Darwin, rather than dealing with Darwin and ending with Freud, as is the pattern here. Taken together, the two books will give an almost complete account of the Freudian-Darwinian synthesis that has become my chief aim and remains in my view one of the most interesting and important developments in modern behavioral science.

Because of the association of terms like "neo-Darwinism" with what I have termed version 3.1 and "sociobiology" with Wilson's revision of it, I have tended to avoid them here. In so far as version 3.3 represents a return to authentic Darwinism and a final purging of errors associated with the pseudo-Darwinism which proliferated for the first century or so of the history of evolution by natural selection, avoidance of these terms is wholly justified. "Neo-Darwinism" suggests much more a revision than a resurgence of pristine Darwinism, and the first syllable of "sociobiology" has faint group-selectionist overtones which seem out of place in an authentically individualist reformulation of Darwinism. Consequently, I have used no particular term to designate what I have metaphorically called "Darwin version 3.3," but have presented the latest version of evolutionary theory in this book very much as a return to the essential inspiration of the original, unspoiled version 1, albeit with many additions and extensions unforeseen and unforseeable by Darwin when he first put his theory forward.

I owe a special debt of gratitude to my publisher, John Davey, for his unfailing support, encouragement, and advice and to the 1989/90 class of my Evolution and Social Behavior course at the London School of Economics, whose constant – and occasionally inquisitorial – cross-examination of their teacher did much to improve the content of this book. I must also thank my wife, David McKnight, Keith Sharp, and Alan Lloyd for helpful comments on the manuscript and Randolph Nesse for conversations on a number of subjects which have influenced my views, particularly on oral behavior. I am indebted to Robert Trivers for permission to quote from his works and to Roger Short for the material on which figure

4.2 is based. Finally, I must thank Glenn D. Wilson for his kind permission to quote him, to reproduce figure 7.1, and for bringing some further material to my attention.

Christopher Badcock
July 1990

Introduction:
Darwin's Difficulties

Historical set-backs

Although it is true that Charles Darwin's (1809–82) *The Origin of Species* sold out on the first day of publication in 1859, acceptance did not come easily, despite the fact that it was based on an idea so simple and seemingly obvious that one might easily wonder why no one had thought of it before. Essentially, all that Darwin's theory proposed is that organisms which differ from others in ways which are heritable, but which also increase the number of offspring they might have compared to others, will inevitably leave more descendants in succeeding generations than organisms without such attributes. The gradual accumulation of such heritable differences would constitute a process of gradual change, or what we would today call "evolution" (in early editions of *The Origin of Species* Darwin called it "mutability"). If purely natural factors determine which differences are important for the number of an organism's offspring, they will play a role exactly like the choice exercised by human breeders when they consciously set out to alter a species by selective breeding. In short, the fact that some organisms might possess heritable factors for reproductive success will inevitably mean that they and their descendants are more reproductively successful than others; and this, fundamentally, is all that Darwin's theory asserts.

One of its most important aspects is what the theory does

not say. It does *not* say that life was created by some agency or according to some plan or as a consequence of some necessary life force or law of progression or improvement. As we shall see in a moment, it does not say what many have thought it says: namely, that selection favors the "fittest" in the everyday sense of that word or that there is implicit in Darwin's theory of evolution by natural selection some inevitable "improvement" or "progress" towards more complex, "advanced" forms of life like human beings. Finally, and perhaps most controversially of all, it does not make any reference to God, divine providence, or moral questions relating to "good" and "evil"; and it does not appeal to any human or scriptural authority but rather to scientific observations of the natural world. It merely asserts that heritable tendencies to superior reproductive success are enough to explain evolution without recourse to any of these other factors previously thought relevant to the issue, and in this respect it was an enormous advance over previous views.

Darwin himself seems to have realized that so simple an idea would rouse considerable controversy. Just as Copernicus had delayed publishing his revolutionary book arguing for a sun-centered, rather than an earth-centered, universe until he was on his deathbed, so Darwin seems to have been content to delay publication of his great work on evolution by natural selection until the last possible moment. But, unlike Copernicus, his hand was forced. In 1858 Alfred Wallace (1823–1913) independently hit on the supremely simple insight that Darwin had been keeping to himself (and a few friends) for years, and finally Darwin was prevailed upon to announce what was now a joint discovery to the world.

One reason why no one else had thought of such a simple and apparently self-evident idea before Darwin and Wallace did so in the mid-nineteenth century may have been that up until then most people did not believe that the earth was old enough for such slow evolutionary change to have taken place. Only the new and uncertain science of geology suggested the contrary. Geologists claimed that sedimentary rocks like sandstones had been laid down and compacted over millions of years out of grains originally produced by the equally slow process of natural erosion of other rocks by wind, ice, and water. Admittedly, many rejected the concept of evolution because they believed in Biblical accounts of creation and the calculations of the age of the earth based upon them; but by no means all of those who contradicted Darwin on this point did so out of religious credulity. On the contrary, some of the most effective critics of evolution took a stand based, not on scriptural authority, but on what seemed at the time to be the soundest scientific fact.

One of the most notable of these attacks on evolution was that of Lord Kelvin (1824–1907), one of the greatest scientists of the time, and was based purely on physics, the epitome of exact, mathematical science. Repeating a calculation originally made by Isaac Newton, Kelvin purported to show that evolution could not possibly have occurred as Darwin proposed because the earth was simply not old enough.

It was known that temperature rises with increasing depth as one penetrates into the earth, and it was clear that the heat in question could not be derived from solar radiation falling on the earth (which heats the surface more than the interior). Since the rate of cooling of the earth could also be estimated, it followed that a relatively simple calculation could show how long it would take for a molten, red-hot earth unable to sustain any form of life to cool to its present temperature. Just as someone who comes upon the warm embers of a fire could estimate how long ago it had been burning by the residual heat, so Kelvin interpreted the internal heat of the earth to be residual and believed that he could use it to calculate how long it would take for the earth to have cooled to its present temperature and, consequently, how much time had been available for life to evolve.

Unfortunately for Darwin, the answer proved to be too short: Kelvin's first estimate put the maximum age of the earth at about 400 million years, and later refinements reduced it to 20–40 million years at most. And Kelvin was not alone. The great German physicist Hermann von Helmholtz and the American astronomer Simon Newcomb independently carried out another, comparable calculation for the age of the sun, setting the upper limit for the age of the earth – assumed to be no older than the sun, and certainly dependent on it where life is concerned – at 100 million years.[1]

There was just no way that evolution by natural selection, starting from nothing, could produce the profusion of advanced species seen on earth today in so short a time. Furthermore, these estimates of the age of the earth cast doubt on the observations of geologists, on which Darwin had relied heavily. Darwin's theory, supported only by the observations and arguments of a very new and inexact science was defeated by the precise calculations of the epitomes of exact science: physics and astronomy. Even if his evolutionary theory made biological sense – which most people also doubted – it was physically impossible: the earth was too young; evolution could not have taken place!

Of course, Kelvin, Helmholtz, and Newcomb were wrong. Unknown to them or anyone else at the time, radioactive isotopes in the interior of the earth heat it considerably, thereby slowing down the overall cooling process, while the heat of the sun derives, not from gravitational contraction assumed by Helmholtz and Newcomb, but from nuclear fusion in its core, which again has the effect of heating it considerably and thereby extending its lifetime by many orders of magnitude. The physicists' calculations, although correct in principle and based on what seemed at the time reasonable assumptions, underestimated the true age of the earth by a very considerable extent. Today the earth is known to be, not 20–40 million, but 4.5 *billion* years old, and this would allow plenty of time for evolution by natural selection to occur.

Genetic puzzles

But the age of the earth was not the only problem that the theory of evolution by natural selection had to face. Critics argued that Darwin's own ideas, if carefully examined, would not have the results which he himself claimed. For instance – and this was certainly one of the most important instances – contemporary critics of evolution pointed to weaknesses in a key concept of the theory: this was Darwin's assumption about the inheritance of what today we could call favorable mutations. By *mutation* we mean some heritable variation which appears in an individual quite by chance. Obviously such chance variations were necessary for Darwin's theory because they provided the raw material of genetic variation on which natural selection could then go to work. Without heritable mutations evolution had no starting point, and without selection and conservation of some of those mutations evolutionary change would not occur in the way Darwin had suggested.

The problem with this idea was that, according to apparently well-founded views of the mechanism of inheritance current at the time, any mutation occurring in any one individual would be diluted by half every time it was passed on. Consider the following hypothetical, but crucial, example. Suppose that a mutation occurs in an individual organism which enhances its reproductive success – the number of offspring it leaves, in other words – by exactly 100 percent. If such a thing were to occur in a species which produced large numbers of offspring as many fish, insects, and plants do, the mutation in question would be beneficial indeed and, according to Darwin's theory, strongly "selected" in the sense that it would have been passed on to many offspring. But if, as is likely in the vast majority of cases, the mutant in question reproduced sexually, only half the mutation would be passed on to its offspring because the other half of their inheritance would come from the other parent. Even if reproduction is asexual, inheritance appears to mean inheriting half the genetic material of the original in the sense in which someone leaving their fortune to two descendants could not possibly leave all of it to both. Irrespective of the means of reproduction, then, the enhancement in the reproductive success of the offspring would consequently not be 100 percent as was that of the parental mutant, but exactly half that, 50 percent.

Admittedly, this could still mean a lot of extra offspring in the case of some species, but the problem is that each time the mutation is inherited, its contribution to its own reproductive success – the number of offspring its possessors have – is seemingly halved. In the second generation, the grandchildren of the original mutant, it will already be down to 25 percent, and in the third to 12.5 percent, in the fourth to 6.25 percent, and so on. In only eight generations the percentage contribution to increased reproductive success of a mutation which originally conferred a very significant 100 percent advantage will be down to less than 1 percent, and beyond that its contribution will be negligible. What chance, asked contemporary critics of the theory, would a mutation have of becoming fixed in the species as a whole? After all, even organisms with large numbers of offspring can hardly dominate an entire species probably numbering millions of members in just a few generations!

In short, the numbers just did not work. The general conclusion was that Darwin's mutations would always be diluted to the point where their effects on evolution were minimal and that, consequently, the natural selection of favorable mutations could not occur to anything like the extent the theory required. Once again, precise analysis seemed to have defeated a mere theory; rigorous mathematics had refuted a purely speculative idea.

The irony of all this is that the foundations of the true science of genetics had been discovered and published as early as 1865 by Gregor Mendel (1822–84), but Darwin – and just about everyone else who ought to have known about it at the time – unfortunately remained totally ignorant of his work. Indeed, Mendel's findings remained unknown to the wider world of biology until the early years of the twentieth century, and Mendel, having made one of the greatest discoveries in the history of science, grew dispirited and lost interest in it himself. This is yet another instance of the fact that the progress of science is by no means as straightforward as one might think. On the contrary, it seems that in Mendel's case a period of latency intervened lasting the best part of half a century between the original discovery and its recognition by the wider scientific community.

What Mendel discovered in the course of his meticulous breeding experiments with peas was that inheritance does not dilute all heritable traits in the manner erroneously assumed to be the case by Darwin's critics. Partly by dint of good luck in choosing to study the characteristics of peas which he did, Mendel realized that the traits in question were not diluted in themselves, but inherited as a whole – as if there were "atoms" or "particles" of inheritance which could not be subdivided. Today these "particles" of inheritance are called *genes*. He showed that in a sexually reproducing plant like the pea it was not a question of any gene being half inherited by all the offspring of the parent, but rather a question of *all of that particular gene being inherited by half the offspring*.

Immediately this solved the problem of the apparent dilution of beneficial mutations, because what Mendel showed was that such a mutation would not be diluted, but handed on complete. Admittedly, it might only be handed on to half the original mutant's offspring, but in those offspring where it was expressed it would retain its entire effect. So to return to our original example, we can see that although only some offspring might inherit a gene which would enhance their reproductive success by 100 percent, those offspring would gradually become more numerous in each generation, thanks to the fact that the gene's effect was not being diluted and that the numbers of its bearers constantly increased.

Even today one sometimes encounters a lingering version of this early objection to Darwinism in the form of the supposition that Mendel's findings apply only to single genes. Since many traits in large, complex organisms like human beings are encoded in a large number of genes, it seems as though Mendel's discovery cannot apply to them, but that, on the contrary, dilution of the kind expected by Darwin's critics is bound to occur. In fact, our modern understanding of genetics shows that this objection has much less force than it might seem to have. For example, it is wrong to claim that the inheritance of single genes cannot account for complex and far-reaching effects on the organism as a whole. There are a number of examples which disprove this, but by far the best is the case of sex in many organisms, human beings included. Here it is undoubtedly true that many genes are involved in creating males as opposed to females, but the fact remains that recent research has found a single gene which acts as a biochemical "switch," "turning on" numerous other genes which then produce the observed result (see below, pp. 143–87). In other words, the fact that many genes may be involved in creating the whole organism does not mean that single genes may not be in control of many of the other genes, suggesting that Mendel's discovery, although based on traits coded by single genes, still explains much, even where large numbers of genes may actually be involved in the final outcome. Although much is still unknown about the inheritance of complex traits, the fact that genes do not appear to be exchanged entirely randomly when sex cells are constituted suggests that often they may be inherited as whole groups, again lending further force to Mendel's finding and reducing the scope for random dilution. As a consequence, whenever I speak in what follows as though single genes were involved in complex matters such as altruistic behavior, I do not necessarily mean to imply that there really is such a thing as a single gene for altruism. Such a way of putting things should be interpreted in the light of the observations above: that although many genes are almost certainly involved in producing the final outcome in a complex organism like a human being, such genes may be strongly correlated in inheritance or under the control of a few other genes, so that random dilution by inheritance cannot necessarily be assumed to be an obstacle to their evolution by natural selection. Indeed, the very fact that inheritance does follow Mendelian principles may be nothing more than a consequence of the fact that mutations which were not inherited along these lines would be less likely to be subject to evolution by natural selection, making Mendelian inheritance itself a naturally selected trait.

Mendel's discovery also solved another thorny problem for evolutionary theory. This was the observation that there appeared to be some inherited traits which were obviously detrimental to their possessors, such as hemophilia, a disorder present in some European royal families which resulted in its victims being at risk from bleeding to death because they possessed blood which would not clot in the normal way. Admittedly, this gene seemed to be inherited in a very odd, irregular fashion, but its occurrence in family lines suggested that it was indeed a heritable trait, but one which could hardly be accounted for by evolutionary selection. So not only could Darwin not explain how desirable traits could be conserved, he could not explain why undesirable ones like hemophilia were inherited, albeit in a mysterious and intermittent manner.

But Mendel could explain it. His experiments showed that each parent seemed to contribute a complete set of genetic material to the offspring, only one set of which was actually expressed in that offspring, the other remaining latent but heritable by that offspring's offspring. Indeed, some genes, present in one set, called *dominant*, seemed to be able to suppress corresponding genes in the other, called *recessive*. Hemophilia turned out to be such a recessive trait. As long as it was paired with a dominant, normal gene, it remained entirely latent, and its possessor was safe from its effects. But if an individual was unfortunate enough to inherit the recessive gene for hemophilia from both parents, there was no dominant, normal gene to suppress it and safeguard against its effects. In these unlucky individuals hemophilia became an *expressed*, not merely latent, trait. The fact that offspring of one generation in an inbred line will tend to share the same forebears in an earlier one dramatically increases the probability that an individual would receive two copies of the hemophilia gene if it were present in any of the common ancestors.

Later work accounted for Mendel's findings by showing that genes were conveyed in so-called *chromosomes*, which were found in the nucleus of most of the body's cells. In a *diploid* species, like human beings and most other sexually reproducing organisms, each individual has two complete sets of chromosomes, one from each parent. The exact number of chromosomes varies between species, being two sets of twenty-three, or forty-six in all, in the case of human beings.

An exception to the rule that cells are diploid is the sex cells. Egg and sperm cells contain only a single set of chromosomes and are termed *haploid* as a consequence. Mendel's findings could be explained elegantly by showing that in a typical diploid species like sweet peas or human beings each parent contributed one haploid sex cell to the offspring, which became diploid as a result. In other words, a human sperm and ovum, each with a single set of twenty-three chromosomes might come together as a fertilized egg with a double set of chromosomes, forty-six in all. Since the parent had originally been diploid also, any diploid offspring would receive only one half of that parent's genes in the haploid sex cell donated to it, explaining why dilution of the kind assumed by Darwin's critics does not necessarily occur. As we have seen, this insight also explained how recessive genes like that for hemophilia could evolve, because, being recessive, they could "hide," as it were, behind the dominant genes in whose shadow they survived. Only in the rare event of two recessives appearing in the same individual might the deleterious gene be expressed and, in all probability, selected against by natural factors.

It was not until the 1920s that Mendelian genetics was fully integrated with Darwinian evolutionary theory and not until 1953 that Francis Crick (b. 1916) and James Watson (b. 1928) finally showed what genes actually were. For some time before it had been known that chromosomes seemed to be largely constituted of *deoxyribonucleic acid*, or DNA for short. Crick and Watson proposed a model which suggested that DNA comprised two sugar-phosphate' helical spirals linked together by four chemical bases. They explained the ratios in which these bases always seemed to appear by suggesting that one of them on one strand was always paired with another on the other, so that a base on one strand would correspond to a complementary one on the other in the same kind of way that the interlocking teeth of a zip fastener do. If the two helical strands were unzipped and collected new complementary bases and sugar-phosphate chains corresponding to them, complete duplication could occur, and this, presumably, was the mechanism by means of which genetic information was copied and transmitted from cell to cell and generation to generation.

Later work showed that this was indeed the case, and that the genetic code consisted of sequences of three bases, each corresponding to a particular constituent of the proteins out of which organisms are ultimately made, or to "punctuation marks" in the code. Genes were found to be "transcribed" one triplet of bases at a time at *ribosomes*, subunits of the cell responsible for the assembly of proteins. A gene was now conceived as the sequence of base-pairs on a strand of DNA which coded for any one particular protein and was typically found to be thousands or millions of base-pairs long and not necessarily all in one piece. Overall, the total complement of DNA in a human being – what is termed the *genome* – is believed to be about three billion base-pairs long. Laid end to end these would be about five feet in length, although far too fine a thread to be seen with anything but the most powerful microscope. If imagined as a rope about two inches in diameter, the total complement of DNA in a human cell would be approximately 32,000 miles in length!

Since nearly all known organisms appear to encode their genetic material in DNA (or the very similar RNA), and since similar genes for similar things are found in organisms as diverse as yeasts, human beings, and plants, it seems very likely that all organisms are descended from originals which used a DNA-like genetic code. Evolution can be seen as occurring by means of chance changes in this code – mutations, in other words – which have gradually accumulated in countless organisms over immense periods of time. But the fact that DNA-like substances are highly vulnerable to chemical attack and certainly cannot survive in an oxygen atmosphere like that which now exists on earth means that ever since the oxygen atmosphere developed, and probably long before, DNA had to be packaged, or enveloped, in some kind of protective covering. To account for this, nothing more than natural selection need be supposed: genetic information which could survive and leave more copies of itself because it included genes for containment and protection would probably be the only genetic information to be selected once real competition among life-forms began. Indeed, we might go further and conclude that essentially this is *why* organisms as such exist: as the temporary containers or packaging, of the genes which they contain. Mendel's discovery, along with that of Crick and Watson and the whole science of molecular biology which has followed from it, leaves little doubt that the essence of life is the containment and transmission of genetic information encoded in an organism's genes. Without such genes an organism could not develop, and without developing as the vehicle for such genes, an organism could have no evolutionary future.

With billions of years at its disposal, thanks to the true age of the earth, and a means of transmitting favorable mutations in the genetic code, evolution could indeed have produced the results which Darwin claimed for it. But a true understanding of evolution was a long time coming and has emerged in its essential simplicity only in recent decades. In order to understand both that essential simplicity and why it was so long delayed, we need to examine the errors and exaggerations, not of Darwin's critics, but of some of his ostensible supporters.

Fallacies of fitness

If ignorance of genetics was a difficulty for Darwin and a gift to his critics, one or two other misunderstandings contributed as much or even more to the past problems of evolutionary theory and, indeed, still bedevil it today. Nowhere is this more clearly seen than in the notorious slogan "survival of the fittest." Although often attributed to Darwin, it was in fact coined by Herbert Spencer (1820–1903) seven years before the publication of *The Origin of Species*. As we shall now see, Darwin's theory of evolution by natural selection does *not* necessarily and primarily predict "the survival of the fittest" in Spencer's use of the term. This and most other rival theories of evolution add other assumptions or draw other conclusions besides the simple, single, and supreme insight of Darwin: namely, that natural selection is ultimately a matter of differential reproductive success *and nothing else*.

In order to understand how Darwin's concept of differential reproductive success as the final arbiter of natural selection differs from Spencer's notion of the survival of the fittest, consider the following paradox. It is now known that men die more readily than women at all ages from all causes which can affect both sexes, something which is seen from conception to death and can be reversed only by castration. In early adulthood men are approximately 400 percent more likely to die from accidents, wounds, and stress than are women and remain at least 100 percent more prone to death from these causes up to age 75.[2] Where violent death is concerned, a man is twenty times more likely to be murdered by another man than is a woman by another woman (see below, pp. 144–65). However, marked differential life expectancy can also be found between male and female members of celibate, nonviolent, and abstemious religious orders, and a similar finding is also reflected in the leading cause of death for both sexes in the United States, heart disease, where women have only 30 percent the mortality of men between the ages of thirty-five and fifty-four. Nevertheless, castrated tomcats live longer than their intact male counterparts, and so do human castrates. Detailed comparisons standardized for age, intelligence, and category of mental deficiency among castrated and intact inmates of a mental institution in Kansas demonstrated that the median age at death of intact men was 55.7 years, as compared to 69.3 years for castrates, and that the earlier the castration was performed, the more life expectancy was increased.[3]

These data suggest that it is being male and being subject to the effects of male sex hormones which actually shorten male life spans. Nor can such observations be explained as the consequence of social causes, since, as we shall see later, the greatest rate of male wastage occurs before birth (see below, pp. 201–2), and in some societies male mortality is lowest when male and female sex roles are most differentiated in early adulthood. We shall have to return to this important point again later when considering the whole question of sex (see below, pp. 197–200), but, for the time being, let us provisionally accept that it appears to be a biological, evolutionary effect, deeply embedded in fundamental factors affecting the evolution of sex differences and not one explicable in terms of culture or limited to recent human experience.

But if natural selection selects for individual health, longevity, and fitness understood in the colloquial sense, how could this have come about? How could evolution possibly discriminate against males in this way? How does it come about, for example, that when the reindeer population of an island in the Bering Sea crashed from 6,000 to 42 as a result of starvation, only one of the survivors was male? Nature may be feminine by gender but surely not feminist by conviction! Consider the paradox: if selection selects for personal survival because the "fittest" survive best, how could human males – not to mention males of other species – have evolved to be less fit in the sense that they survive less well than females?

If we go a little deeper into the problem, we find that one reason why males generally survive less well than females is the direct and indirect consequences of the male sex hormone, testosterone. This also seems to explain why castrated males survive better. For instance, one known effect of testosterone is to raise the resting metabolic rate of males by approximately 5 percent as compared to females. Effectively, this means that the male biochemical "engine" is running about one-twentieth faster all the time than is that of a woman, perhaps explaining why it wears out sooner. Again, a major factor in enhanced male vulnerability to death, disease, and injury is the greater aggressiveness and readiness to take risks characteristic of males; and this, too, seems to be an effect of testosterone.

But how could this possibly have evolved? After all, if selection selects for personal survival and individual longevity, any male born with a mutation which gave him less testosterone would, in all probability, survive longer and better. But, according to this interpretation of evolutionary "fitness," this is only another way of saying that such a fitness-promoting mutation would be selected. In no time at all – at least, by evolutionary standards – men would adapt personal fitness equal to that of females: the fittest would survive because the survivors were the fitter.

Yet, for all that, males do not survive as well as females. The reason is easily seen and returns us directly to our original – and correct – formulation of the true basis of selection. The reason is that whatever costs testosterone may exact in terms of personal well-being, survival, and safety, it confers greater benefits in terms of personal reproductive success. In other words, what wastes individual males is exactly the same factor which promotes their personal reproductive success, so that males with the right – albeit life-shortening – levels of testosterone leave more offspring than males with lower – if, nevertheless, life-extending levels. As we shall see when we come to consider the whole question of male sexual behavior later, it appears that the very factors which reduce life expectancy in a male, such as greater aggressiveness, faster metabolic rate, heavier body weight, greater readiness to take risks, and so on, are those which are normally likely to enhance a man's ultimate reproductive success in competition with other males (see below, pp. 143–9).

To reduce the point to total absurdity, consider the crudest possible version of this paradox. If castrated males survive better than sexually intact ones, as they are indeed known to do, and if evolution does in fact select the fittest in the sense of personal survival, why has natural selection not selected males without testes? Put in bald terms such as these, the answer is obvious. Males without testes would do somewhat better in terms of individual survival and resistance to all causes of death at all ages, but they would leave no descendants who could enjoy those advantages! From this we can draw the correct conclusion, insufficiently appreciated until astonishingly recently: *selection selects ultimately for reproductive success, not necessarily or primarily for personal survival.* If it does select for the latter – and, of course, it usually does so in practice – the only reason is that personal survival, health, longevity, or whatever are necessary factors in promoting an individual's ultimate reproductive success, rather than being factors selected in themselves, irrespective of reproductive success.

If natural selection selected primarily for personal survival, rather than reproductive success, death and reproduction in general – but sexual reproduction in particular – would be very difficult to explain. After all, why reproduce at all if what is selected is individual survival ability? Even if death and reproduction existed early on as evidence of the failure of natural selection to perfect survival to the point where it was the norm for organisms to exist for long periods and seldom if ever die or need to reproduce, one is still left wondering why, after billions of years of evolution, lifetimes are so short in so many otherwise successful organisms (such as bacteria and insects) and why death and sex are so common.

Sex in particular seems very strange from this point of view because it fails to reproduce an organism with the exactness of asexual reproduction, which produces clones, genetically identical with their progenitor. These might be regarded as the result of selection for individual survival if we take the view that genetically identical individuals are identical as far as selection for survival is concerned; but we can hardly hope to explain why sexual reproduction is by far the most common kind of reproduction especially among many of the longest-living organisms, such as trees, tortoises, and human beings. Since sexual reproduction does not reproduce an individual exactly, but constantly throws up new genetic combinations, it would hardly seem to serve the interests of the survival of the individuals who reproduce by this means. On the contrary, the final, definitive form of organisms which undergo metamorphic change as butterflies and moths do is adapted purely for reproduction, suggesting that sexual reproduction is the point of life, not personal survival in and for itself. This is not a difficulty for Darwin's theory, but must always remain a paradox if individual survival, rather than reproductive success, is considered the primary aim of natural selection. Furthermore, as we have already seen, differential survival related to sex seems totally incomprehensible if selection selects for anything other than reproductive success.

Perhaps some readers will object that it is really a chicken-and-egg situation, with survival being necessary for reproductive success and vice versa. To a large extent this is true, but it is untrue if we interpret such a remark to mean that personal survival and well-being have exactly the same significance for natural selection as ultimate reproductive success. To return to the point I made at the end of the last section, we can see that if organisms as such are essentially the packaging and vehicles of the genetic information which they contain and originally evolved to carry and protect it, then *organisms must be able to survive in order to reproduce*, rather than be able to reproduce in order to survive. If it is indeed a chicken-and-egg situation (and it certainly is for chickens!), we can say that it is not the egg that is the chicken's way of making another chicken, but rather that the chicken is the egg's way of making another egg: "the organism is only DNA's way of making more DNA."[4]

The mistake made by those who think that natural selection selects fitness first and foremost as understood in the everyday sense is rather like the mistake which alien observers might make if their spaceship landed in a super-market parking lot where they could observe people taking away cartons, cans, and bottles. The aliens, unfamiliar with human shopping habits, might assume that it was the packaging in itself that human beings valued and be astonished to find those same cartons, cans, and bottles being thrown away later. However, if they looked inside our kitchens and tracked individual packages, they would soon find out that it is not the packet or container as such that human beings select in the supermarket, but what is inside it. Once the contents are consumed, the carton is usually discarded because it has no further useful function. It seems that natural selection selects organisms in much the same way that we choose cans and cartons, using them as purely temporary containers for something more vital inside: the DNA. Early evolutionists like Spencer who thought that selection selects for the benefit of the fitness of the organism, rather than for its ultimate reproductive success, committed the same error that the aliens might make in mistaking the packaging for the goods, the carton for the contents.

Another factor militating against this correct view of the relationship between the organism and evolution by natural selection is the fact that, if true, it ought to apply with equal force to human beings. It suggests that each one of us is – at least as far as evolution is concerned – a biodegradable piece of packaging for our genes, and this is hardly an insight likely to appeal to human vanity. However, what distinguishes science from other kinds of knowledge is that it is pledged to accept reality as its final and only court of appeal and cannot be expected to take human preferences into account in formulating its conclusions. Nevertheless, human beings never seem to stop trying to recast reality in a more agreeable form, and one cannot escape the impression that the appeal of Spencerian "survival of the fittest" evolution lay partly in its implicit concept of evolution as a process which improved and perfected the organism, perhaps human beings especially. Unfortunately, the modern Darwinian view of evolution by natural selection sees no necessary ultimate benefit to the organism in evolution, but only to its genes.

Some readers might have been tempted to observe that the general conflict of interest between reproductive success and personal survival and the apparent paradox regarding male survival and male reproductive success in particular were instances of distinct types of selection: what Darwin termed *sexual selection*, as opposed to purely *natural* selection. In these terms, it would be tempting to think that, whereas natural selection selected for individual survival, sexual selection selected for reproductive success. According to this view, adverse male survival would be a consequence of increased sexual selection among males, which to this extent was working against natural selection in its prime role of safeguarding survival.

Of course, it is perfectly true that Darwin did indeed use the term sexual selection and that he did regard it as an adjunct to natural selection, somewhat in the manner suggested in the paragraph above. But Darwin's use of the term was more descriptive than analytic, and he himself pointed out that "in most cases it is scarcely possible to distinguish between the effects of natural and sexual selection."[5]

Today we would probably go further and say that it is scarcely possible to distinguish between the principles of selection involved if we wish to avoid confusion regarding the true meaning of "fitness" and ambiguity about what natural selection actually selects. Since sex is natural and since naturally selected traits can be passed on only by sexual reproduction in sexually reproducing species, it follows that the two types of selection are not conflicting principles so much as different descriptions of the same basic process. This process is the selective one which decrees that organisms which have heritable traits for greater relative reproductive success will pass those traits on to more descendants than will those not so endowed. "To be selected" means to have enhanced reproductive success, and so both "natural" and "sexual" selection must come ultimately to the same thing. However it comes about, "selected" traits are reproductively successful ones, and reproductively successful traits are those which are selected. Whether they are naturally or sexually selected is really little more than a detail regarding the specific adaptation involved, not the basic evolutionary principle at work.

Another possible view is to assert that natural selection seems to select for personal survival, health, and well-being until reproductive age is reached, and thereafter sexual selection selects for reproductive success. Although this is very often true, it is by no means always so and cannot explain why some organisms in certain circumstances seem to postpone reproduction or never undertake it at all. The latter, rather paradoxical situation exists, for instance, among the social insects, where sterile castes are found. In this case we would have to say that, whereas the sterile worker castes were naturally selected, sexual selection affected only the reproductive castes, the queens and the drones. But this seems a very strange situation, to say the least, and immediately poses the question as to what could have selected this equivocal situation: sexual or natural selection? Again, this way of looking at things suggests that queens and drones should be less "fit" in terms of personal health and survival than workers, something hardly warranted by the facts which, if anything, suggest the contrary. All in all, it seems safest to avoid drawing too sharp a line between natural and sexual selection and to see both as ultimately reducing to reproductive success, whether unproblematically linked to personal survival or otherwise.

During the nineteenth and early twentieth centuries, the common misunderstanding of the meaning of "fitness" in evolution was perhaps understandable. After all, this was the era when the populations of Western countries like the USA, Great Britain, France, and Germany were undergoing both rapid expansion in numbers and rapid rise in living standards, health, and general welfare. Life expectancy rose, infant mortality fell, and the population in general increased, so that, in dramatic contrast to the traditional family, the Victorian family often numbered six, eight, or even ten or more surviving children. At that time it must have been easy to confuse evolution with general health, welfare, and survival of the population.

But had the Victorians been alive today, they would have confronted an altogether different picture and one which might well have seemed highly paradoxical. In today's world the countries whose populations are increasing most rapidly are not those of the advanced, Western industrialized nations, but those of the Third World, where poverty, ill health, and disease are more often the accompaniments of rapid population growth than anything else. Today no one could be forgiven for confusing affluence and general health and welfare with population expansion and for naively assuming that the two were practically synonymous.

Comparable errors about the meaning of "fitness" underlie the worst excesses of some other nineteenth-century views of evolution. For instance, Spencer's concept of "the survival of the fittest" was applied to social inequality, suggesting that the powerful, wealthy, and able-bodied members of society were products of a social equivalent of natural selection which determined that the fittest should succeed and the less fit should fail. It was an inevitable consequence of this view that those who were poor, ill, or disadvantaged in any way were not among the elect of evolution and were neither fit nor fitted to share the privileges enjoyed by those who had beaten them in the struggle for survival. Indeed, some argued that even to support or to succor such evolutionary failures was perverse and worked against the grand plan of evolution: it would weaken the race and dilute the "fitness" of society as a whole. Here was "survival of the fittest" perfecting, not merely individuals, but entire social classes!

These absurd views seem to be the inevitable consequence of errors about what natural selection actually selects and a natural outcome of the belief that evolution is primarily concerned with increments to individual health and welfare, rather than anything else. But if we take the correct view that true, Darwinian fitness is only another term for *reproductive success*, there is no way in which we could make these mistakes. In other words, Darwinian fitness implies a purely *quantitative* measure, differential reproductive success; it does not necessarily imply any other kind of necessary *qualitative* improvement, superiority, or enhancement of an organism's individual attributes.

By contrast to Darwin's quantitative and objective, as opposed to subjective and qualitative, concept of natural selection, such odious value-judgments about certain classes being "more fit," and thereby more worthy, than others or certain races being "more highly evolved," and thereby more human, than others (because further from their pre-human origins) can now be seen to be what they really are: nothing in the least to do with Darwin's essential insight. On the contrary, if "fitness" had meant what it was almost always fallaciously taken to mean, then Herbert Spencer, and not Charles Darwin, would have been the true originator of the modern theory of evolution when he used the term "survival of the fittest" seven years before Darwin's theory was published. Indeed, where the strict Darwinian definition of natural selection is concerned, phrases like "more advanced" or "less evolved" are meaningless, and certainly cannot be used to justify the claim that modern, Western nations are at a "higher" or "more advanced" stage of evolution than others, any more than the concept of natural selection can be used to justify social inequality.

Because of these common fallacies about the meaning of "fitness," I propose to avoid the term from now on wherever possible, even when qualified with the adjective "Darwinian," and instead follow the precedent set by the best modern literature on evolution and refer only to *reproductive success*. For, essentially, this is what Darwin's true, original discovery was: that evolution is a process directed by differential reproductive success, and nothing else.

The problem of altruism

Quite apart from errors and confusion regarding the meaning of "fitness," yet another muddle bedeviled evolutionary thinking until quite recently. This was confusion over the *level* at which selection operated. This is important, because the question of the level at which selection operates becomes absolutely critical to any discussion of social behavior, especially of cooperative behavior or *altruism*. The latter is a term which will be used a great deal in what follows so it is important to be clear from the beginning what is meant by it. At first sight, it might seem that any use of "altruism" in the context of animal behavior is misplaced and that it is a term which should be reserved for describing human behavior, where motive, intention, and meaning can be assumed. We might argue that since altruism in human affairs implies an altruistic motive, it cannot be applied to organisms such as insects or fish, whose level of cerebral development calls strongly into question any attribution of conscious motive to them. For example, if I give someone some money because I want that person to have it rather than to keep it myself, everyone would agree that I have performed an act of altruism. But if someone gets some of my money because I inadvertently lost it, for instance, most people would not regard my losing it as altruistic, because I did not intend it to pass out of my possession. On the contrary, they would probably regard the recipient's keeping it as evidence of selfishness on the latter's part, rather than altruism on my part. Here it seems that it is my altruistic motive which defines the altruism of my act, rather than the mere transfer of the benefit to another person.

All this is perfectly correct, but it will not get us very far with altruism in an evolutionary context. Here it must be more strictly defined, so much so that we must regard it as a technical term. It is in that sense that I shall always use it, unless I qualify it in some way to the contrary by the addition of adjectives like "human" or "humanitarian," "pure" or "ascetic." As to the question of whether this purely technical, scientifically defined use of the term "altruism" has anything to do with human altruism, I must ask my readers to suspend their judgment for a while. As we shall see, altruism is a deep and perplexing issue.

Nowhere is it more perplexing than in evolution. The view of nature as "red in tooth and claw," which many associate with Darwinism and which was popularized by some of the so-called Social Darwinists, tended to emphasize self-interest, as opposed to altruism. After all, if selection selects for personal survival, health, and well-being, why should any organism help any other? Socialist critics of Social Darwinism in particular made much of this and portrayed evolution as a theory which glorified selfishness, greed, and aggression. In the "struggle for survival" it seemed that only a fool would help anyone else. In terms of natural selection, it seemed, only the selfish could win. According to this view, "evolution" and "cooperation" were contradictions in terms.

Of course, the moment we recall that it is erroneous to believe that natural selection selects primarily for personal well-being, we can see that this cannot be correct. At best, it is a question not of a struggle purely for survival so much as a struggle for reproductive success, with survival being a means to that end rather than an end in itself. But here we see immediately that one particular kind of altruism becomes obvious and self-explanatory. Because reproductive success means having offspring, self-sacrificing acts by parents towards those offspring seem predictable and will presumably be selected. Such self-sacrifice will be selected in the way in which any other behavior or trait is selected: because it confers reproductive success on those who possess it. It is not difficult to understand that a parent who is selfish to the point of neglecting his or her offspring might leave fewer of them than one who is prepared to make sacrifices for their benefit.

In part, then, correcting the cruder mistakes about "fitness" helps to explain altruism in animal behavior. Unfortunately, it will not completely solve the problem by any means. To understand why, we must be more specific, and, in particular, we must define what we mean by "altruism" much more carefully. After all, most people would hardly regard self-sacrifice for one's own children as archetypically altruistic, even if it might be altruistic in a weak sense. True altruism seems to suggest something much less self-interested than this.

For the purposes of a discussion of altruism in a purely evolutionary context, let us define "altruism" as *any behavior which promotes the reproductive success of the recipient at a cost to the reproductive success of the altruist*. Immediately, we can see that there is a real problem here. If we insist that selection selects for reproductive success rather than personal survival, it becomes immediately obvious that any act which promotes the reproductive success of one organism at a cost to another cannot be selected. By definition, an act which confers a benefit in terms of reproductive success on another, but at a cost to the reproductive success of the altruist, cannot be selected if, by "selection," we mean anything which promotes reproductive success. It seems, in short, as if our definitions of both natural selection and altruism have ruled out altruism as anything which could possibly be selected because, by definition, altruism *reduces rather than enhances the reproductive success of the altruist.*

To make the situation completely clear, consider the following "thought-experiment." Imagine a species of entirely selfish individuals among whom, by means of a mutation, a gene for altruism appears. By definition, that gene seems to have no reproductive success because we have already defined altruism as something which promotes the reproductive success of others at a cost to its own reproductive success. If the others are selfish, as they are in this example, genes for selfishness will benefit, not those for altruism. Contrariwise, consider the opposite state of affairs. Imagine a species in which all members have genes predisposing them to altruism. It will require only the chance appearance of a gene for selfishness for all the altruistic genes to be driven into extinction, since, by definition, they must promote the reproductive success of the gene for selfishness at their own expense.

This might not be such a problem if notable acts of altruism were not common in animal behavior. However, altruism, even if strictly defined as it is above, is surprisingly common. For instance, alarm calling is commonly found among birds and small mammals who are vulnerable to sudden attacks by predators. But why should the individual who gives the call bother to do so? After all, it must already have noticed the danger; so why expend energy for the benefit of others? Why risk drawing attention to oneself in this ostentatious way? If this seems problematic, consider the most monumental problem of all: the social insects. Here we find sterile castes of workers, always female, who altruistically promote the reproductive success of the queen at their own very significant cost. Indeed, in terms of reproductive success – the only factor which our definition of evolutionary altruism recognizes – sterile workers make the ultimate sacrifice, because they forgo their own reproduction altogether in the interests of others. Finally, even if we have a lingering attraction to the idea of fitness, rather than reproductive success, as promoting survival, consider the extreme altruism of soldier castes in some termite species. In this case, the soldiers in question sacrifice their very existence by literally making themselves explode in the path of invaders of the nest, who subsequently become bogged down in their sticky viscera. Suicidal self-sacrifice of this kind cannot be bettered even among human beings, where we have it on good authority that, "Greater love hath no man than this, that he lay down his life for his friend."

But however that may be, some who associated themselves with Darwinism thought that they had a ready answer. Darwin, to his credit, was more circumspect and wondered whether his theory could really deal with what we might call "the problem of altruism." If we recall our thought-experiment above, we can see why. Any correct understanding of natural selection as something which selects on the basis of reproductive success must make behavior which by definition reduces the reproductive success of the actor something of a paradox. It certainly seemed so to Darwin, who could not fully explain it, although he correctly intuited that an answer must lie somewhere in considerations of genetic relationship or reciprocity. But the true solution lay in the future. As far as the contemporary popularizers of Darwin, like Herbert Spencer, were concerned, a ready answer could be found in what we can now see was yet another evolutionary fallacy. This was an aspect of the view of evolution as a cumulative process, one which gradually created larger, more complex and more complete entities, and which assumed that selection selected not merely individual organisms, but groups of organisms too: families, societies, perhaps even entire species.

Although Darwin explicitly stated that he believed "in no law of necessary development,"[6] many assumed that "evolution" was a term synonymous with "biological progress" and that selection for "fitness" implied selection for organisms which were more complex and complete, "more advanced" or generally superior to those which went before them. This was the view of Herbert Spencer, who, as we have already seen, anticipated Darwin's theory of evolution with one of his own and was one of the chief founders of Social Darwinism. Spencer applied the term "evolution" to the development of the cosmos as a whole and did not base his concept on natural selection. On the contrary, Spencer believed that there was an inevitable tendency for all things to evolve towards a more complex, unified state out of simpler, separated beginnings.

As applied to biological evolution, the argument goes like this. In the beginning, there were single cells, the most primitive form of life, today represented by bacteria and such-like organisms. Later, multicellular forms of life evolved. At first these were simple, small, and poorly coordinated. But in time they evolved into the complex multicellular organisms we see gradually dominating the earth. The first complex organisms were entirely confined to the sea, but gradually they colonized the land. At first, they were slow-moving, dim-witted, cold-blooded, and lived alone. Gradually these primitive forms were superseded by faster, more intelligent, warm-blooded, social species who could exploit the environment much more effectively. Now societies emerged, and social groups could be seen as "super-organisms" – a higher level of evolution, selected as units more complex and "advanced" than what had gone before them. Just as individual cells, themselves once dependent units, are organized into multicellular organisms, so individual organisms in social species are organized into social super-organisms. Furthermore, just as the first multicellular organisms were simple and relatively undifferentiated, so were the first societies, including the first human societies. But in the course of time the cosmic process of evolution developed, enlarged, and elaborated these simple, primitive societies into vast, complex, super-organisms with much internal division of labor, especially in modern human societies. Such societies represent the pinnacle of evolutionary development, something even more "evolved" than an individual human being: a human super-organism.

This view nicely rationalized Victorian social prejudices by suggesting that Western, industrial nations with complex division of labor and high population density were "more advanced" or more "highly evolved" than others. Such an erroneous view of evolution was explicit in Spencer's idea of the "super-organism," and it seemed immediately and completely to solve the problem of altruism for evolution. It did so by assuming that selection can operate at various levels and that altruism might be selected if the family, group, society, or species were selected *as a unit*. Since altruism, by definition, benefits others, it can indeed be selected if the others are part of some larger group, or super-organism, to which the altruist belongs. Indeed, if selection ultimately aims at perfecting the race or species, as Social Darwinist views of it generally suggested, then altruism could be selected for that very reason alone. In other words, altruism benefited the species, society, or family because natural selection selected for the perfection, elaboration, and enlargement of the family, society, or species.

Not only does this appear to solve the problem, it seems to suggest that the very existence of extensive altruism – for instance in insects like bees and ants – argues that insect societies, so notable for their elaborate organization and impressive cohesion, are indeed super-organisms which are selected as units by evolution. What individual cells are to the multicellular organisms which they comprise, individual organisms are to the societies which they constitute. In other words, just as individual cells make up organisms like ants or human beings, so individual ants or human beings comprise the "cells" making up the more complex super-organisms represented by their societies. Once constituted as such, societies become subject to natural selection just as individual organisms do. If worker bees, ants, or termites sacrifice their personal reproductive success, it is because they serve the reproductive interests of selection at this higher, more complex level: the social. According to this view, altruism in these cases is not a problem for evolutionary theory so much as a proof of a particular evolutionary theorem: selection can operate at the group, family, or social level, as well and perhaps even in preference to the level of the individual.

As applied to evolutionary theory in general, the proposition which we have just derived is nowadays known as *group selection*. As an indication of the problems involved in it, consider the following example. Many animals equipped with lethal weapons in the form of teeth, horns, or whatever are vulnerable to the effects of unrestrained conflict among themselves. If fights were carried through to the finish, there would soon be few left to enjoy the fruits of victory; species constituted by lethally aggressive individuals would simply decimate themselves. However, a similar species in which individuals possessed some innate constraint on their aggression with their own group members would benefit. If such a constraint prevented fighting to the finish, but ritualized it short of doing real damage, such a species would prosper relative to one without such an adaptation.

At first sight, this might seem to make good evolutionary sense, but consider the following argument. Suppose that the reasoning above were correct and that a species with a gene for ritualized, rather than lethal, aggression did evolve by group selection. Suppose that a mutant emerges lacking that gene, one which, instead of stopping short at relatively mild aggression, carries it through to lethal effect. What will happen? Obviously, such a mutant will win nearly all the fights it starts, because, where its opponents will hold back from inflicting lethal bites or blows, it will not. If, as is usually the case, conflict with other members of the same species is over access to scarce resources critical for survival and reproduction, the lethal aggressor is likely to be reproductively much more successful than its nonlethal competitors. Its own descendants will inherit the gene for lethal aggression to their advantage and that of their offspring, and so on. Before long, only lethal killers will be found in a once more peaceful species.

Immediately we can see that this is just another version of the thought-experiment above, but one in which a gene for lethal aggression has been substituted for one for simple selfishness and where genetic constraints on aggression have been put in place of altruism. Nevertheless, such genetic constraints on aggression would be an instance of altruism, as defined above, and lethal aggression is self-evidently selfish. In order to begin to understand how constraints on aggression in lethally armed species actually evolve – because there is no doubt that they do, in fact, exist – we must look at the whole question of cooperation with, or defection against, the interests of groups. We will begin with the smallest possible group and with the most finely balanced cooperation we can find. As we shall now see, the outcome of the following analysis is completely revolutionary and suggests that, contrary to first appearances, cooperation in general and altruism in particular can indeed evolve on an individualistic, genuinely Darwinian basis.

1

The Evolution of Cooperation

Prisoner's Dilemma

Two bank employees have been cleverly embezzling large sums of money by means of a computer fraud for some months. The fraud requires the conspiracy of the two, but no one else, and both know that neither could be convicted without the testimony of the other. One morning as they arrive for work they are dismayed to be called up to the president's office, but in the elevator on the way up, each pledges to cooperate with the other in keeping the technical details of the fraud secret, so that no evidence will be found which could be used against them. On arrival in the president's office, both are further disconcerted at being addressed by the code-names under which they operated: "Bold" and "Italic." Each is taken to a separate office.

Bold is seen by a vice-president of the bank, who makes the following accusation: "We know that you, under the code-name 'Bold,' have been defrauding the bank for some time with your accomplice 'Italic.' We know that each of you has transferred money to foreign bank accounts, and we know how much and where. What we do not know is how you carried out the fraud. We are prepared to offer you complete immunity from prosecution if you tell us the full technical details of the operation. As a further inducement, you will be allowed to keep your ill-gotten gains."

For a moment Bold is delighted. The prospect of immediate

release with his plunder appeals to him, now that he knows the game is up. But then he thinks a little further: "What will happen to Italic?" he asks.

"He will be prosecuted on your testimony," responds the vice-president.

"But we agreed never to incriminate one another," says Bold.

"Very good," replies the vice-president; "you do, of course, have the right to remain silent."

"Then that is exactly what I will do." With this, Bold sits back, smiling smugly.

There is a long silence. Bold is disconcerted to see that the vice-president's expression has not changed. A look of menace lurks behind an impassive countenance. Finally, the vice-president breaks the silence. "There is just one other thing you should know. In your own interest you must be advised that 'Italic,' as you call him, is being presented with exactly the same offer."

"Then perhaps I could discuss this with my colleague?" asks Bold.

"I am afraid that will not be possible," replies the vice-president; "you must both make up your minds without consulting one another."

"And what happens if neither of us agrees to tell you anything?" responds Bold.

"In that case," replies his superior, "you will both be released immediately, but your foreign bank accounts will be frozen, and the money will be retrieved by the bank."

There is another long silence. Bold continues to think that he will remain silent. After all, he will still have his freedom, even if he will never enjoy the proceeds of his crime, and he knows that, without evidence which could bring about the conviction of at least one of them, the bank will probably want to keep the fraud a secret and could be relied upon not to pursue them later. And then again, there is the question of his promise to cooperate with his accomplice: a question of loyalty among thieves.

But suddenly he breaks out in a cold sweat. A terrible thought crosses his mind: suppose that Italic succumbs to temptation and provides information to incriminate *him*. Now he realizes the danger of silence. Even as he is thinking this, Italic could be telling all, and he, Bold, could be prosecuted, jailed, and ruined while Italic escapes with his proceeds from the crime!

Now he begins to reconsider his first reaction. Perhaps he should not remain silent after all. A thought occurs to him. "Supposing," he asks, "supposing we both tell all. What happens then?" He is told that the bank's legal advice is that if both voluntarily provide full details of the fraud, both will be tried, but both could plead for mitigated sentences on the grounds that they had helped the bank protect itself against future frauds of a similar kind and that the prosecution would support such a plea. The resulting sentences of both would be much shorter than the sentence of the one who was incriminated by the other, but, of course, both would have to return the cash they had stolen. Abruptly, the vice-president leaves, telling him that he has one hour in which to make up his mind. Ominously, Bold hears the key turn in the lock.

What is he to do? What would you do? Consider the problem. Each conspirator knows that if he incriminates the other, there is a chance that he may go free and keep the proceeds of his crime. This would be an ideal solution, were it not for the fact that his fellow conspirator would be left to serve a long sentence and face the confiscation of his ill-gotten gains. On the other hand, if he remains silent and cooperates with his fellow criminal in this respect, both can go free, albeit without their gains. But if he does that, there is a real danger that the other might not cooperate in keeping silent, and he himself might end up the sucker, serving a long sentence because his confederate in crime had turned traitor on him. Finally, if both turn traitor and incriminate each other, both will suffer a prison sentence, although shorter than in the former case. Soon both realize that the fiendish dilemma they are in results from the fact that the outcome of whatever one does is determined by what the other does; and yet neither has any way of knowing what the other will do.

This anecdote is meant to illustrate the fundamental problem which we posed at the end of the last chapter, that relating to whether individuals should cooperate with a group or do otherwise. In general, we must assume that group membership implies some cost to the individuals who constitute it, as well as some benefit. However, it is a fundamental principle of social science that in a group of any size where this is true, *individuals will always have a self-interest in obtaining the benefits of group membership without paying the initial costs or, alternatively, will have an interest in not paying an additional cost of membership from which they will obtain no more benefit than any other member.*

This is often termed "the free-rider theorem," for obvious reasons. It sets out in terms of social theory what we all already know from bitter experience of the world: namely, that there will always be free-riders who, at others' expense, try to get advantages for which they have never paid. Were this not a fact of life, public transport systems, markets, and society in general would not have to be policed by various means, and sanctions would not have to exist to punish those who take without giving, benefit without contributing, or ride without paying.

The conspirators in my anecdote constitute the smallest possible group, a group of two people. The "cost" of membership is their pledge of loyalty and cooperation with one another in seeing that their fraud is never discovered and, if it is, in never divulging anything which could be used in evidence against the other. The benefit is the proceeds of the crime. As long as it remains undetected, the benefit of cooperation vastly outweighs the cost: only a fool would confess all to the authorities if nothing were suspected. But my anecdote has been contrived to illustrate the essential dilemma in any social interaction: when to cooperate with the group interest and pay one's dues, as opposed to when to defect in one's own self-interest and benefit without paying.

What I have done is to imagine a situation in which there is a very real temptation to free-ride by getting the benefit of the conspiracy – the loot plus immunity from prosecution – by means of not paying the cost represented by continuing loyalty to the other conspirator.

I have contrived the inducements to illustrate this in the simplest and most direct way possible. As we have seen, if one of the conspirators defects by confessing and thinking only of himself while the other cooperates by remembering their pledge to mutual support by means of staying silent, the defector gets both immediate freedom and the proceeds of the crime. Let us call this the pay-off for succumbing to temptation, or T, for short. In this case the other, the unrequited cooperator, gets the worst possible pay-off, the long jail sentence and no proceeds, what we may call the sucker's pay-off, S. But, in order to make the dilemma as to whether to cooperate or to defect in the joint interest of the conspirators real, we must recognize that there is also a real incentive to cooperate, because, if both stay silent and faithful to their pledge, both get immediate freedom. This pay-off is less than T, which also allows one of them to retain the loot, but is still very significant. Let us call it R, the pay-off for reciprocity. Finally, if both defect by trying to incriminate the other, both suffer, but not as much as they would if either had been the sucker. Let us call this pay-off for mutual defection P, for punishment. Although both get a jail sentence for this in my anecdote, it is a shorter one than the sucker's.

What is important here is not the details of the story, but the basic logic of the dilemma and the relative values of the pay-offs. What is essential is that T, the pay-off for defection if the other cooperates, has a greater value than R, the pay-off for mutual cooperation because, were it the other way round, there would be no incentive to defect. On the contrary, if the pay-off for mutual cooperation were greater than any pay-off for defection, no one would ever be tempted to defect, and so there would be no dilemma about cooperating. However, R, the pay-off for mutual cooperation, must be greater than P, the pay-off for mutual defection in order to maintain the reality of the incentive to cooperate, given that there is also an incentive to defect (because T is greater than R). Obviously, if the pay-off for both unilateral and mutual defection were greater than any other, there would be no incentive to cooperate and, again, no dilemma. Finally, P, the pay-off for mutual defection, must be more than S, the pay-off for cooperating if the other defects, because cooperating when the other defects must be the worst possible outcome for the cooperating player if defection when the other cooperates is to remain a real temptation. We may summarize the situation by saying we have the following ranking of pay-offs: $T > R > P > S$ (where $>$ means "greater than").

However, we must also assume that the pay-off for random defection and cooperation – or for the players resolving the dilemma by taking turns at exploiting each other, which comes to the same thing – is less than the pay-off for mutual cooperation, R. Clearly, were this not so, each player would realize that the outcome was essentially a game of chance, with the average pay-off for successful detection, T, and unsuccessful cooperation, S, exceeding R, the pay-off for mutual cooperation. As a game of chance, there would be no dilemma and no point in agonizing about one's decisions. Consequently, we must add to the inequalities listed at the end of the previous paragraph the requirement that R should be greater than the average of T and S: that is, $R > (T + S)/2$.

We can summarize the dilemma in a table and assign arbitrary numerical values to the pay-offs on the basis of the rules set out above. In table 1.1 I have indicated cooperation by means of the symbol of two fish swimming around one another and defection by a dagger. T, which corresponds to immediate freedom and the defector's share of the loot in my anecdote, gets 5 points; R, corresponding to immediate release for both Bold and Italic following their cooperation in protecting one another, wins 3; P, corresponding to commuted sentences for both in the event of each defecting and incriminating the other, gets 1; finally, S, the long sentence with the loss of loot, gets 0. We can also see that the average pay-off for random cooperation and defection works out as the average of T and S, which is 2.5, and that this is indeed less than the pay-off for mutual cooperation, R, which I have set at 3.

Table 1.1· Prisoner's Dilemma

		Italic		
		cooperates 🐟		*defects*
cooperates 🐟	🐟 (3)	🐟 *(3)*	🐟 (0)	*(5)*
Bold				
defects	(5)	🐟 *(0)*	(1)	*(1)*

My anecdote also illustrates the other fundamental conditions which make the dilemma unavoidable. There is no way that the players can communicate with one another, thereby making threats, commitments, or choices determined by the other player's decision impossible. Furthermore, there is no way to avoid the interaction or to dispose of the other player. Finally, there is no way to change the pay-offs, which are fixed and imposed equally on each. Under these conditions, only actions count, and the only action open to each player is the choice to cooperate or defect.

Of course, this is an abstract mathematical game. Some may be tempted to argue that it is not relevant to real life. Two replies can be made to this. The first is that, abstract and contrived or not, it does portray in an elemental and fundamental way the basic dilemma of social interaction: cooperate in the mutual interest of yourself and others or defect in your own self-interest. Furthermore, we have already seen that it is basic to the whole question of the evolution of cooperative behavior. Secondly, one sometimes comes across situations in real life which are astonishingly like the game.

For example, some years ago my wife made an agreement with another woman to cooperate in taking the children of both to school. The agreement was that one mother would take the children to school at the beginning of the day and the other would collect them at the end. Obviously, both had a real incentive to cooperate in this way because it meant halving the time spent .taking and collecting, petrol consumed, and so on. At first, all went well, but then, towards the end of the first term, the other lady's car began to let her down, and my wife did significantly more journeys than she did. The holidays came and went, and the next term things got going on an equitable footing again. However, as the end of the term approached, the other lady's car once again began to be afflicted with mechanical problems. Finally, when exactly the same thing occurred at the end of the third term, my wife made a polite excuse and established another – and more successful – arrangement with another mother for the next school year.

Although a real-life situation, this was also a classic Prisoner's Dilemma, with an implicit pay-off matrix like that in table 1.1. T, the pay-off for successful defection is represented by one mother having her children transported to school free of the very considerable cost represented by the time, petrol, and general wear and tear on one's car and nerves involved, while S represents the corresponding cost to the other mother of taking both her and the other's child to school each way. P represents the cost to each woman of taking just her own child to school without any help from the other and is less than S, since it does not include the very real cost of collecting, waiting for, and delivering the other's child. R, mutual cooperation, represents exactly half S, unilateral cooperation, since it means taking both children only half the time, but is clearly less costly than P, taking only one's own child both ways all the time. In other words, T, no cost at all, is a greater benefit than R, half the cost of taking both children; this in its turn is a greater benefit than P, the cost of taking one's own child both ways; and the latter, finally, is less costly than S, taking both children both ways each day. In short, $T > R > P > S$.

Admittedly, R, the saving in cost of having one's own child taken half the time, is equal to the average saving of having one's own child taken every time, T, and always having to take both children oneself, S. But such random cooperation and defection as would produce such an averaged result was hardly a realistic option for the women concerned, who either had a cooperative arrangement or did not. If they were indeed to cooperate in taking their children to school, the value to each of reciprocity, R, had to be greater than purely random, day-to-day cooperations and defections, whose cost in terms of general hassle and inconvenience would be considerable. In practical effect, then, $R > (T + S)/2$, since we would have to add to $(T + S)/2$ the extra costs involved in not having a cooperative arrangement with pay-off R.

This real-life situation also illustrates another dimension of Prisoner's Dilemma interactions: what happens when they are *iterated*, or repeated over a period of time. As we shall see in the next section, it was modeling of such iterated interactions made possible by modern computer technology that produced results which have revolutionized social theory and put the modern, evolutionary understanding of social behavior on a surprising new basis.

Computing cooperation

From time to time, new publications appear in fields of science which instantly make everything previously published on the same subject obsolete. An obvious example would be Charles Darwin's *Origin of Species*, but a more recent one is the series of publications culminating in Robert Axelrod's book *The Evolution of Cooperation*. At first sight, nothing could be more surprising, because the book's ostensible purpose was to report and comment on nothing more significant than the results of two computer tournaments. Yet, as we shall now see, the consequences of how and why the winning program won ramify throughout social and biological science, making Axelrod's book a landmark publication in the modern study of social behavior.

What Axelrod did was to invite participants to submit computer programs to play iterated Prisoner's Dilemma. We have already met a real-life example of this at the end of the last section, where we saw that, effectively, my wife was playing a game of Prisoner's Dilemma when she participated in the arrangement to share school journeys. As we have also already seen, Prisoner's Dilemma boils down to a simple choice either to cooperate or to defect. The computer programs entered for Axelrod's tournaments each had to make such a choice with knowledge of the previous choices of its opponent (although obviously not of the current choice). Programs were played against each other in a round robin tournament (meaning that each entry was played against every other entry), and scores were totaled. Points in each round were allocated as in the previous example: 5 for successful defection, 3 for mutual cooperation, 1 for mutual defection, and 0 for unsuccessful cooperation.

Two tournaments were played. In the first, fourteen entries were submitted by individuals with experience of Prisoner's Dilemma from five disciplines: psychology, economics, political science, mathematics, and sociology. Axelrod also entered RANDOM, a program which made its choice to cooperate or defect a matter of chance and which came last in the first tournament and second to last in the second, indicating that some strategy was better than none. The winner was the shortest, simplest program submitted. Called TIT FOR TAT, its strategy was to cooperate on the first move and thereafter do exactly what its opponent had done on the previous move. This was despite the fact that TIT FOR TAT was known beforehand to be a good strategy, and a number of the programs submitted were attempted improvements on it. Analysis showed that neither the discipline of the author, the length of the program, nor its brevity could account for the result.

The first point which must be grasped about iterated Prisoner's Dilemma is that, given a sufficiently large number of interactions, *there can be no best strategy independent of the strategy of the other player.* To illustrate this, consider what one would do on meeting DEFECTOR (called "ALL D" in Axelrod's book), a strategy which defects every time (and which, for obvious reasons, was not entered in either tournament). If DEFECTOR will never cooperate, there is no point in doing anything except defect oneself, and so the best both players can do is repeatedly to win P, the pay-off for mutual defection. If playing against FRIEDMAN, however, a program submitted in the first tournament which begins with a cooperation but switches to permanent defection after just one defection by its opponent, one can do much better by cooperating every time, gaining both players, R, which, as we already know, is always greater than P.

Of course, many of the programs submitted were more sophisticated than this. In the case of the first tournament, what distinguished higher- from lower-scoring programs was that the former were the *nice* ones. Here "nice" means *not being the first to defect*. For instance, one of the most interesting programs entered in the first tournament was DOWNING (named after its author). This program monitored its opponent and tried to get away with defections, but would cooperate if the opponent responded by defecting itself. However, although DOWNING played an important part in the overall success of a number of other programs played against it, it made the mistake of beginning with a double defection and found itself among the lower-scoring "not nice" competitors. The nice rules, by contrast, did well in the tournament, largely by virtue of their interactions with one another and because there were enough of them to raise their individual scores. FRIEDMAN was the lowest-scoring of the nice programs, but, as we have already seen, also the most unforgiving, because it switches to permanent defection after only one defection by its opponent.

Unforgivingness was also the undoing of another interesting program entered in the first tournament, JOSS. This program is a sneaky version of TIT FOR TAT, which always defects after the other player does so, but cooperates only after the other player has done so with a 90 percent probability. In other words, every tenth time or so that TIT FOR TAT would mirror the cooperation of its opponent's previous move, JOSS would defect. To see the unfortunate consequence of this, consider what happens when JOSS plays TIT FOR TAT. Both players begin by cooperating, but after five moves JOSS sneaks in one of its occasional defections. TIT FOR TAT defects on the next move in accordance with its invariable rule, but JOSS cooperates because TIT FOR TAT did the time before. For the next 17 rounds both programs alternate, each mirroring the move of its opponent on the previous occasion. Eventually, on the twenty-fifth move, JOSS defects again instead of cooperating, but now both programs are locked into defection for the remainder of the match because this defection causes TIT FOR TAT to defect twice, causing JOSS to defect permanently (see table 1.2).

Although TIT FOR TAT won the first tournament, a number of programs entered in the second would have won. TIT FOR TWO TATS, a strategy which begins with a cooperation but defects only after two consecutive defections by its opponent is a case in point. This suggests that, even though the contestants in the first tournament knew about the strength of TIT FOR TAT-style strategies, "expert strategists from political science, sociology, economics, psychology, and mathematics made the systematic errors of being too competitive for their own good, not being forgiving enough, and being too pessimistic about the responsiveness of the other side."[1]

Following the first tournament, the results and their analysis were circulated widely, and a second tournament was held. This time sixty-two entries were submitted from six countries, and contestants ranged from a ten-year-old computer hobbyist to professors of computing, biology, and physics. Despite the success of TIT FOR TAT in the first round and the fact that entrants could submit any program, even one authored by someone else and entered by others in either tournament, only Anatol Rapoport, who entered TIT FOR TAT the first time, did so again. The sixty-three programs (including RANDOM) were paired in 3,969 different ways, and over a million rounds were played; once again, TIT FOR TAT won.

In a variant of the basic round robin tournament, an "evolutionary" or "ecological" variant was played, made possible, like the main tournament, only by the speed of modern computers. In this tournament, programs were "selected out" as they fell to the bottom of the score sheet, and their representation was weighted according to their past success. Once again, TIT FOR TAT emerged as the winner and went on winning by a steadily growing margin. Interestingly, one or two programs did not conform to the

Table 1.2   TIT FOR TAT versus JOSS

Move	Score	TIT FOR TAT	JOSS	Score
1–5	3			3
6	0			5
7	5			0
8	0			5
9	5			0
...	...	...	...	...
25	1			1
26–200	1			1

Scores after 200 moves: TIT FOR TAT 236, JOSS 241.

general pattern of gradual failure and deletion over the many hundreds of "generations" over which the tournament was played. One in particular, named HARRINGTON after its author, did well at first, staying up with the leaders. Then, at approximately the two-hundredth generation, it suddenly began to fail and soon became "extinct." Analysis showed that it was a program whose success relied on its ability to exploit programs inferior to itself. Once these dropped out, its own success ended, and this predatory program followed its victim to extinction.

How is the astonishing success of TIT FOR TAT in these tournaments to be explained, given that there can be no best strategy? Fundamentally, its success seems to rely on three principal attributes. First, it was notably *robust*. This means that *it could not be easily exploited and could hold its own against many different opponents.* For instance, if it meets DEFECTOR, TIT FOR TAT's strategy is to begin with a cooperation, but of course, DEFECTOR defects. So TIT FOR TAT loses the first game, gaining no points to DEFECTOR's 5. On the next move, TIT FOR TAT also defects because DEFECTOR did so the time before, and DEFECTOR goes on defecting. Both programs get 1 each, the pay-off for mutual defection, and this continues indefinitely. After 200 games TIT FOR TAT has scored 199 $(0 + (1 \times 199))$ and DEFECTOR has scored 204 $(5 + (1 \times 199))$. TIT FOR TAT loses, but not by a large margin (see table 1.3).

Table 1.3   TIT FOR TAT versus DEFECTOR

Move	Score	TIT FOR TAT	DEFECTOR	Score
1	0	🐟	⇧	5
2	1	⇧	⇧	1
3–200	1	⇧	⇧	1

Scores after 200 moves: TIT FOR TAT 199, DEFECTOR 204.

Significantly, TIT FOR TWO TATS, which, as we have already noted, would have won the first tournament had it been entered there, did much less well when it was entered in the second. Here it finished in twenty-fourth place, mainly because it was much less robust than TIT FOR TAT. In particular, it was vulnerable to programs run in the second tournament like TESTER. This was a variant of TIT FOR TAT which begins with an initial defection in order to test its opponent's response. If the other player defects, it apologizes by cooperating and plays tit for tat for the rest of the game. Otherwise, it cooperates on the second and third moves but defects every other move after that. When meeting TIT FOR TWO TATS, TESTER finds that the initial defection is tolerated and proceeds to exploit it mercilessly because, while defecting on every other move, it never defects twice in a row and so does not provoke the too-forgiving TIT FOR TWO TATS to defect itself. The consequence is that after 200 moves TIT FOR TWO TATS has only 300 points, whereas TESTER has 800 (see table 1.4).

Table 1.4   TIT FOR TWO TATS versus TESTER

Move	Score	TIT FOR TWO TATS	TESTER	Score
1	0			5
2	3			3
3	3			3
4	0			5
5	3			3
6	0			5
...	...	...	...	...
199	3			3
200	0			5

Scores after 200 moves: TIT FOR TWO TATS 300, TESTER 800.

TIT FOR TAT, by contrast, resists by means of immediate retaliation on a single defection by its opponent and is not vulnerable to TESTER which apologizes by cooperating and playing tit-for-tat for the rest of the game. Again, another sneaky strategy, aptly named TRANQUILIZER, exploited programs which were less robust than TIT FOR TAT by lulling its opponents into a false sense of security by appearing to be nice and cooperative, but slipping in unpredictable defections, albeit without pushing its luck too far.

Secondly, TIT FOR TAT, like the majority of winning programs in both tournaments was "nice," which, as we have already seen, means that it would never be the first to defect. To see how TIT FOR TAT could elicit cooperation by being initially cooperative itself, consider how it plays against the worst possible strategy of all (even worse than RANDOM), one which cooperates unconditionally, what we might call SUCKER. Against its opposite, DEFECTOR, which defects every time, SUCKER must score no points at all in any number of games, while DEFECTOR gets 5 points each time. However, if SUCKER meets TIT FOR TAT, both score R, the pay-off for mutual cooperation on the first round, and continue to do so indefinitely. The consequence is that, in 200 moves, SUCKER, the worst possible strategy, wins 600 points playing TIT FOR TAT, the outright winner, which is much more than the 204 points which DEFECTOR, the most predatory strategy, could manage against TIT FOR TAT! Again, if TIT FOR TAT meets TAT FOR TIT, a similar reciprocating strategy, but which is not "nice" in that it begins with a defection, each defects and cooperates alternately and wins 500 points in 200 games, which is also less than SUCKER got when it met TIT FOR TAT (see table 1.5).

Finally, and perhaps most important of all, TIT FOR TAT was ideally *reciprocating*: in other words, *it immediately and unfailingly rewarded cooperation with cooperation and defection with defection*. The latter is the secret of its robustness, the

Table 1.5   TIT FOR TAT versus TAT FOR TIT

Move	Score	TIT FOR TAT	TAT FOR TIT	Score
1	0	🐟	↑	5
2	5	↑	🐟	0
3	0	🐟	↑	5
...	...	...	...	...
200	5	↑	🐟	0

Scores after 200 moves: TIT FOR TAT 500, TAT FOR TIT 500.

former that of its niceness. This also gave it clarity and predictability. Unlike sneaky variants like JOSS, its decision rule was clear and simple, building confidence in its reliability. Astonishingly, its success was based on the fact that *it never won any more points than any competitor it played against.* "It won," as Axelrod points out, "not by doing better than any other player, but by eliciting cooperation from the other player. In this way TIT FOR TAT does well by promoting the mutual interest rather than by exploiting the other's weakness. A moral person could not do better."[2]

The rewards of reciprocity

At this point it is important to correct a common misunderstanding relating to the question of the role of reciprocity in establishing and maintaining cooperation. This is the view that the success of TIT FOR TAT represents a return to Old Testament-style "eye-for-an-eye" and "tooth-for-a-tooth" retaliation, the kind of thing which perpetuated the blood feud or vendetta and which, while it may sometimes encourage cooperation, also maintains violence, once started, in a self-perpetuating cycle.

A first observation might be that Old Testament-style retaliation is more a case of TAT FOR TIT than TIT FOR

TAT. This is because, as we saw earlier, TAT FOR TIT begins with a defection, rather than a cooperation as with TIT FOR TAT, and blood feuds and vendettas also begin with the equivalent of a defection since they aim to avenge some wrong or to return some insult. We also saw that TAT FOR TIT did less well against TIT FOR TAT than SUCKER did – an observation which in itself goes far towards correcting the view that TIT FOR TAT-style stragegies necessarily inflict harm because they reciprocate it just as they do cooperation (see above, pp. 47–8). The point is not that TIT FOR TAT was indiscriminately reciprocating, but that it was a "nice" strategy which began with a cooperation and encouraged further cooperation with it, punishing defection more as noncooperation than as an attack which had to be avenged.

A case which shows that reciprocity does not necessarily breed self-perpetuating cycles of violence is provided by one of the most dramatic real-life examples of the role of TIT FOR TAT-style reciprocity in establishing cooperation that one could wish to find. Historical accounts from World War I show that an astonishing live-and-let-live cooperation between the opposing armies emerged. A British officer who discovered it in a French sector recounted that it was maintained by virtue of the French only firing if fired on, but always returning two shots for every one fired at them. The fact that they retaliated with twice as much force as was directed at them shows that they were not following a crude eye-for-an-eye tactic, and the fact that their policy appeared to have established a surprising degree of peaceful cooperation suggests that it was not an example of blood feud or vendetta mentality.

On the contrary, what the French were doing in this sector was what TIT FOR TAT did in the tournaments: not merely hitting back for the sake of some primitive law of talion, but *reciprocating, not for its own sake, but in order to bring about continuing cooperation.* This is why the French responded to the Germans with twice as much force as the Germans

directed towards them. But this is also why the French were
never the first to shoot. What they were attempting to do
was to induce peaceful cooperation in the enemy by
punishing their belligerent defections. Here reciprocity did
not exist as an end in itself, but as a means to the end of
cooperation with the other side, and, essentially, this was
how TIT FOR TAT behaved in the tournaments. Its
immediate and discriminating reciprocity was added to its
other attribute: it was never the first to defect. TIT FOR
TAT was not the Prisoner's Dilemma equivalent of primitive
talion; it was a program which began by cooperating and
which succeeded by encouraging its partners to cooperate,
just as the French soldiers did with their two-for-one
retaliations but parallel reluctance to start any shooting.

The live-and-let-live system, whereby one side would
inflict damage on the other only if the other punished it,
relied in large part on the fact that trench warfare produced a
situation in which small, evenly matched units faced one
another for considerable periods of time. In other words, it
was an iterated Prisoner's Dilemma, comparable to my
wife's situation in the shared school run described earlier. As
Axelrod points out in his discussion, cooperation in this
situation was equivalent to avoiding damaging the enemy,
while defection meant shooting to kill.[3] In the short run, it
will always be preferable to do damage to the enemy
irrespective of what he is doing in these situations, because
damage inflicted now can weaken him in future conflicts.
This results in P, the pay-off for mutual defection, being
greater than S, that for unilateral restraint (represented in this
case by taking casualties without firing back). It also means
that T, the temptation to inflict casualties while the other side
does not do so, is greater than R, the pay-off for mutual
cooperation in not inflicting any casualties. Again, the pay-
off for mutual restraint, R, is greater than that for mutual
punishment, P, since the latter implies that both sides take
casualties in roughly equal numbers. Taken together, we
have the classical set of inequalities required for Prisoner's

Dilemma set out earlier: $T > R > P > S$ in the sense that killing all the enemy now is always better than mutual survival, which is in turn always better than mutual casualties, the latter always being preferable to destruction of our side without damage to the enemy. Finally, since both sides would prefer continuing mutual restraint with no casualties to random alternation of attack and restraint with inevitable casualties on both sides, R is likely to be greater than the average of T and S: that is, $R > (T + S)/2$.

The consequence was an astonishing and exquisite example of how cooperation can emerge spontaneously and be maintained, motivated purely by the self-interest of the cooperating parties. Like the triumph of TIT FOR TAT in Axelrod's computer tournaments, the emergence of the live-and-let-live system suggests that *cooperation can emerge spontaneously in a world of egoists motivated solely be self-interest.* Peaceable restraint, which originally began on both sides during mealtimes or bad weather, became extended to the point where open fraternization became possible and where on occasions soldiers on one side would actually apologize to the other for unintended breaks in the informal truce. Sniper or artillery fire, ostensibly intended to inflict damage on the other side, was in fact used as a means of maintaining the peace. Snipers would demonstrate their skill by repeatedly shooting at the same place on a wall to bore a neat hole, while artillery would show off their accuracy by hitting nonmilitary targets. These apparently ritualized expressions of the conflict served to maintain the overall pattern of cooperation because they showed that, if necessary, the other side could be provoked into telling retaliation.[4]

What is truly astonishing about this situation is the way in which it totally contradicts the widely held view that social order can emerge only if it is imposed or policed in some way. The cooperating parties involved in the live-and-let-live system were not subject to any external authority enforcing the peace. They did not belong to the same society and did not share a common language or set of values. They had not been socialized to cooperate with their enemies, and their cultural backgrounds did not promote such fraternization. On the contrary, the cooperating parties came from different cultural backgrounds, which were at the time dominated by appalling nationalistic jingoism. Most outstandingly of all, the fact that the participants in this astonishing display of international cooperation were subject to their respective High Commands and military disciplines, which were diametrically opposed to what they were doing, demonstrates that, even where external authority attempts to impose one kind of social order, order of a quite different kind can nevertheless emerge spontaneously, naturally, and with greater effect.

It is a sobering thought that the imposed social order so popular with conventional social thought was the very thing which worked against the live-and-let-live system and which eventually destroyed it. The institution of unexpected raids, often carried out by troops not familiar with the local conventions, did much to undermine the implicit truces which had come to dominate long tracts of the front line. These sudden and vicious defections roused the enemy to retaliate in kind and undermined the trust and mutual confidence which had earlier been built up so that eventually live-and-let-live was replaced by kill-or-be-killed.

Another aspect of the misunderstanding which sees the success of TIT FOR TAT as basically negative and retaliatory is found in the mistaken supposition that true reciprocity can occur only in the context of a *zero-sum game*. This is one in which anything gained by one side is a loss for the other (so that the sum of the minus points on the losing side and the plus points of the winner add up to zero). Most competitive games are like this, and so are all races in which competitors win or lose by their final placing. Just as the triumph of TIT FOR TAT demonstrated that cooperation can indeed emerge spontaneously in a world of egoists, so it also demonstrated that *cooperation is not a zero-sum game, but that, on the contrary, both parties can gain more by mutual cooperation than either can gain by unilateral defection.* An example almost as astonishingly counter-intuitive as the spontaneous live-and-let-live co-operation of World War I is provided by recent experience of tax deductions in both Britain and the USA.

On the face of it, nothing seems more obviously a zero-sum game than does taxation. After all, more for the government means less for the citizen and vice versa: the revenue service's income is the taxpayer's loss. Yet, contrary to superficial appearances, taxation has some profound similarities to a Prisoner's Dilemma. To see why this is so, we have to realize that paying and collecting taxes does involve free choices and is a form of cooperation.

If the government sets tax rates at 100 percent of citizens' income, taxpayers have absolutely no incentive to earn any income which could be taxed because they get nothing. However, if the tax rate is set at zero, the government gets nothing, and the citizens retain all their income. Actual tax rates are always somewhere between these two extremes, so that in reality the incentive to earn or not to earn and to pay or not to pay taxes varies. In Prisoner's Dilemma terms, earning money on which taxes must be paid can be seen as the citizens cooperating with the government. Contrariwise, avoiding paying tax by not earning or by withholding or evading taxes can be seen as defection on the part of taxpayers. Correspondingly, as far as government is concerned, reducing taxes can be seen as cooperating with the citizens, whereas increasing them can be seen as defecting.

Obviously, both taxpayers and government have an incentive to maximize their respective forms of income. Citizens would like to have all their income and pay no taxes, while government tax revenues would reach their absolute maximum where all pay was taken as tax. In other words, both parties rank T, the pay-off for unilateral defection, above R, that for mutual cooperation. This is because mutual cooperation implies both that citizens pay some taxes (and therefore have less than all their income to spend) *and* that government should take less than all the citizens' income in taxation. If T for both parties is 100 percent of income, R must therefore be somewhat less than this. However, R must also be more than P, the pay-off for mutual defection, because, if both parties defect as defined above, taxation will both be levied at a high proportion of citizens' income *and* be a small actual amount of money remitted to the government. This is because we have defined defection by the government as increased tax *rates* and because we have defined defection by taxpayers as reduced payment of *monies* to the government.

At first sight, this seems impossible. How could high tax rates produce little actual tax revenue? The answer is contained in my earlier observation about marginal tax rates. At punitive marginal rates of taxation there is a strong incentive not to pay the tax, and plenty of perfectly legal means usually exist which allow the citizen not to do so, the most obvious being not to earn that particular form of income in the first place. The consequence is that P, the pay-off for mutual defection by both taxpayers and tax collectors, is going to be more than S for both parties, which, as we have already seen, is zero, even though it is not likely to be anything like as much as R, what both would gain from moderate rates of taxation.

This establishes that, in terms of my definitions of cooperation and defection in taxation of income, $T > R > P > S$, as demanded by classical Prisoner's Dilemma. But is R, the pay-off for mutual cooperation, actually greater than the average of T and S? This amounts to asking if 50 percent marginal tax rates produce less income for both government and taxpayers than lower ones because T has been defined as 100 percent share of income for tax man or citizen and S as zero percent, producing an average of 50 percent. Recent experience certainly suggests that the pay-off to both government and citizens from marginal tax rates below an average of 50 percent may indeed be greater than the pay-off to both at or above 50 percent, at least for some groups of taxpayers. For example, in Great Britain in financial year 1978–9 the top rate of tax levied by the government was a punitive 83 percent of "earned" and a staggering 98 percent of "unearned" (investment) income. In that year the best-paid 10 percent of the population contributed 34 percent of all income tax collected. In 1989–90 the top rate of tax had fallen to 40 percent, but the top 10 percent of earners now contributed 42 percent of total income tax revenue in real terms. Exactly the same effects are found if one concentrates on the top 5 percent or 1 percent of income earners.[5] Not all taxpayers, it seems, are the passive victims of government policies; they can respond actively in various ways, depending on the degree of cooperation with their income-raising activities shown by governments and their revenue-collecting services.

This is an important point in itself because critics of this approach to the analysis of cooperation often claim that real-life cooperative relationships are seldom comparable to the abstract, mathematical model represented by iterated Prisoner's Dilemma. For instance, I can well imagine some readers objecting to the foregoing discussion of taxation on the grounds that many taxpayers in reality have little choice, because tax is deducted from their pay irrespective of their wishes, and that their freedom to choose among forms of income is very limited, if not completely absent in practice.

I will readily grant that my argument probably applies with special force at the extremes of income distribution. People with high incomes can and do afford legal, financial, and other opportunities which allow them to arrange their affairs to minimize their liability for tax. Again, at the bottom of the scale, marginal rates of taxation may be sensitively reflected in workers' readiness to earn taxable income, as opposed to accepting untaxed payments in cash, not working at all, and so on. Nevertheless, even people on middle incomes with apparently inescapable pay-as-you-earn tax liabilities show a surprising degree of resourcefulness in response to taxation. For instance, I know of a number of middle-income academics who could hardly consider another form of employment but who nevertheless have taken advantage of government grants for home improvement and tax concessions on mortgages to devote much time to buying, improving, and then reselling houses. Because proceeds from the sale of one's own home are tax-free in Britain, such incomes, although not realizable every year, can nevertheless be very considerable when they are earned. Indeed, one colleague openly admitted to me that he had costed the income-generating effect of spending time building, as opposed to writing to further his career, and had found that, given the taxation regime applicable at the time, it paid him to build rather than write! It seems that if governments can defect by raising taxes, citizens are not without means of defection of their own.

I have found that some people react to the argument above – not to mention the fact that tax cuts have produced big increases in tax revenues – with something of the consternation with which the military and political authorities greeted the live-and-let-live cooperation in World War I. My guess is that what really scandalizes them are the surprising, counter-intuitive truths which such examples reveal. These, as we have seen, are essentially two: first, that cooperation can and will emerge spontaneously in a world of egoists motivated solely by their self-interest and requires no necessary outside force or innate altruism either to begin or be maintained; second, that social cooperation is not necessarily a more-for-one-means-less-for-another affair, but that, on the contrary, cooperation can and does produce more for all those cooperating than any one could have realized by not cooperating. Finally, we have also seen that fundamental to both these effects is reciprocity, but not Old Testament, retaliatory reciprocity; rather, reciprocity which exists, not for its own sake, so much as to make cooperation possible, to maintain it in a stable equilibrium, and to guarantee worthwhile pay-offs for all the cooperators. As we shall now see, these are the insights which have definitively resolved the problem of altruism and provided the foundation for a new, scientific theory of social behavior.

The solution to the problem of altruism

Having looked closely at Axelrod's abstract analysis of cooperation, let us now go on to consider its relevance to our original problem: that of trying to understand how altruism in particular, and cooperation in general, could evolve by natural selection. To remind ourselves of this problem, we might recast the thought-experiment of the last chapter in terms of an iterated Prisoner's Dilemma.

Essentially, the apparent impossibility of any kind of altruism or cooperation being naturally selected boils down to two possible situations, both of which seem totally hostile to the evolution of cooperation. First, we may imagine a population of selfish organisms programmed by their genes to play DEFECTOR. A pure altruist playing SUCKER, who might emerge by mutation, cannot survive. If we accord degrees of reproductive success using the same pay-off values as before, we find that, in interactions with DEFECTORs, SUCKERs have zero reproductive success, while the DEFECTOR organisms reproduce five times. Clearly, this is the first version of the earlier thought-experiment, that in which a gene for altruism could not invade a population of selfish organisms.

Similarly, we saw that a popultion of pure altruists playing SUCKER could not resist the intrusion of DEFECTOR. As long as the population contains only SUCKER strategists, all is well, with each individual earning R on each interation. If R is set equal to three degrees of reproductive success, the population trebles each generation. However, if a mutant DEFECTOR strategist appears, it wins a reproductive success not of three but of five and begins to out-reproduce its victims. Before long, DEFECTOR is the dominant strategy in the population, and SUCKER an increasingly tiny minority, finding its reproductive success reduced to zero in repeated interactions with DEFECTOR.

Once again, we see that spontaneous evolution of cooperation seems an impossibility, at least as long as we limit ourselves to considerations of pure, indiscriminate cooperation on the one side and unremitting selfishness and defection on the other. But what of other strategies? Let us consider the evolutionary prospects for TIT FOR TAT in the conditions set out above.

At first sight, its prospects are not much better. We can see that if a single TIT FOR TAT mutant appears in a population of DEFECTORS, it is bound to cooperate the first time, so that the DEFECTOR it first encounters will see its reproductive success enhanced by a factor of five, and TIT FOR TAT will have no reproductive success at all. Thereafter it can do no more than defect itself, but does no worse in terms of reproductive success than DEFECTOR. Although the TIT FOR TAT organism holds its own after the first encounter and does not do any worse than any other, it seems that, once again, cooperation as such cannot evolve even though individuals who could cooperate, if given the chance, already exist in the population and even though we allow interactions between individuals to last long enough to make cooperation likely.

But now let us turn to the second situation: that in which a TIT FOR TAT mutant appears in a population dominated by SUCKERs. As we know, TIT FOR TAT will cooperate every time that a SUCKER cooperates with it. Its degree of reproductive success will be the same as that of SUCKER, both reproducing three times in each interaction. But now imagine that organisms playing DEFECTOR attempt to invade the mixed population of SUCKERs and TIT FOR TAT strategists. What will happen? As far as the SUCKERs are concerned, what happened last time: namely, reproductive success of zero, thanks to interaction with DEFECTORs. But what of TIT FOR TAT strategists?

At this point, something startling occurs. We notice that, as SUCKERs become a more and more negligible part of the population, thanks to the success of DEFECTORs, the latter tend increasingly to interact only with each other or with

TIT FOR TAT players, of whom, we assume, there must now be a good number. When a DEFECTOR meets a TIT FOR TAT organism, it benefits on the first interaction by scoring five in terms of reproductive success, but thereafter both score one, the pay-off for mutual defection. Any TIT FOR TAT individual surrounded by DEFECTORs can do no better than they, but, equally, does no worse after its first encounter. It continues to enjoy reproductive success of one, just like the DEFECTORs, and so does not become a shrinking proportion of the population, like the SUCKERs.

But let us assume that, just as a TIT FOR TAT individual can become grouped with DEFECTORs, so it can interact regularly with its fellows who are also playing TIT FOR TAT. Immediately we see that a TIT FOR TAT-playing group has greater reproductive success than a DEFECTOR-playing, or mixed, DEFECTOR versus TIT FOR TAT group. The TIT FOR TAT group finds its population growing by three times each generation as each individual scores R, the pay-off for mutual cooperation. DEFECTORs, by contrast, score only P, one point of reproductive success, in interactions with each other. The consequence is that the all-TIT FOR TAT population grows three times faster than the DEFECTORs, while the TIT FOR TAT players marooned among DEFECTORs hold their own.

If DEFECTORS try to invade local populations of TIT FOR TAT cooperators, they can make no real progress, because their pay-off drops after the initial interaction to no more than they would get with other DEFECTORs. TIT FOR TAT individuals, as we saw, hold their own after the initial encounter, even when outnumbered by DEFECTORS. Groups of TIT FOR TAT cooperators, by contrast, continue to enjoy high reproductive success as long as they interact sufficiently frequently with one another. Indeed, Axelrod comments that if interactions between individuals last the approximately 200 moves which were standard in the tournaments, only one interaction out of a thousand with a fellow TIT FOR TAT player is enough to invade a world of

DEFECTORs. Even with a median game length of only two moves, anything over a fifth of interactions with another TIT FOR TAT individual is enough for cooperation to emerge.[6]

The consequence of this is that, whereas a population of SUCKERs cannot resist invasion by DEFECTORs, and DEFECTORs cannot be invaded by SUCKERs, DE-FECTORs are vulnerable to invasion by TIT FOR TAT, at least if the latter does not come one at a time, but in a group. Correspondingly, TIT FOR TAT is not vulnerable to invasion by DEFECTOR to anything like the same extent that DEFECTOR is vulnerable to invasion by it.

Here, essentially, is the solution to the problem of altruism. In Axelrod's words, "Cooperation can emerge even in a world of unconditional defection. The development cannot take place if it is tried only by scattered individuals who have no chance to interact with each other. But cooperation can emerge from small clusters of discriminating individuals, as long as these individuals have even a small proportion of their interactions with each another."[7] In other words, we can advance the general proposition that *cooperation can evolve by natural selection if cooperators cooperate with other cooperators but defect against defectors.* Clearly, cooperating with other cooperators wins the gains of cooperation, while not cooperating with defectors protects against the costs of one-sided cooperations. Even though we have defined altruism as any behavior which promotes the reproductive success of the recipient at a cost to that of the altruist, we can now see that, in general terms, *altruism can evolve if altruists benefit other altruists but do not benefit non-altruists.*

2

Three Kinds of Cooperation

Kin altruism

So much for the abstract, general solution to the problem of altruism. Yet the question still remains of how, in the real world, such self-perpetuating clusters of cooperators could evolve. One possibility is that an individual organism, living in a world in which cooperation had not yet evolved, might possess a mutant gene for cooperation. Assuming that the costs of being cooperative did not lead to the gene's immediate distinction, it might pass that gene on to a number of its offspring. Since its offspring might be both spatially and temporally clustered, for instance by means of living in the same, quite small place, they might interact preferentially with one another, as kindred organisms often do. If the benefits of cooperation to the closely related organisms concerned outweighed any costs, altruistic cooperation could emerge. Indeed, in such circumstances as these, one can readily imagine that it would not even be necessary for the individuals concerned to gain a benefit; only the copy of the gene for self-sacrifice which they shared would need to be favored.

Let me give an example. Suppose that I am the original, altruistic mutant. Let us also assume that the altruism concerned is of the most extreme and unmistakable kind. Let us imagine that it is a gene for cooperation with others to the point that I will sacrifice my own life for theirs. As we have already seen, such quintessential altruism posed a major problem for Darwin and remains a paradigm of self-sacrifice however we look at it. But could such a thing evolve? Certainly it could. If I possess such a gene, and it causes me to sacrifice my life, saving three or more of my children from some life-threatening danger such as a predator, fire, or flood, the gene in question would have been selected, at least in this instance.

In order to understand why this is so, we must remind ourselves what natural selection essentially is. As we have already seen, it cannot ultimately select for personal health, well-being, or survival. If it did, there is absolutely no way in which suicidal self-sacrifice of the kind instanced here could be selected, because, by definition, such sacrifice radically curtails my survival, health, and well-being. As we saw, natural selection selects in exactly the same way that artificial selection selects: by bringing about differential reproductive success, so that some organisms leave more copies of their genes to future generations than do others. To see how this comes about in the example under consideration here, we need to remind ourselves about something else which we looked at briefly earlier: namely, the facts of genetic inheritance. In order fully to understand the kind of altruism in question here, we must go a little deeper into the matter.

As we saw in the first chapter, human beings, like most sexually reproducing organisms, are *diploid*. This means that they each have a double complement of chromosomes, in the human case, two sets of twenty-three, making forty-six in all. Suppose that I, as the original altruistic mutant, carry the gene for my altruism on one of my forty-six chromosomes. As we also saw earlier, Mendel's insight into the laws of inheritance showed that such a trait as this would not be half-inherited by all my offspring as some of Darwin's critics wrongly supposed, but would be wholly inherited by half of them.

To understand why this is so, we need only recall the facts of sexual reproduction in a diploid species like human beings

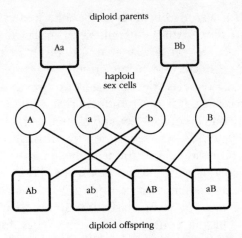

Figure 2.1 In the simplest possible case, diploid parents, each with one gene (A,B) on a paired chromosome (a,b), pass on a haploid sex cell to diploid offspring. Consequently each offspring must share exactly half its genes with each parent and, where large numbers of genes are present, will tend to share the same proportion with other offspring of the same parents.

(see figure 2.1). Although I have forty-six chromosomes in most of the cells in my body, my sex cells contain only one complete set, twenty-three in all. If the mutation for altruism is on one of my forty-six chromosomes, it can only be present in about half my sex cells, because there is an even chance that any particular sperm cell will get that particular gene, rather than the corresponding, but nonmutant, non-altruistic gene on the paired chromosome. Exactly the same would apply if I were female, except that the sex cell in question would be an ovum, rather than a sperm. The consequence is that my altruistic mutation can be inherited only, on average, by half my offspring. What this means for my gene for suicidal altruism on behalf of my near kin is that if I kill myself on behalf of three of my children, 100 percent of my genes have been lost, but 150 percent of them have been saved, because each of the children who survive because of my sacrifice has 50 percent of my genes. If we assume that my gene for altruism is likely to be inherited in comparable ratios, it follows that, overall, such a sacrifice might be "selected" in the sense that it might result in more of the genes for such sacrifice being present in future generations than would have been the case had I not possessed it (and of course, in reality, it is most unlikely that a single gene would be the only one involved – see above, pp. 8–9).

In other words, the evolution of altruism teaches the fundamental lesson about the true meaning of "fitness" that we saw also applied to certain aspects of sexual behavior. We can now see that in this example my personal health and well-being are not particularly important to my gene for altruism. On the contrary, this gene relies for its future existence on the fact that I am merely its temporary carrier. If, by sacrificing me, it can secure a greater representation for itself in the future, it will have been selected just like any other feature, including those which do further my personal health and well-being.

Taking such a "gene's eye" view of things may seem strange; but there are good reasons for arguing that it is a more realistic and objective way of looking at things than is our conventional, rather self-centered attitude to ourselves. It seems that ultimately our genes are not here to serve us so much as we are here to serve them; and if on occasion this means making sacrifices – perhaps even the ultimate one – then, from the individual gene's point of view, that is how it must be. Natural selection ultimately selects, we must not forget, not for human improvement, health, comfort, a balance of nature, advances in complexity, or whatever, but for one thing and one thing only: the reproductive success of genes for which organisms are nothing more than temporary packaging. Only this view of things makes sense of suicidal altruism from the point of view of natural selection without recourse to dubious concepts such as group selection.

Numerous studies of animal behavior strongly support the contention that this kind of altruism – what we might term *kin altruism* – is indeed strongly correlated with close genetic relatedness. Alarm calling, for instance, has been found to be more marked when kin are the beneficiaries; and suicidal self-sacrifice by soldier ants and termites occurs in the context of very high degrees of interrelatedness among the individuals concerned. So common is cooperation with kin among human beings that we have a special term for it – at least, when we disapprove of it. We call it "nepotism," meaning by that term favoritism towards relatives, usually at the expense of nonrelatives. Admittedly, not all acts of human suicidal – not to mention nonsuicidal – self-sacrifice are in fact for the benefit of kin, and so we must not assume that nepotism covers all acts of altruism, or that, even where it does apply, it does so in a simple, obvious manner.

However, the principle should also apply in reverse in the sense that, not only might acts of altruism on behalf of relatives be selected in the way I have suggested, but acts of selfishness which do harm to them might be discouraged for similar reasons. For instance, if I had a set of genes which made me preferentially sacrifice three of my offspring to save my own life (the exact reverse of my previous example), 100 percent of my genes for selfishness would be preserved, but 150 percent of those genes present in my children would have perished. Because more copies of the genes for selfishness would have been destroyed than were saved, we can conclude that natural selection for the reproductive success of individual genes would select *against* such selfish acts which are injurious to kin in precisely the same way that it selects *for* acts of altruism which benefit kin.

Putting the matter another way, we might say that natural selection could favor self-restraint where acts injurious to kin were concerned. Earlier I pointed out that self-restraint in regard to violent conflict seemed unlikely to evolve on an individualistic basis because selection would always seem to favor "free riders" who exploited others' self-restraint without showing any themselves (see above, pp. 35–6). But if a genetic predisposition to self-restraint benefited near relatives who had also inherited it, such a trait could be selected in exactly the same way as one for any other kind of self-sacrifice. Furthermore, there is considerable evidence that such is indeed the case where human beings are concerned.

If one makes the important decision between blood relatives and relatives by marriage, statistical evidence does appear to bear out the prediction that genetic relatives tend preferentially to avoid killing one another. For example, in 1972, 75 percent of all murders of relatives in the city of Detroit were by nonblood-related relations. In the same sample co-residents unrelated by blood were eleven times more likely to be murdered than genetic relatives living in the same household. If the frequency of interaction were the important factor in deciding who murdered whom, genetic relatives would be no different from any other category of persons with whom one had much to do. This would mean that two individuals who carried out a murder together would be just as likely to be related to one another as would victims to their killers. However, figures for collaborative murderers in Miami showed that 30 percent were relatives, as compared with 2 percent of murder victims being blood relatives of their murderers. Nor are such figures exceptional in any way. On the contrary, the degree of relatedness between collaborative killers is far higher than that between victim and killer in every society for which a relevant sample of cases is available, including tribal horticulturalists, medieval Englishmen, Mayan villagers, and urban Americans.[1]

These findings become particularly striking if we compare them with data regarding relatives who have no genetic tie, but a purely social one, such as step-parents. An interview study of middle-class step-parents in Cleveland, Ohio, who were not experiencing any particular kind of stress in relation to their step-children found that only 53 percent of step-fathers and 25 percent of step-mothers claimed any "parental feeling" towards their step-children, and fewer still professed to feel "love" for them. That such subjective reports are not misleading is suggested by the finding that an American child living with one or more substitute parents in 1976 was approximately a hundred times more likely to be fatally abused than was a child living with its natural parents. Nor are such figures a peculiarity of the United States; similar findings are reported for Canada and England. Indeed, a recent study concluded that "Stepparenthood *per se* remains the single most powerful risk factor for child abuse that has yet been identified."[2]

In many pre-industrial societies exactly the same pattern emerges, often even more unmistakably. A study of the Ache hunter-gatherers of Paraguay showed that children whose fathers lived until they were at least fifteen years of age had only a half of one percent chance of being killed after the age of two. However, if the father died before the child reached age fifteen, the chance of its dying after age two rose to a significant 9 percent. The reason appears to be that, with no father to reciprocate food on their behalf, other band members have no incentive to provide for them (see below, pp. 86–7). Thus, whereas 43 percent of children without a father had died by age fifteen, only 19 percent of those with both parents surviving had done so.[3] The Yanamamö and Tikopia are even more robust about it, and men who acquired wives with existing children expected them to kill their children – or, if they would not, did so themselves.

A study of 870 families based on local registers for the years 1668–1879 in the Ostfriesland region of North Germany reveals similar findings, but in much finer detail. Almost half of all children who had lost a parent died before they were fifteen years old, and one-quarter of them died within their first year of life if the parent had also died by then. However, the death of the mother carried a greater risk to the life of the child than did the death of the father, with children who had lost a mother showing almost one-and-a-half times greater risk of dying by age fifteen than those who had lost a father. Since women whose one and only firstborn child had died had a 17 percent better prospect of remarriage than those whose child survived, it is not surprising that the study found that children of widows died more frequently prior to a second marriage than did those of widowers. Firstborn offspring of widows were particularly at risk, while children who had lost a mother died relatively more frequently during the second marriage of their father. In other words, if children of remarrying mothers tended to die prior to the remarriage, those of remarrying fathers tended to die after it – a finding which casts an interesting light on the widely found myth of the evil step-mother. Overall, the study left little doubt that remarriage coincides with increased child mortality.[4]

But even if we accept that doing good or harm to others may be affected by genetic relatedness, a further difficulty seems to remain. For even if we adopt the view that organisms are little more than the temporary resting places of the genes which they carry, to be discarded when their function has been fulfilled, we can hardly expect such an explanation to apply also to the other extreme form of altruistic self-sacrifice, that in which the organism sacrifices not itself so much as its reproductive success. Surely, this is inexplicable. Having proposed that natural selection selects, ultimately, for reproductive success and for that alone, how can we also go on to claim that, in certain cases, it also selects for the complete absence of reproductive success seen in sterile worker castes among the social insects? In the earlier example in which I sacrificed myself for my children, my self-sacrifice could not have been selected if I had had no offspring to inherit my altruistic mutation, and so the selection of sterility seems impossible.

In that particular case, it would indeed seem so; but let us look at the situation more closely before jumping to such conclusions. Supposing that I did indeed have a gene which made me sterile but nevertheless possessed all the other behavioral proclivities for raising offspring. If I were part of a family group, the possibility exists that, lacking offspring of my own, I might instead adopt those of my relatives as recipients of my parental activities. If some of those near relatives also carried my gene for preferring to care for the offspring of relatives in place of one's own, that trait could be selected in just the same way that a gene for suicidal self-sacrifice might be selected. Yet, just as we had to go into genetics a little more closely in order to understand how that might come about, so we have to go into the question even further if we wish to comprehend the present example.

If I did indeed possess a gene for sterility, it is very hard to understand how it might be inherited, given that I could have no offspring if the gene in question were expressed rather than merely remaining latent in me like a recessive trait. Furthermore, it is obvious that if I shared the gene with all my relatives, and we were all sterile, there would be no possibility of it being selected. However, if the sterility were expressed in only some of my kin or expressed in me only some of the time, it could easily be selected. This is because I would also share 50 percent of the genes of near relatives, such as siblings.

To understand how this comes about, let us recall that in diploid inheritance I receive two complete sets of chromosomes, one from each parent. That makes my *degree of relatedness* to them (often represented by the symbol, r) one half, or 50 percent, just the same as it is with my offspring. My full brothers and sisters also receive one set of chromosomes each from my parents. However, because each of my parents has *two* sets of chromosomes themselves, the chances are that any full sibling of mine has received, on average, half the same genes from half of each parent's total complement of genes from which I received mine. This means that, on average, half of one of my sets of genes is the same as the half my sibling inherited from one of our joint parents. Our degree of relatedness through that parent is therefore one-quarter, or 25 percent. In other words, both I and my full sibling have, on average, half of half of our mother's or father's genes. Since the same is true for the other parent, our total relatedness via both parents, is $1/4 \times 2 = 1/2$, or 50 percent (see figure 2.1, p. 63).

We can now see that if I had a gene even for permanent and total sterility, it might still be selected if it made me contribute to the reproductive success of near relatives, such as my parents' other offspring. Since I am just as closely related to my full siblings as I would be to any potential offspring of my own ($r = \frac{1}{2}$ in both cases), any parental care I direct towards them might, in the absence of my own offspring, be just as useful to the genes which I share with them. If some of those genes threw up the occasional sterile uncle or aunt, it could be selected if the benefit it conferred exceeded any cost (such as that of the sterile relative's sterility).

In general, *an altruistic trait might be selected if it conferred more than twice the benefit (as compared to the cost to its copy in myself) on copies of itself present in any relative with whom I shared half my genes.* Exactly the same figures would apply in the event of my foregoing any reproduction of my own because a gene for sterility in me might nevertheless mean that my parents could produce at least two more offspring than they otherwise might have done, each of whom would have, on average, a 50 percent chance of carrying my gene for altruistic sterility. (Putting the matter in simple mathematical terms, we could conclude that kin altruism of this kind might be selected wherever $Br > C$, where B is the benefit to the reproductive success of the gene for altruism in its beneficiary, C the cost to the reproductive success of the gene for altruism in the altruist, and r, as we have already seen, the degree of genetic relatedness between altruist and beneficiary. To go back to my original example, we can see that this means that if I sacrifice my life for three of my offspring, C represents a 100 percent certainty of destruction of my gene for altruism, B represents saving three of my offspring, and $r = \frac{1}{2}$, means that there is a 50 percent chance that my gene for altruism will be present in any of them. Therefore, in terms of the probability of survival of my gene for altruism and substituting these numbers in the formula $Br > C$, the sum becomes: $\frac{1}{2} \times 3 > 1$. Correspondingly, a selfish trait which injured kin might be selected against if its cost to copies of itself in victims discounted by the degree of relatedness between actor and victim were more than its benefit to its copies in the actor: $Cr > B$.)

We can now see that, far from being paradoxical, altruism which reduces an organism's personal reproductive success is to be expected and derives from exactly the same determinants as those which dictate that organisms should on occasion be ready to sacrifice their own bodily health and welfare for their offspring. Even though such acts of altruism may reduce *personal* reproductive success, they may increase the *shared* reproductive success which copies of the gene for altruism may have in beneficiaries of the altruistic act. If we recall the fact that true, Darwinian "fitness" means reproductive success of the individual, we can see that what is usually termed *inclusive fitness* connotes the *reproductive success of individual genes, including that of identical copies which are present in near kin* and are, in this way, positively selected. Following the usage which we have adopted regarding the frequently misunderstood term *fitness*, we might suggest that *inclusive reproductive success* may be a preferable alternative.

In this case it will be readily seen that the "gene's eye" view is the correct one: namely, that whether in the same body or in a near relative, natural selection determines that the benefit to the reproductive success of individual genes should on occasion exceed the cost of sacrifices to personal health or reproductive success of particular organisms who carry them. In a manner which reveals the true character of natural selection with particular clarity, it seems that both the reproductive success and personal survival of some organisms should on some particularly revealing occasions be compromised in the interests of selection at its most fundamental: that of differential reproductive success at the level of the gene.

"Kin selection" confusions

At this point it is necessary to sound a note of caution and to spend some time discussing a number of common errors and confusions found in connection with what is often termed "kin selection." This term was coined on an analogy with Darwin's "sexual selection," and, if used analogously, is perfectly justifiable. However, it is important to notice that it can give rise to misunderstandings and mistakes.

By far the most important of these is the supposition that the term "kin selection" suggests that selection in this case is operating on a kin *group*. If this were so, it would be a clear case of group selection; but, in reality, the term implies nothing of the kind. On the contrary, the concept of kin altruism outlined in the previous section shows that behavior which seems to have evolved to benefit a group of kin can in fact be explained without recourse to the erroneous idea that selection can operate at the level of the group – or, at the very least, that of the family. Indeed, as we have seen, kin altruism can be much better explained as a consequence of the view that selection operates at the level of the individual gene. In order to understand why kin altruism does not imply any kind of group selection, but rather its contrary, let us look at what might, at first sight, seem to be cases which suggest that it does.

Two instances in particular seem to suggest that some kind of group selection is operative. The first is the case of the social insects. Here sterile worker and soldier castes apparently devote themselves selflessly to the interests of the greater society to which they belong and without which they would appear to be nothing: organisms which cannot live and which ostensibly could not reproduce without the whole. The second example is very similar, but even more extreme. This is the case of multicellular organisms, like human beings. Here we have no difficulty in thinking of selection operating on individual organisms, yet they themselves are composed of thousands, millions, or billions of individual cells which, in so far as the individual multicellular organism can be seen as subject to selection, are apparently subject to it *as a group*.

However tempting and seemingly obvious this portrayal of group selection may seem, consider an alternative way of looking at it. If we pursue the line of reasoning embarked upon in the last section, we could predict that reproductive altruism of the kind suggested there would be most likely to evolve under two circumstances. The first would be that in which parental care was critical for reproductive success, thereby necessitating the recruitment of helpers. The second would be that of organisms who are more closely related than usual who might evolve such altruism because of the very high degree to which they share genes. (Recalling the basic formula for kin altruism, $Br > C$, we might say that the need for help in parental care might increase the potential value of the *benefit*, B, compared with the *cost*, C, and high relatedness would raise the value of the factor which discounts the benefit relative to the cost, the *degree of relatedness*, r).

Both these expectations are fulfilled in the case of the *hymenoptera*, the bees, wasps, and ants. Eggs and larvae have to be cared for, fed, and transported, and a peculiarity of their genetic system means that the degree of relatedness can reach unusually high values. This is because the hymenoptera are not diploid, but *haplo-diploid*. What this means is that, while females are diploid in the normal way – that is, have two sets of chromosomes, one from each parent – males are *haploid* – meaning that they have only one set of chromosomes and only one parent. This is because, whereas females develop from eggs fertilized in the normal way, males develop from unfertilized eggs (see figure 2.2).

This strange arrangement has some intriguing consequences. For one thing, it means that a male cannot have any male offspring, because these develop from unfertilized eggs and therefore have no father. In other words, a male's sperm cells carry exactly the same set of genes that all his other cells do, and his daughters each receive exactly the same set of genes

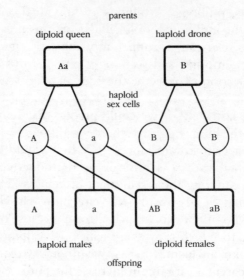

Figure 2.2 In the case of the social insects, males possess only one set of chromosomes and hatch from unfertilized eggs, whereas females, both sterile workers and fertile queens, hatch from eggs fertilized by a drone and have two sets of chromosomes. All females with a common father share one identical set of genes, making their relatedness through him one-half, and half of half of their mother's diploid genes, adding one-quarter to their average overall relatedness, making three-quarters, or 75 percent, in all.

from him, meaning that through him their shared relatedness amounts to one half of their total complement of genes. However, since their mother is diploid, daughters share, on average, only the normal quarter of their genes derived from this source (sisters inherit half of one half of their mother's genes, because she has a double set). Consequently, the total relatedness to one another of females who share the same parents is half via their common father and a quarter via their mother, making three-quarters in all (see figure 2.2, above).

If we were to take the counter-intuitive "gene's eye" view of things, rather than seeing it in terms of some kind of group selection of organisms sharing common genes, we might come to a remarkable conclusion. Looking at these figures, we might conclude that, from the point of view of any individual gene, it might be best if females in these species did not have any offspring of their own but, instead, helped their mother produce more sisters for them. This is because sisters with the same father share three-quarters of their genes, whereas a mother and daughter share only half. In other words, *females with the same parents are more closely related to each other than they would be to any offspring which they might have themselves.*

If selection selects for reproductive success of individual genes, it follows that a gene for sterility in some females could become established, because, paradoxically, it enhanced those females' reproductive success rather than reduced it. We should therefore expect to find castes of sterile female "helpers" farming their joint mother for sisters. The fact that this is exactly what we do find suggests that the "gene's eye" view is not a mere artifact of theory, but a fact of life in many haplo–diploid species. It also suggests that attempts to explain these facts by recourse to some form of kin-group selection is unnecessary at best and actually misleading at worst.

Exactly the same reasoning applies, albeit with even more force, to the other instance of apparent group selection suggested above, that of the selection of individual organisms. Although evidently not a case of group selection as such, because the individual is, by definition, an individual and not a member of any group, the fact that a multicellular organism is itself a group of cells suggests that selection of such individuals is implicitly a form of group selection, at least at the level of the cell. That it is no such thing is revealed by a consideration of the same factor that explains the kin altruism of insect societies: the degree of genetic relatedness. Because all the cells in multicellular organisms which carry genes carry the same genes, we can see that their degree of relatedness is one, the maximum possible. Because all cells contain the same genes, there is no internal conflict over allocation of resources, and because the sex cells are also related by the same factor of one to the body, or somatic, cells, the latter are content to let the gametes undertake reproduction on their behalf, just as worker bees might allow the queen bee to lay eggs on their behalf.

Indeed, we can use this same insight to give yet another compelling reason why we should not suppose that natural selection ultimately selects for the survival of individual organisms as such. This is because, if it did, it would be a covert form of group selection: one which treated the cells of a multicellular organism as a group selected for its own sake rather than for the reproductive success of the genes which it contains. The fact that cells which undergo a spontaneous genetic change for any reason often begin to proliferate at the expense of the rest – in the form of cancers, for instance – reminds us that it is the genetic identity of the cells in a multicellular organism which promote its survival as a unit, not group selection of cell societies which promote the survival of the organism they constitute, as Herbert Spencer and the Social Darwinists erroneously thought.

So pervasive has group-selectionist thinking become that it frequently reveals itself in other, similar errors. For instance, people sometimes think that "kin selection" means that a high degree of genetic relatedness is itself enough to "cause" altruism and social cooperation and, at the very least, must prevent competition and conflict. Furthermore, we have already seen that there is an element of truth in this and that relatedness does indeed seem to be a factor which rather markedly reduces risk of homicide among human beings. But nevertheless, as Robert Trivers wisely points out and our own experience of life ought to teach us, "close association permits more altruism but also throws individuals into closer competition, thus engendering more opportunities for selfishness."[5] In other words, genetic relatedness is a *necessary* condition for the evolution of kin altruism – how could we speak of *kin* altruism otherwise? – but not a *sufficient* one. It can also be a sufficient condition of conflict, as we shall see later when we consider the whole question of conflict and cooperation between parents and offspring (see below, pp. 188–207).

A simple logical proof exists which makes the situation unmistakable. Imagine a group of individuals with identical genes by common descent equally present in all of them. Is this in itself enough to make them cooperate? By no means – the gene codes for solitariness, causing individuals to disperse, never to interact again. As an example, consider the case of the cheetah. Genetic research suggests that all living cheetahs may be descended from as few as seven individuals who constituted a kind of genetic bottleneck through which the species passed. This means that there must have been a time when there were only a few cheetahs who were to be the ancestors of the modern population, and that the degree of relatedness among these inbred individuals was very high. Yet this does not seem to have made female cheetahs evolve to be cooperative hunters, as lions are. On the contrary, they are adapted to be solitary hunters, and this explains their incredible turns of speed, something which they need far more than lions do because a cheetah, usually hunting alone, must overtake its prey early in the chase if it is to have any success. High degrees of relatedness in the past have not, it seems, predisposed this species to cooperation in its prime adaptation.[6]

This example also suggests another common misunderstanding. Notice that I did *not* say that the present high degree of genetic similarity of cheetahs ought to predispose them to cooperation on the argument above; but it is sometimes argued that such ought to be the case. The fact that one can take a skin graft from any modern cheetah and find it accepted by the immune system of any other suggests to some people that degrees of *overall* genetic similarity are what matter. For instance, the fact that all human beings evidently share at least 90 percent of their total genome suggests that the degree of relatedness, r, as we have been calculating it here, applies only to the remaining 10 percent, and that the overall degree of relatedness is at least 90 percent. Again, the high degree of genetic similarity overall between chimpanzee and human genomes should mean that the degree to which human beings are related to chimpanzees overall is much more significant than the degree to which a child is related to its parents.

This fallacy, like the preceding one, fails to take account of the fact that it is not individuals' sharing of genes in general which matters, but rather the likelihood of their possessing an identical gene for altruism which counts. As we saw, mere genetic relatedness is not enough to account for altruism. On the contrary, if we recall my original examples and the thought-experiment discussed earlier, we will see that the problem is to explain how altruism can evolve in the first place. Even if it begins to evolve in a world of closely related individuals, we have to assume that all those individuals would act selfishly if not motivated to the contrary by genes for various kinds of altruistic sacrifice. Since the sacrifices concerned must ultimately benefit copies of those genes in the recipients, it follows that it is the common inheritance of those altruistic genes which is critical, not the general sharing of genes in the genome as a whole.

One can appreciate the same point by putting it the opposite way round. Suppose that an individual evolved who had a gene which motivated its possessor to perform acts of altruism based not on the probability that the recipient of their altruism possessed a copy of the same gene but on their overall, general genetic similarity. Such an individual's behavior would be almost indistinguishable from generalized, indiscriminate altruism. We might term it the "90 percent sucker" strategy if we conservatively assume an overall 90 percent similarity of genome. But, as we have already seen, SUCKER is the worst possible strategy for cooperation, and if a 90 percent TIT FOR TAT strategy like JOSS could not succeed in Axelrod's tournament, there is little hope for a 90 percent SUCKER in real life (see above, pp. 45–7). Inevitably, defectors would spring up all around it, and such an indiscriminate altruist would soon be exploited to extinction.

Finally, the term "kin selection" can lead people to think that it is something exactly analogous to what "sexual selection" is often taken to be: namely, a special, extra kind of selection alongside natural selection, which selects for altruism, just as sexual selection "selects" for sex. The difficulty here is that, as we shall now see, there are two other fundamental forms of altruism which the term "kin selection" cannot possibly cover because neither has any necessary relationship with kinship. It is to a consideration of these that we must now turn.

Reciprocal altruism

Another consideration worth bearing in mind when observing that genetic relatedness is not in itself enough to explain altruism is the fact that many altruistic relationships, often of a very stable, long-term kind, have evolved between organisms which are not in the least closely related but are members of different species or even of different kingdoms. An example of the latter is the astonishing relationship which exists between certain species of ant and acacia trees. The fact that one of the parties is an animal and the other a plant has not prevented an altruistic relationship developing between them. On the acacia's side, this is represented by food, specially and exclusively produced for the benefit of the ants which colonize its thorns and branches; on that of the ant, by a readiness both to defend the tree by attacking any animal which attempts to browse off it and to cut down saplings which begin to grow within an area which would make them potential competitors to the tree.

However, the best example of altruistic relationships between totally unrelated organisms is provided by *cleaners*. Many animals, particularly fairly large ones, are vulnerable to attack and infestation by micro-organisms, tics or whatever, and have to be periodically cleansed of these parasites. Many small- or medium-sized mammals can perform this task themselves; for example, primates like monkeys and apes have hands with which to do it. But even in their case, much grooming is mutual, being performed as a service by one animal for another, which then usually reciprocates. However, many fish and some of the larger reptiles and mammals are simply too large or the wrong shape to be able to clean themselves. Such cases often give rise to relationships with other species who specialize in the cleaning function.

In the case of fish at least forty-five species of specialized cleaners are known, and there are almost certainly more. A number of shrimps and crabs have also taken up cleaning as a way of life. Sometimes the relationship is casual and fleeting, sometimes much more intensive and long-term. In many cases the large fish which is to be cleaned adopts unusual behavior to indicate that it is ready for the service. Typically, cleaners, who are, of course, usually smaller than their clients, will find that the latter stop dead in the water, suppress all movements except those necessary for station keeping, and hold their mouths and gill slits wide open, ready for them to enter. Some fish which have laterally narrow but deep and rounded body shapes adopt a bizarre posture, inclined at 45 degrees to their normal vertical orientation. Others change color. For their part, the cleaners advertise themselves by distinctive stripes and coloration and by performing ritualized movements. Some are territorial, setting up shop at a particular place where they can always be found, their clients sometimes patiently lining up while they await their turn for attention.

These displays, along with the territoriality of some cleaners, become explicable the moment we take notice that genuine acts of altruism are involved. Large fish which hang stationary in the water, their mouths and gill cavities wide open, inviting other fish to swim inside, are taking something of a risk, as are even more evidently the cleaners who venture into those open mouths. At any moment a client could simply close its mouth and swallow a cleaner. The fact that they do not normally do this but, on the contrary, signal to cleaners inside their mouth cavities when they are about to depart (if, for instance, a predator suddenly appears) shows that the client is at real pains to protect its cleaner. Again, the fact that the cleaners do not take advantage of their clients to attack them suggests that they too are making a sacrifice for the benefit of the client.

In terms of our original, basic definition of "altruism" which defines it as any act which promotes the reproductive success of the recipient at a cost to that of the altruist, we can see that genuine acts of altruism are involved: the clients are quite evidently promoting the reproductive success of the cleaners by providing them with meals and are reducing their own by foregoing one – the cleaner. The cleaners, for their part, are promoting the reproductive success of the clients by removing life-endangering detritus and parasites from them while foregoing the opportunity for an even more nourishing meal – some part of the client.

This is dramatized and brought sharply into focus by the realization that, besides genuine cleaners, like the cleaner wrasse, false cleaners also exist. Similar in size, shape, and coloration (despite being a blenny and not a wrasse), the false cleaner even mimics the strange, head-down "dance" which the true cleaner uses to advertise to its clients. The false cleaner is so-called because it does not make the sacrifice that true cleaners do in not exploiting the client. On the contrary, having lured a large fish into vulnerable immobility, it darts in and takes a big bite out of it before disappearing, never to be seen again!

It is the reality of the altruism involved, along with the very real possibility of deception and injury, which explains the elaborate displays, the ritualized behavior, and the territoriality often found in genuine cleaning relationships. True cleaners need to make their special adaptation completely clear and fully convincing to their clients for their own safety;

and clients need to be just as sure for their own. Characteristic, unmistakable markings and special, out-of-the-way displays and behavior all work to that effect. So does territoriality, because clients who have been satisfactorily serviced once at any particular cleaning station can usually expect to find the same reliable service offered by the same cleaners on subsequent occasions. False cleaners, by contrast, do not hang around!

If we conclude that acts of genuine altruism as defined here are involved in the activities of cleaners and their clients, it is obvious that they cannot be covered by the theory of kin altruism, because the two parties are not in the least closely related and in fact belong to quite different species. They are examples of a second fundamental form of altruism, what we may term *reciprocal altruism*. The parties to reciprocally altruistic interactions do not need to be related because, ideally, the cost and benefit to the gene for such altruism should be at the very least equal. Furthermore, the benefit should be almost immediate. In the case of the cleaner wrasse and its clients, both parties benefit at the same time; but, perhaps even more important, both parties benefit more than they would if they did not cooperate. Experiments in which large fish are deprived of cleaners show that they sicken quickly; and cleaners deprived of clients find life harder trying to compete as just another small fish.

The situation is in fact a classic Prisoner's Dilemma, with T being the temptation to act as a false cleaner in the cleaner's case and the temptation to eat the cleaner in the client's; S, the sucker's pay-off, obviously being to be eaten, either whole in the case of the cleaner or in part in that of the client; R, the pay-off for mutual cooperation, honest cleaning and no cheating by the client; P, the pay-off for mutual defection, the situation clients face if they eat all their cleaners and end up full but uncleaned and what cleaners would face if they all became false cleaners and destroyed their own business in so doing. Evidently $T > R > P > S$ and $R > (T + S)/2$, since random alterations between cooperation and defection on

both sides would be so damaging that the cleaning relationship would hardly be likely to develop very far and certainly
could not become the dependable, localized and advertised
service that it often is. In other words, the two stable
strategies in iterated Prisoner's Dilemma, TIT FOR TAT
and DEFECTOR, are both seen, with true cleaners playing
the former and false cleaners the latter. The fact that true
cleaners are in the majority attests to the fundamental fact
already noted that the mutual pay-off for cooperation is
greater in the long run than that for selfish defection.
Evidently, in cases of reciprocal altruism, reciprocity pays.

But how could this get started? As we saw at the beginning
of this chapter, kin altruism could be expected to evolve
because the cooperating altruists would naturally be grouped
together by the fact of kinship and so cooperation could
evolve and become stable, even in a world of defectors. If we
now propose a form of altruistic cooperation which does not
rely on kinship, how can we suppose that it could evolve? If
this general question seems awkward, consider the even
greater problems involved in trying to explain how genes for
reciprocal altruism could have evolved in cleaners and their
clients simultaneously! Surely, this strains credulity. Indeed,
it has even been claimed that so incredible is this coincidence
that it discredits Darwinian evolution as a whole and argues
for life having originated in outer space!

How anyone could think the latter a less incredible
hypothesis amazes me, but the fact remains that it is not
difficult to propose how behavior of this kind could have
evolved, evolution from space notwithstanding. Although
we shall probably never know the actual means by which
cleaning symbioses of the kind discussed here first evolved, it
is by no means far-fetched to suppose that, for instance, the
ancestors of today's cleaner shrimps or wrasses were, like
many other brightly colored and gaudily striped organisms,
poisonous, or at least bad-tasting. This might have made fish
intent on eating them have second thoughts and could have
been the means by which the cleaning symbiosis began to

evolve. Fish who found that the ancestors of the cleaners were not good to eat but tolerated them inside their mouths for a while might have achieved slightly greater reproductive success than others not so disposed, thanks to the beneficial effects on them of what the cleaner ancestors did eat while they were there.

But however that may be – and we shall probably never know for sure – the fact remains that this kind of explanation points, in all probability, to the right general conditions whereby reciprocal altruism could evolve among unrelated organisms. This is nothing more than the supposition that chance factors (like being a small, inedible fish) might draw otherwise unrelated organisms into sufficient proximity for mutual cooperation to evolve (such as being inside the mouth of a larger fish who could benefit by being relieved of matter which might constitute a meal for the intruder). In this kind of way mutual cooperation could easily begin and, once established, could gradually become more elaborate and pronounced, perhaps especially if, again as in the cleaner case, the activities of defectors as well as cooperators contributed to the development of the critical behaviors.

Although I have used examples featuring reciprocity between partners of different species up to this point, there is clearly no reason why reciprocal altruism should not evolve among those of the same species. On the contrary, we might predict that the greater likelihood of similar organisms being found together in similar places and conditions would be especially likely to encourage the evolution of reciprocity. An exquisite example is provided by vampire bats. Despite their unprepossessing way of earning a living, sucking blood from sleeping animals under cover of darkness, vampire bats are highly cooperative and frequently regurgitate a meal for the benefit of a bat who has not eaten. As flying mammals, bats cannot afford to carry too much weight in the form of fat, and field studies show that bats who do not procure a meal will starve to death in just three days. The studies also show that about 30 percent of immature bats under two years of age and 7 percent of mature ones fail to feed in any given night and that failure appears to be random. Computer predictions show that the annual mortality rate for adults in the absence of food sharing would be about 82 percent. In fact, it has been measured at 24 percent, which suggests that foodsharing has been strongly selected and plays a critical role in vampire bat survival.

Although bats frequently regurgitate meals to partners to whom they are related, making their sacrifice an instance of kin, rather than reciprocal, altruism, a significant number of regurgitations are made to partners unrelated to the donor. However, although unrelated, such partners must associate with each other for at least 60 percent of the time at the roost and, as theory would predict, tend to regurgitate exclusively to one another. Although this means that overall the cost and the benefit of the relationship to both partners should tend to equalize, we may also predict that reciprocating individuals would be discriminating, not merely about *whom* they benefit, but *when* they provide the benefit. This is because two partners who have both fed would gain nothing by regurgitating to one another; neither would two partners who were starving to an equal extent be able to aid one another. However, a bat who has just fed loses less than twelve hours of life expectancy by regurgitating to a starving partner and still has two nights of hunting left before starving itself. Such individuals should only regurgitate a meal to a partner who will gain a greater benefit from it than they would themselves, and this is exactly what the field study showed. Returning bats replete with blood might lose six hours of life expectancy by regurgitating it to a starving partner with only twelve hours left, but the latter would gain a further eighteen hours as a result. Observation also showed that partners saved by such timely aid were much more likely to repay the original donor than chance association would predict.[7]

Those who may have thought that only human beings were capable of making discriminating sacrifices to unrelated individuals whose need was greater than theirs are clearly contradicted by these Draculas of the animal world; but reciprocal altruism remains a prime human adaptation. A study of the Ache hunter-gatherers of Paraguay reveals a situation closely comparable to that of the vampire bats. Although women gather mainly vegetable matter, Ache men provide 87 percent of the calories consumed when a group is hunting in the forest, and 60 percent of all game is taken during cooperative, rather than individual, hunts. The game in question mostly comprises small and medium-sized items such as monkeys, armadillos, and deer. Significantly, a man is unlikely to eat much of a kill which he has made himself, and no kinship bias was found in the kill's distribution. This suggests that the large element of chance in hunting operates in the same way that it does in the case of vampire bats and encourages reciprocity. Since no individual man can guarantee to feed himself and his family all the time because of the element of chance related to both quantity and quality of available game, men appear to exchange kills on the basis that the hunter seldom consumes much of what he himself has caught but instead relies on the catches of others. However, better hunters did have more surviving offspring than poor hunters and also enjoyed more extramarital liaisons. As we saw earlier, children whose fathers lived until they were fifteen years of age had much better chances of survival thanks to the fact that they had a hunter to reciprocate food on their behalf (see above, p. 67).[8]

These facts strongly suggest that Ache hunting is a mainly cooperative affair and that reciprocal, rather than kin, altruism underlies it. Evidently hunters reciprocate, not merely each other, but each other's families and, as the finding regarding extramarital affairs indicates, enjoy more than merely economic benefits. Since human beings appear to have led a hunter-gatherer way of life throughout at least 98 percent of the million-odd years they have existed on earth, it follows that the Ache case may not be unrepresentative of primal human adaptations. Indeed, recently published observations of cooperative hunting by chimpanzees in a forest habitat suggest that the hunting style of the Ache may go back to the very beginnings of human evolution and that reciprocal altruism in the sharing of kills is fundamental to it.[9] Finally, we shall see later that, where human psychological adaptations are concerned, reciprocal altruism in particular, and cooperation and defection in general, seem to have left deep and lasting impressions on the human mind and behavior (see below pp. 99–117).

Induced altruism

Having discussed kin and reciprocal altruism, it might be thought that we had exhausted the subject and that no further fundamental forms of altruism remain, at least if we ignore for the moment the whole question of the alleged existence of a separate, "pure" or "ascetic" form of human altruism. However, this is not the case. A third – and almost certainly final – form of altruism does indeed exist and, as we shall see here but more particularly in the next chapter, has much to do with the question of allegedly "pure" altruism in human beings and so cannot be ignored in any discussion of the problem which puts human affairs at the center of the stage.

In order to see how this comes about, let us go back to the false cleaner and his hapless client. In my discussion of the cleaning relationships I claimed that both sides make sacrifices which, in terms of our objective, behavioral definition of altruism, are genuinely altruistic. That of the client consists in not trying to eat the cleaner and in laying itself open to possible attack by adopting the characteristic, immobile, open attitude necessary for cleaning. So far, so good. But now a strange conclusion emerges. To reach it, we must ask ourselves if the client who is exploited by a false cleaner has performed an altruistic act. The answer is inescapable – it must be "yes!" This is because the client does exactly what it would do if it were being serviced by a genuine cleaner; and if the behavior of not eating the cleaner and laying itself open to attack is altruistic in that case, then it must be in the case of the client who meets a false cleaner, since exactly the same behavior is involved.

Of course, at this point some readers may balk and say that the whole use of the term "altruism" is misleading here and that it should only be applied to human altruism. But this does not help. Even in this case, the outcome is the same. If I donate a sum of money to charity with due care and attention that it will reach its proper destination, most would agree that I have performed an act of altruism. But if my cheque, unbeknown to me, is stolen or misdirected so that it benefits some criminal who is exploiting the charity, the altruistic nature of my act is not affected. I still gave the money altruistically. Admittedly, I did not intend that outcome, but if the desirable nature of outcomes defined altruism, much apparent human altruism would have to be redefined, and a major element of subjectivity would enter our definition, because we could argue endlessly about whether, for instance, international aid really helps the Third World, whether providing formula and feeding bottles saves more babies than it kills, and so on.

It seems that if we are to avoid these endless and irresolvable controversies, we must stick to our original concept of altruism as something defined by its benefit to the reproductive success of the recipient at a cost to that of the altruist. Looked at from this objective point of view, it seems that we must conclude that if clients serviced by true cleaners have performed an altruistic act, those exploited by false cleaners must also have done so. The fact that they would not have wished to have done so had they known what the outcome would be makes no difference, and, even if it did, who would feel secure in attributing such human attributes as forethought and intention to a fish? Unless we are to take the view that "altruism" is a term which can be properly applied only to human behavior, we must conclude that in the case we are discussing an act of altruism was indeed performed. Furthermore, to those who might take the view that all talk of "altruism" outside human behavior is illegitimate, I would merely ask for patience, for, as we shall see in the next chapter, there are interesting conclusions to be drawn on this very issue where purely human behavior is concerned!

Perhaps we would like to say that in this case the altruism concerned in the client's behavior, although real, is negligible and marginal. Perhaps. But consider the following, parallel case. Cuckoos, as we know, lay their eggs in other birds' nests. Other birds who raise cuckoos as if they were their own offspring must have performed an act of altruism on the basis of our definition above. Indeed, since cuckoos never raise their own offspring and so could have no reproductive success without the help of others, we can conclude absolutely without hesitation that the hosts perform notable acts of altruism where cuckoos are concerned. Furthermore, when one considers the considerable labor and effort involved in raising cuckoos – which are sometimes much larger than the host parents' own offspring – we can hardly dismiss it as an insignificant kind of altruism.

But what kind of altruism is involved here? It is not kin altruism, as it would be if exactly the same behaviors were being directed towards the host's own offspring. Similarly, the altruism of the duped client in the case of the false cleaner can hardly be reciprocal, since there is no reciprocation. We could perhaps say that these were instances of pathological, parasitized, or manipulated kin or reciprocal altruism, and indeed they are. Nevertheless, so important is the type of altruism involved here and so distinct in some of its characteristics that at least two authors have thought it important enough independently to invent the same term for it: namely, *induced altruism*.[10] Induced altruism can be defined as *any behavior which promotes the reproductive success of the recipient at a cost to that of the altruist without any consequent benefit to the altruist or its kin.* In other words, it is *a form of altruism which does not qualify as kin or reciprocal altruism and is* consequently one which must be carefully distinguished from them.

Fundamentally, there can be only four types of social action involving two persons. An action can be *altruistic* if the actor pays and the recipient benefits, *reciprocal* if both benefit, *selfish* if only the actor benefits and the recipient pays a cost, and *spiteful* if both actor and recipient pay and neither benefits. A glance at table 2.1 shows that this exhausts the possibilities of this way of looking at things.

Table 2.1   Four fundamental social behaviors

	ACTOR	RECIPIENT
Altruism	*pays*	*benefits*
Selfishness	*benefits*	*pays*
Reciprocity	*benefits*	*benefits*
Spite	*pays*	*pays*

Spite benefits no one and so does not enter into our consideration of altruism, because neither does anyone make any sacrifice. *Reciprocity* and *altruism* correspond to reciprocal and kin altruism discussed above. Selfishness, equally, has nothing to do with altruism. But what of the recipient's or victim's point of view? According to the table above, the entries under *altruism* and *selfishness* are mirror images of one another: in both cases someone pays and someone benefits, but the roles are reversed. In altruism the actor pays; the consequence of selfishness is that the recipient pays. The recipient would also qualify under our definition above as having performed an act of altruism, albeit induced.

This becomes unmistakably clear if we map the idea onto our previous consideration of Prisoner's Dilemma. Clearly, *spite* corresponds to both actor and recipient defecting, *reciprocity* to both cooperating, *selfishness* to the one who benefits by defecting when the other cooperates, implying

Table 2.2 Social behaviors as a Prisoner's Dilemma

| | *ACTOR* | |
	cooperates	*defects*
cooperates	**reciprocity** *reciprocity*	**altruism** *selfishness*
RECIPIENT		
defects	**selfishness** *altruism*	**spite** *spite*

that *altruism* must apply to the converse: one cooperating when the other defects (see table 2.2).

If all this seems a little abstract and far from reality, let us look at some examples from real life. Ants are paradigms of altruism, as we have already seen. But not all ants labor for their kin. Some are captured and put to work as slaves in the colonies of other species. Yet the tasks which the slaves perform are exactly the same as those they would perform in their own colony and for the benefit of their own kin. Again, if ants can be induced to act altruistically for the benefit of other ants, they can also be induced to comparable behavior sometimes by organisms more distantly related to them. For example, the liver fluke which infects sheep requires ants to act as a "vector" for it in the following way. Liver fluke cells get into ants from sheep droppings on the grass and penetrate their central nervous systems. There, they induce the ant to climb to the tip of a blade of grass and wait to be eaten by a sheep, thereby transporting the liver fluke back into its principal host. When soldier ants sacrifice themselves for their colonies, they are performing archetypical acts of kin altruism; when they sacrifice themselves for liver flukes, they must also be acting altruistically, but their altruism is induced by a parasite which infects them, not programmed by their genes.

Indeed, all cases of parasitism and even predation qualify as instances of induced altruism, because, in the last analysis, one organism has made a sacrifice for another and received no compensating benefit to itself (which would make its altruism reciprocal) or its genes (which would make it a case of kin altruism). The fact that organisms wholly killed and eaten by predators or only partly injured and consumed by parasites have no wish to perform the acts in question cannot figure in our deliberations if it is the objective consequences of the behavior which qualifies it as altruistic.

From all this we can reach a further conclusion: *that induced altruism describes selfishness of the actor from the point of view of the victim.* Admittedly, this is not the usual way we look at selfishness, and even if we do notice the sacrifice of the victims of parasites, predators, and other exploiters, we seldom think of it in terms of the altruism of their victims. Nevertheless, the fact remains that a selfish gain by one implies a personal loss by another, and we have no right to ignore the cost to the one in favor of the benefit to the other if an objective approach to social behavior is our aim. On the contrary, it seems a virtue of modern evolutionary theory that it reminds us of the interests of individuals even when those concerned are not the aggressors but their victims and confronts us with their sacrifice even when it is one extorted from them by deceit, error, or superior power. Perhaps it is because we seldom take an objective, evolutionary, and evenhanded view of selfishness and its consequences for others that this way of looking at things seems so strange, and perhaps we ought to ask ourselves why this is so. After all, who benefits from such a view of selfishness? Hardly the exploiter, it seems.

One final point remains to be made which will serve as an introduction to the chapter which follows and which we will take up again in its final part. This is the observation that the characterization of induced altruism which I gave just now sees it essentially as a form of self-sacrifice from which the altruist benefits in no way whatsoever. The birds who raise cuckoos believing them to be their own offspring have absolutely no self-interest in doing so; nor do ants who obligingly wait at the tip of grass blades to be eaten by sheep gain the slightest advantage to themselves or their kind by such behavior. In this, objective respect they are exactly like human altruists of the purest kind, whose lack of personal or family benefit proves the probity of their altruism and is the foundation of their claim to transcend self-interest in the interest of others. Yet, if there is no fundamental difference as far as objective cost and benefit is concerned between an animal that is duped, coerced, or manipulated into benefiting another with no advantage to itself or its genes and a human altruist who makes sacrifices for others out of an intention to act altruistically, then the difference can lie only in the subjective motivation of the human altruist. As we saw earlier in considering the paradox of gifts which are stolen, it is the intention of giving which distinguishes a genuine gift from something which is merely taken. If I give someone something with a conscious intention that they should have it, I have performed an act of altruism; but if someone gets something from me which I did not intend them to have, they have committed an act of misappropriation. Objectively, both gift giving and being robbed may be the same, but in intention they are unmistakably different.

When thinking of our own altruistic acts, we readily realize the force of this distinction. We know that it is the purity of our intention which guarantees our altruism and makes it genuine. But the moment we think of the altruism of others, we notice the fundamental problem. Politicians, to quote just one example, routinely claim to act in the public interest, but does that necessarily mean that voters should always believe them? Are saints of all religions really always righteous? And can parents who conscientiously claim to act in their children's best interests really be trusted to do so on all occasions? We shall see later that the answer to the last question must be a rigorous "no," at least if the central theorems of modern evolutionary biology are to be believed (see below, pp. 188–97). In the next chapter we will consider the fundamental issues which lie at the heart of these questions: free will, self-consciousness, and the psychology of morality and human altruism.

3

Evolution, Cooperation, and Human Nature

The issue of free will

In the past many have claimed that it is the existence of human freedom and particularly the presumed fact of rational self-consciousness (or, at the very least, some measure of self-awareness of the consequences of our actions) which make us different from animals – moral beings with the ability to choose, rather than mere creatures prevailed upon by biological drives. On the issue of free will, the evolutionary considerations relating to altruistic behavior which we have already reviewed would suggest some degree of agreement as well as some disagreement with these views, depending on just how the term "free will" is understood. If we take an extreme view of it and regard the term as implying total emancipation from any kind of restraint, so that human behavior is regarded as totally unconstrained, uncaused, unpredictable, and so on, we would obviously have to be skeptical. This is because behavior can powerfully promote or reduce reproductive success and is often affected by heritable factors. Indeed, even our commonsense understanding of everyday life suggests that if someone asks me, for example, whether I want tea or coffee to drink, my choice will be conditioned by some kind of pre-existing preference. Only in encounters with totally trivial or completely new and unknown factors are people likely to be totally unconcerned about their final choice.

In terms of an evolutionary understanding of behavior, it seems most unlikely that natural selection would produce human beings with behavioral tendencies to totally unpredictable, indiscriminate behavior. This would be the biological equivalent of RANDOM in Axelrod's tournament, a program which, it will be recalled, did very nearly worst of all (see above, p. 44). A moment's reflection is enough to show that if human choices were genuinely unconstrained by anything whatsoever, they could not be limited by factors affecting ultimate reproductive success. If final reproductive success were affected – accidentally, as it were – we could predict that if choice were genuinely free, as many outcomes would promote reproductive success as would hinder it, leaving the overall effect exactly zero. It would take only the appearance of a mutant with a predisposition to favor more reproductively successful behavior for natural selection to take a hand and alter human nature in the direction of promoting ultimate reproductive success, thereby destroying true freedom in this sense.

However, if by the term "free will" we mean something less extreme and more equivalent to "self-determination" or "free choice," the situation is quite different. This is the sense in which I am free to choose tea or coffee because the outcome is entirely left to me, rather than being decided without reference to my preferences and desires by someone or something else. If selection operates on individuals and their individual genes, selection should select for individual choice and free will in the sense of self-determination and self-referential choice. Of course, this does not mean that choice, if left to the self, will be totally unconstrained. On the contrary, evolutionary, heritable constraints will probably exist; but they will work in the context of self-interest rather than in that of the interests of some group or large assemblage of individuals. An example may make the situation clear.

Designers of mobile probes intended to explore the surface of other planets realized early on that such vehicles would have to be able to control themselves to a large extent, simply because it was impractical to think that they could be operated remotely from the earth. This is because signals would take time to transmit to and receive from the vehicle, which might be on Mars, for instance. If a vehicle attempted to cross Martian terrain under remote control from earth, it would have to move very slowly in order to allow for the two-way transmission time of several minutes before it could be stopped so as to avoid an obstacle, for example. Under these conditions it would obviously be much better if the vehicle could make its own decisions about whether to go over or round an obstacle it encountered.

It seems that evolution acts in a comparable way. Natural selection cannot constantly intervene in an organism's activity to dictate the best behavior for the situation. On the contrary, all that natural selection can do is to provide general parameters likely to enhance ultimate reproductive success, like "Avoid fire or deep water," and leave it to the organism to decide for itself what to do if it encounters fire or flood. Indeed, since natural selection could hardly foresee each and every specific instance in which fire or flood might endanger ultimate reproductive success, it is in exactly the same position as earthbound designers of vehicles to explore distant planets. It must allow the individual considerable latitude to react to the given circumstances and cannot possibly control every action.

This is presumably why organisms capable of self-propelled movement and self-selected action are normally found to have nervous systems. These systems fulfill the same function that on-board computers would in planetary probes designed to dispense with total reliance on remote control from earth. What is normally called Artificial Intelligence is specifically designed to deal with such situations, and naturally evolved intelligence presumably arose in the same kind of way. Indeed, we could predict that the greater the degree to which natural selection has allowed free will in the sense of self-determination to an organism, the greater the development of the nervous system or its equivalent. Here it is tempting to see human beings as a kind of pinnacle of evolution and to conclude that because we have some of the largest brains found in nature, we therefore have some of the widest choice.

However, we would also have to notice that natural selection could be expected to set limits to such free choice and that most kinds of choice would in fact have some kinds of constraint placed on them. The restraints in question could be predicted to be those which, in most cases and all other things being equal, would promote ultimate reproductive success rather than reduce it. Furthermore, the constraints in question could normally be expected to be of a generalized nature, since the more complex the choices facing an organism, the less specific naturally selected determinants like reflex actions could normally be. In the case of human behavior, for example, we might suggest that Sigmund Freud's (1856–1939) discovery of what he termed *the pleasure principle* might be an important instance of this general effect. This is because it does not seem far-fetched to suggest that most of the things which most people experience as pleasurable are things which, in the conditions in which our species originally evolved, might have tended to maximize the ultimate reproductive success of those who found them so. Examples such as pleasure in eating, being warm and comfortable, and having sex make immediate sense from this point of view. It is self-evident that a person who felt no pleasure in these things – or, in the most extreme case, actually enjoyed starvation, cold, discomfort, and abstinence – would probably leave fewer offspring than one who did enjoy them. Admittedly, it is conceivable that pleasure could sometimes lower, rather than enhance, ultimate reproductive success, but it is important not to fall into the trap of crude adaptationism and commit the error of imagining that normally adaptive traits must always be adaptive. In the real world it is most unlikely that this should be so and quite unnecessary that it should be so for our argument. All we need to assume is that, *on average and in most circumstances and all other things being equal*, pleasure would probably tend to promote behaviors more conducive to ultimate reproductive success than the contrary in the circumstances in which human beings originally evolved.

Pain, by contrast, can be imagined to have evolved in exactly the same way, but by means of exactly the opposite feelings. Burns, abrasions, and incisions to the body are presumably registered as painful because they tend to be associated with things which reduce, rather than enhance, reproductive success. Of course, this does not mean that a human being cannot overcome pain and its purely psychological equivalent, anxiety, if they are sufficiently strongly motivated to do so, any more than that we must assume that pleasure can always succeed in motivating behavior. However, it is not unreasonable to hold that overall and on average, human freedom to choose is broadly constrained by subjective human sensations of pleasure, pain, satisfaction, and anxiety. Nor is it unreasonable to assume that, even though free in the sense of self-determining, human action may be constrained by such subjective factors because those who possessed the genes which produced them left more descendants than those who did not.

Furthermore, we might also expect that the degree of pain or pleasure involved might generally reflect the importance of the associated behaviors to ultimate reproductive success. For example, if I have to choose between tea or coffee, I may usually choose coffee, but having to drink tea would not be very much less pleasurable. Presumably this is because the significance for my ultimate reproductive success of drinking one as opposed to the other may be very slight, so that a strong stimulus has not been selected. However, the intensely pleasurable sensations which accompany some activities – notably sexual ones – may be explicable in terms of their crucial bearing on reproductive success, and much the same may apply to pain and anxiety. It is understandable that I might be only slightly apprehensive about a cat jumping onto my lap, but much more concerned if it were a tiger.

Such naturally selected parameters as pain and pleasure (and I am by no means assuming that these are the only ones, or even the most important) would correspond to the parameters laid down by an Artificial Intelligence program for a planetary probe, within which it was free to make its own choices. Here "free" would mean, not necessarily able to do anything, but free in the sense of being allowed some considerable latitude of choice within certain definite limits. This is the sense in which we might imagine that human freedom had been naturally selected.

The question of consciousness

Following on from the previous discussion of free will and biological determination, we must now go one step further and consider another, related attribute of human nature: the question of consciousness. We might begin with the observation that it would be a serious mistake to imagine that *self-determination* in the sense just discussed and subjective, human *self-consciousness* were one and the same thing. A bee may be free, in the sense just described, to select blossoms from which to harvest nectar, but it can hardly be assumed to "know" what it is doing in the same way that a human being gathering something might know what they were doing. Furthermore, it would also be wrong to imagine that everything a human being does which is self-determined involves self-consciousness. On the contrary, many of our actions, although wholly self-determined and therefore "free" in the sense in which we are now understanding the term, are also almost totally unconscious. For example, running quickly downstairs involves a complex choreography of movements of legs, feet, and arms, but it is one of which we are normally quite unconscious. Indeed, efforts to monitor such actions consciously invariably result in one having to slow down, merely to allow time to think about what one is doing, and can be distinctly dangerous if conscious control turns out to be too slow or too inept to manage the situation. As a less dangerous, if painful, experiment which teaches the same lesson, I suggest paying conscious attention to the no less intricately choreographed movements of one's tongue while chewing. We seldom notice how expert we are at avoiding our own teeth until we perform an experiment such as this, which almost always results in biting oneself. Yet the tongue normally avoids the teeth without any need of conscious intent on the part of the person chewing, so automatic and wholly instinctive are its operations. It seems that even so humble an organ as a tongue can be self-determining to the point that it does not require conscious direction by the managers of our mental mission control to carry out its functions. Indeed, in the light of these considerations one might even begin to wonder why we are conscious at all and to ask exactly in what human consciousness consists, given that it is not the critical element in carrying out many complex actions.

Few matters have received so much attention, yet with such meager results, as the question of human consciousness. So it is all the more surprising that the very insights we are pursuing in regard to human nature, altruism, and self-determination should cast a revolutionary new light on the matter. To understand how this can come about, let us return to the considerations left at the end of the last chapter relating to reciprocity, deception, and the induction of altruism in others to the benefit of the inducer.

Up to this point, I have concentrated on the problem of altruism: the cost to the altruist of an act which benefits another. I have taken the benefit to the recipient of the altruistic act as self-evident and not in need of further comment. However, it is clear that, in the case of reciprocal altruism especially, any net benefit of an altruistic interaction to one side rather than the other must, by definition, promote the reproductive success of the beneficiary and therefore be selected. Of course, selection will also operate on the other partner, whose reproductive success will be promoted by not letting the exploiter get away with it. Situations of this kind, with major selective advantages operating on both sides of a competitive encounter – because this is what reciprocal altruism becomes, if it is not truly reciprocal – often result in what students of animal behavior call "arms races." The term seems apt, because any advantage won by one side will tend to provide the selective pressure for a compensating advance by the other, and so on in a self-perpetuating cycle of competition.

In other words, cheating pays; but it also pays to detect cheats. Now comes the surprising insight, first clearly formulated in evolutionary theory by Robert Trivers: in an organism with complex reciprocal interactions and a psychology to go with it, like a human being, the best, least detectable cheats are likely to be those *who do not themselves know that they are cheating.* This is because successful cheating will encourage successful detection of cheats in terms of a psychological arms race related to deception in reciprocal interactions. However, if some cheats become so subtle in their cheating that even they do not know that they are doing it, the chances of others knowing are correspondingly less. Furthermore, not knowing that one is cheating allows one to make completely sincere denials of deception and much more convincing claims to the contrary. An analogy will make the situation clear.

Let us suppose that the management of a large organization has been involved in some dishonesty or disreputable behavior which it cannot afford to admit. If it wishes to keep the matter a complete secret, it might prefer that its public relations department does not know the truth. This is because those called upon to make public statements will have to do so in the full glare of publicity and public scrutiny. Anyone knowing one thing, but saying another, might give the truth away by mistake, such as by means of a slip of the tongue, a nervous appearance, or an ambiguous remark. All in all, it is much better that those exposed in this way should not know anything, so that they can make their disclaimers and assertions in complete sincerity. After all, if the information department does not know about it, what chance does the public have?

It seems that human consciousness may have evolved in part to fulfill a comparable public relations function. Where creditable, unimpeachable motives and behavior are concerned, it will pay consciousness to know what it is doing and why. It will then be able to say, "I am doing this or that for you, for the public good, for others' benefit," and so on. If it is true, so much the better. However, this facility also means that if an individual is doing something which is in their own interests by being deceptive, it can also function to hide the truth and to make disclaimers – disclaimers and deceptions which will be all the more impenetrable to others because totally sincere, at least insofar as consciousness knows the truth. Like the public relations department which has not been told the truth, consciousness can lie and deceive without the slightest awareness that it is doing so.

If this is the case, we might wonder about the fate of the truth. Is it totally expunged, so that it could never be recalled? In fact, this is most unlikely. To see why, let me suggest another analogy, based on an actual incident. Some years ago, a round-the-world single-handed sailing race was held, with the competitors circumnavigating the globe in the Southern Ocean. Once in the South Atlantic from the starting line off Western Europe, the sailors would not see land again until near the finish. One of the leading contenders had some bad luck early on and arrived in the South Atlantic with little chance of winning. Here he hit upon a clever deception. Reasoning that no one would see him until he was back in nearby waters after the circumnavigation of the Southern Ocean and that no radio transmission by him could be used to fix his true position, he gave up the attempt to follow the leaders and instead circled where he was, waiting for them to return. Then he rejoined the race and crossed the finishing line first. In order to do this, he had to falsify his official log to show that he had in fact completed the prescribed course, even though he had not done so. However – and this is the point relevant to this discussion – in order to carry out the fraud, he had to start a second, true log in order to navigate at all. It was the eventual discovery of this second, hidden log which finally unmasked him as the cheat he was.

Essentially, the point is that such deception as this should be something which is contrived for the benefit of others, not for oneself – or, rather, it should be something which might benefit oneself only if it succeeds in misleading others. It need not be intended, first and foremost, to mislead oneself. To revert to my earlier analogy, it is obvious that there too it is not in the interests of the top management of an organization involved in deceiving the public not to know exactly what it is doing. Only the public relations people need critically to be kept in ignorance; senior management needs to know what kinds of frauds it is undertaking and what the facts are, just as the cheat in the sailing race needed to know where he was in reality in order to be able to mislead others about where he ought to be and to be able to rejoin the race again at the right time and place.

Similarly with mental deception. If what is being hidden is one's self-interest, it is not in one's self-interest to be completely unaware of it, just consciously unaware. The point is not to deny being a defector by actually playing SUCKER, but to appear to play SUCKER while actually defecting. In other words, we might predict the existence of a second kind of consciousness, analogous to the true log in the analogy above, in which consciously disavowed information was stored, inaccessible to consciousness, but present to oneself in some other kind of consciousness. In the words of Robert Trivers, "The mind must be structured in a very complex fashion, repeatedly split into public and private portions, with complicated interactions between the subsections."[1]

If this were merely an interesting speculation, unsupported

by any kind of observations or factual evidence, we might be justified in noting it but leaving it at that. In fact, of course, an entire field of psychology, psychoanalysis, has grown up, based on Sigmund Freud's discovery of exactly what this line of reasoning predicts: a stratified human consciousness, with an unconscious to which publicly unavowable thoughts, wishes, and motives have been consigned by an active force of conscious repudiation which Freud called *repression*. Unlike the everyday, pre-Freudian, purely descriptive meaning of "unconscious" as anything of which we are not presently aware, both psychoanalysis and recent evolutionary biology suggest a further, more specific, and essentially *dynamic* concept: that of the unconscious as not merely not conscious, but that which is *actively and involuntarily excluded from consciousness*. Like Freud's concept of the unconscious, that of recent Darwinism is both dynamic in this sense and *topographical* in the sense that it envisages consciousness as stratified and subdivided.[2]

This is all the more significant an observation because it is noteworthy that, just as key Darwinian concepts like "selection" and "fitness" were extensively misunderstood and misconstrued for the best part of a hundred years after Darwin first put forward his theory, so comparable Freudian concepts like "repression" have been widely mistaken and misapplied. In particular, "repression" has been conceived more on a Marxist, political model, where it connotes something done to one by another for the other's benefit, rather than in Freud's original sense of something which one does to oneself for one's own good reasons.[3] Unlike the Marxist model of repression which is so frequently confused with the psychoanalytic one, both recent evolutionary and Freudian insights into repression see it as concerned primarily with *self-deception* and involved essentially with language. As Trivers observes:

> With the advent of language in the human lineage, the possibilities for deception and self-deception were

greatly enlarged. If language permits the communication of much more detailed and extensive information – concerning, for example, events distant in space and time – then it both permits and encourages the communication of much more detailed and extensive misinformation. A portion of the brain devoted to verbal functions must become specialized for the manufacture and maintenance of falsehoods. This will require biased perceptions, biased memory, and biased logic; and these processes are ideally kept unconscious.[4]

One of the principal reasons for this is that words are cheap and by no means the same thing as actions. So whereas we would predict that a person's actions might reflect their hidden, cryptic self-interest much more reliably, their words could be expected to be much more misleading. The fact that a door-to-door salesman begins by denying that he wants to sell you anything does not mean that you may not end up buying something nevertheless! Since words are cheap, self-deception with regard to them is likely to be particularly easy and will seldom carry the costs involved in action, so that conscious, verbal thought can be expected to be particularly misleading where reality is concerned. But this is only true from the point of view of the person practicing the self-deception. For others, the costs of deception can be very great indeed. In reciprocal interactions, for example, self-deception which successfully deceives others may rebound to the self-deceiver's benefit, but will cost those on whom it is practiced an equal but opposite amount. Here we encounter the other side of the arms race and another important aspect of the evolution of human consciousness.

Quite apart from self-deception, self-consciousness understood as a self-referential ability may have evolved as a counter to deception as practiced by others and would essentially be the introspective equivalent of the naturally selected ability for self-determination within broad limits which we reviewed in the previous section. In this respect it is worth recalling that if Freud discovered repression and the dynamic unconscious, he also found that repressions could be undone and the inner conflicts occasioned by them resolved by means of making such self-deceptions *conscious*. Here the implied ability to overcome self-deception could be understood as likely to have evolved as a means of dealing with the consequences to oneself of the self-deceptions of others. In short, if self-deception pays, an ability to see through the self-deceptions of others would certainly pay those likely to be the victims of the self-deceivers.

This is all the more likely because such self-deceptions are by no means necessarily undetectable merely because they are unconscious. In a famous passage addressing this point Freud remarked:

> When I set myself the task of bringing to light what human beings keep hidden within them . . . I thought the task was a harder one than it really is. He that has eyes to see and ears to hear may convince himself that no mortal can keep a secret. If his lips are silent, he chatters with his finger-tips; betrayal oozes out of him at every pore.[5]

Recent laboratory research has shown how true this is. Subjects set the task of detecting false stories from true ones told to them improved their ability to detect the untrue ones the more they could see of the storyteller, with the result that those who only listened did less well than those who could also see the storyteller's face, while those who could see the upper half of the storyteller's body did less well than those who could see it all.[6] (Perhaps this is why, when broadcasting of the sessions of the House of Commons began, only radio was admitted at first and then, when television followed, only head-and-shoulders shots of speakers were permitted!)

Indeed, it has even been suggested that the human capacity for enjoying music originated this way, with sensitivity to pitch, rhythm, and tone evolving long before music itself because of the importance of these parameters in assessing the true value of something being heard.[7] Furthermore, the purely aesthetic enjoyment which seems to come from recognizing harmonious patterns in visual, verbal, and auditory communications and which underlies our appreciation of the visual arts, theater, literature, and music may originate in the essential harmony which exists in communications which are truthful, as opposed to deceitful. This is because a truthful expression, gesture, or speech would not usually be one in which there was much internal contradiction or discrepancy between the ostensible message and the underlying signals. Deceptions might be revealed by such disharmonies and internal dissonances, however, causing us to feel unease at them, but to appreciate the contrary.

Being able to look at oneself as if one were someone else would be especially valuable in the circumstances we are considering, because one of the greatest dangers implicit in self-deception is the extent to which some of one's own self-deceptions might increase one's vulnerability to the self-deceptions being practiced on one by others. An example would be a belief in bargains and the kind of deceptions likely to be practiced by those selling cheap goods; another would be self-deceptions feeding religious credulity which others could exploit to their benefit, for instance by seeming more religious than oneself. However, if one could occasionally stand back from oneself and see oneself as if with others' eyes, one might realize that one was deceiving oneself and that one's self-interest was no longer being served.

In conclusion, if self-deceiving lies can be an effective weapon against truth, then self-revealing truth can be just as effective against lies – especially the lies of others to which one is vulnerable. To the extent that this is true, human consciousness may well have evolved to be just as much a weapon against self-deceit as it evidently is in its service. If human beings like to portray themselves as passionate pursuers of the truth, the truth is likely to be that this is because they are such habitual practitioners of lies that they do not always know when they are lying. For us, consciousness may be in large part both a lie to ourselves and an insight into the lies of others.

Altruism and identification

The lesson of the previous section was that, in the human case at least, we can envisage situations in which individuals both defect and cooperate at one and the same time – or, to be more exact, *seem* to cooperate at a conscious level while actually defecting at an unconscious one. As we noticed, this is most likely in the context of reciprocal altruism, where any inequity in reciprocation pays the partner who gains as a result. However, not all altruistic interactions are reciprocal, nor are defection and deceit the only important factors in human cooperation. In particular, we might ask if there is any psychological adaptation comparable to divided consciousness specific to kin altruism as such and to cooperation, rather than defection, as a motive.

If we think back to the earlier arguments relating to the evolution of cooperation, we will recall that cooperation can evolve and become stable on a tit-for-tat basis, one in which altruists cooperate with other altruists but defect against defectors. We will also recall that tit-for-tat strategists must be localized in some way, or at least interact with one another sufficiently often to benefit from their cooperative propensity. We saw that a natural basis for this is the fact of kinship. But how could such behavior evolve in the human case? Three requirements must be met:

1 Individuals must be able to identify their kin or other cooperators.
2 They must be motivated to cooperate with kin or others who cooperate with them.
3 They must be motivated not to cooperate with noncooperators.

Let us take the first requirement: *identification of kin and other cooperators*. Fundamental to such kin recognition as this is the basic process known as *phenotypic matching*. An animal's *phenotype* is the totality of its anatomy, physiology, and behavior. The phenotype is the expression of the genome or *genotype* in interaction with the environment, a term which, as we have already seen, describes the totality of the individual's genes, both expressed and latent, in the total complement of the chromosomes. Comparison of phenotypes is therefore an indirect way of comparing genotypes. Similarity of appearance, behavior, or, in many cases, smell is probably the best evidence an individual can have of deeper, genetic similarities to its kin. In the human case the great elaboration of behavior and psychology and apparent reduced reliance on chemical clues like smell suggests that phenotypic matching may be carried out at an unconscious, psychological level. In the small-scale societies centered round groups of kin thought to be characteristic of human origins, a positive comparison with the self would tend to confirm genetic similarity, and the extent of the similarity would reflect the degree of genetic relatedness, reaching a maximum in identical twins ($r = 1$). Another name for such positive self-matching is *identification*. In other words, identification of kin may have evolved originally in human beings by means of the psychological mechanism of identification, because in primal, hunter-gatherer societies in which most groups would consist of small-scale networks of kin *the extent to which individuals could identify with others would be an indirect index of the degree of relatedness between them.*

This is important, because psychological studies of altruism suggest that identification with the recipient of the altruistic act is a key factor, even though it is often unconscious. For instance, a classic psychoanalytic study by Anna Freud (1895–1982) demonstrated that such identifications are facilitated by *projections* of self-interest onto the individual identified with. A woman who as a child had wanted beautiful clothes and many children had lived an intense fantasy-life fulfilling these wishes and had become so insistent about these urgent desires that she had annoyed her elders; nevertheless she grew up to be a rather shabby and inconspicuous spinster. However, closer inspection showed that these infantile wishes had not vanished, but had merely undergone an extraordinary transformation. They had been projected onto others, so that, while careless of her own clothes, she took a lively interest in those of her friends; without children of her own, she became a governess and took a great delight in the children of others; unmarried herself, she was an enthusiastic matchmaker, having many love-affairs confided to her. "She gratified her instincts by sharing in the gratification of others, employing for this purpose the mechanisms of projection and identification."[8]

On the face of it, this finding, like many Freudian findings, seems counter to evolutionary logic. After all, if an individual forgoes her own gratification in life – still more, her own reproduction – in the interests of others to whom she is in no way closely related, her sacrifices look much more like pure, unalloyed altruism than they do the kin or reciprocal versions discussed earlier. Whereas these latter forms of altruism can indeed be selected, because they ultimately or indirectly promote the reproductive success of the altruism in question, the form of altruism described by Anna Freud seems to violate all the principles of evolution and carry no means by which it could contribute to its own reproductive success.

But such Freudian insights as these seem much less incomprehensible once we set them against their probable evolutionary background. If we interpret this example of apparently pure altruism in terms of the suggestion which I made just now regarding identification and phenotypic matching, we can readily see that a psychological mechanism which today might result in altruistic sacrifices being made for individuals to whom the altruist might not be related almost certainly would have been made on behalf of kin in primal human societies. This would have been simply because such societies are known to have been much smaller and much more significantly based on kinship than most modern urban ones are. As I remarked above, in such primal conditions there is a very good chance that the extent to which others reminded one of oneself would have been a direct and reliable guide to one's degree of genetic relatedness to them; consequently, projection of one's own wishes onto such individuals would almost always have followed pathways already marked out by the pattern of inheritance of one's genes. Psychological projection would follow genetic propagation guided by psychological phenotypic matching, the identification *of* kin by identification *with* them.

What I am proposing, then, is that the solution to the particular problem of altruism posed by modern psychological case studies like that instanced above is likely to be the same as that provided by the concept of kin altruism for many forms of self-sacrifice in general. Indeed, even in the cases cited by Anna Freud, one cannot help noticing that many of the most immediate beneficiaries of the altruism described were indeed kin – siblings, parents, or their children. As we saw in more general terms earlier, the forgoing of reproduction is not inexplicable by Darwinism if the net result is enhanced reproductive success of the genetic determinants of such self-sacrifice, and such may be the ultimate, evolutionary foundations of the behavior described by Anna Freud.

Identification may be the means, then, by which individuals satisfy the first of our conditions set out above, the requirement to identify kin as the preferential recipients of acts of altruism. But this is probably only the most specific expression of the more general effect which we have already seen underlies the evolution of cooperation. Whether by means of kin recognition of other individuals who have inherited identical genes for altruism by common descent or not, altruism can evolve and become a stable strategy on a tit-for-tat basis if cooperators preferentially cooperate with other cooperators. We have also seen that genetic relatedness is not a necessary condition for such altruistic cooperation if the form of altruism in question is what we earlier termed *reciprocal* altruism. In the case of reciprocity, it is not a question of making a sacrifice which benefits copies of the gene for such sacrifice in the recipient to an extent greater than the cost in the altruist, but one of securing a return benefit which compensates for the cost of the benefit to the other participant. In this case altruism is exchanged: a benefit provided is compensated for by a benefit returned.

TIT FOR TAT achieved this feat by *mimicry*: it simply copied the move the other player had just made. If the previous move was cooperative, it cooperated; if defecting, it defected; and, as we saw, this was the key to its success. Obviously, mimicry is a major factor in identification: one tends to behave like the persons with whom one identifies. At an even more basic level it may be that a tendency to identify with others mobilizes human tit-for-tat behavior in the sense that identification may be the means by which an individual mimics the cooperative behavior of others by cooperating on their own part. Here the identification would be not so much with the individual cooperator but with the latter's cooperation. In this case, projection would probably play little or no role since there is no question of genetic relatedness; but the mimicking aspect of identification would probably be enhanced.

Nevertheless, the distinction is to some extent purely theoretical. In practice, much human reciprocal altruism occurs in contexts defined by kinship, and we have already seen that in principle kin altruism is founded on a deeper kind of mutual cooperation revealed by the success of TIT FOR TAT. Because tit-for-tat cooperators must interact with one another sufficiently often to gain the benefits of cooperation, grouping by genetic descent is likely to form a common and widespread basis for preferential interaction with other cooperators, even if it is unlikely to be an exclusive one. In either case, it seems that identification mobilizes and controls the expression of human altruism by confirming relatedness and facilitating projection of what would otherwise be self-interest in the case of kin altruism and by confirming cooperation with the cooperation of other cooperators in the case of reciprocal altruism.

But what of our final requirement set out above, that which requires individuals to discriminate against non-cooperators? Is there some corresponding psychological adaptation to identification and projection here too? If the foregoing line of argument were to be relied on, we would certainly expect there to be such a thing, quite probably, closely allied to the other mechanisms. The sad fact of ethnic, religious, and political prejudice suggests that if human beings are predisposed to act more altruistically towards those with whom they can identify, then, by contrast, they may also be predisposed to act less altruistically, or even aggressively, towards those with whom they could not easily identify. Yet a closer look at the problem reveals an altogether more complex and more interesting reality than those immediately visible to commonsense, everyday observation. In particular, we might wonder if, having discovered deep, unconscious propensities towards altruism in the human psyche, psychoanalysts might not also have discovered evidence of the converse. Indeed they have.

Along with the study of altruism from which I quoted above, Anna Freud published another classic finding regarding the workings of the strange phenomenon of identification. This, she called *identification with the aggressor*. Again, this is something which seems bizarre on the surface and certainly does not appear to have anything to do with the evolution of human altruism. Nevertheless, a closer look reveals that it does have something to do with it and almost certainly corresponds to our third, so far unsatisfied expectation.

She opens her account with a case related by August Aichhorn (1878–1949). It concerned a schoolboy who could not stop grimacing at his teacher. When Aichhorn had the opportunity to see teacher and pupil together, he noticed that "the boy's grimaces were simply a caricature of the angry expression of the teacher and that, when he had to face a scolding by the latter, he tried to master his anxiety by involuntarily imitating him." Far from being a peculiarity of the boy in question, Anna Freud's vast experience with children convinced her that identification of this kind "is really one of the most natural and widespread modes of behavior on the part of the primitive ego." However, a notable peculiarity of this kind of identification is that it does seem to be "not with the person of the aggressor but with his aggression."[9] Identification with the aggressor evidently follows this prior process of identification with the aggressor's aggression. By contrast to altruistic identification, with its tendency to project the self-interest of the subject onto the recipient, identification with the aggressor involves *introjection* of the aggressor's aggression by the subject and the latter's transformation from a passive victim of aggression into an active aggressor.

In the psychoanalytic literature this process is regarded mainly as a defensive one, but, from our point of view, we can readily see that identification with the aggressor might be more generally and perhaps meaningfully retermed *identification with the defector*. This, as we saw earlier, is an exact description of what TIT FOR TAT did when it encountered DEFECTORs and was the secret of its robustness and survivability. But it is also what we would expect the mechanism of identification to bring about if it had indeed evolved as the means by which much human altruism was facilitated. If *cooperate with cooperators, but defect against defectors* is the fundamental maxim for the evolution of cooperation, and if identification and projection of personal identity can bring about altruistic cooperation with other altruists, then identification with other's defection makes perfect sense.

Perhaps this explains the so-called imitative violence which some analysts have discerned in homicide statistics. As a recent review of the literature points out, there is some evidence that homicide rates in the United States rise in the immediate aftermath of a prize fight, but not a year earlier or later. But however this may be (and the question remains controversial), the authors conclude that:

> If we wish to predict the present level of violence in a given society, our estimate will not be greatly improved by knowing the unemployment rate or the modes of production or how Draconian are the laws or even the population's demographic structure; far and away the best available predictor of that present level of violence is the level in the recent past. The likely implication is that present violence is itself a causal determinant of future violence.[10]

Identification with the aggressor – or, rather, as we have already seen, with his aggression (and here the masculine pronoun is not out of place because most homicidal aggression in all societies is the work of men) – seems an apt description of the mechanism of such imitative violence if, as the authors of this review suggest, we consider "the impact of the local prevalence of violence upon a rational man's readiness to resort to violence." If human beings have indeed evolved to apply unconsciously a tit-for-tat strategy to social interactions, it follows inevitably that raised levels of local violence will tend to trigger raised levels of violence in response, if only because, as the authors of this study point out, "Violence can beget violence, for example, by raising the perceived risk of behaving *non*violently."[11]

If projection can be discerned alongside identification with the defector – and it often can – it is significant that what is projected is usually better described as tendencies to defection in the subject, rather than, as in the case of altruistic identifications, tendencies to cooperate. An excellent example of this, mentioned by Anna Freud, is the common psychoanalytic finding that delusions of jealousy and the accompanying reproaches made against a partner almost always originate in the accuser's own repressed wishes to be unfaithful. The evolutionary considerations of the previous section showed us why such wishes would tend to be repressed. Indeed, in the case of unfaithfulness they represent obvious desires to cheat, but desires which are hidden from detection by one's partner by also being hidden from oneself. If we regard such unfaithfulness as a very real instance of defection, then we can see that what is effectively happening is that unconscious wishes to defect oneself are being justified by finding imagined evidence of defection in one's partner. Presumably the same applies to the often very obvious element of delusional projection in racial, ethnic, and other forms of prejudice. If one wants to defect against strangers, what better justification than the certainty that they are already defecting against you!

But however important identification and projection may be in facilitating human altruism, there seems little doubt that other psychological mechanisms have also evolved to control and exploit reciprocal interactions. Moral indignation and self-righteous anger seem obvious candidates for emotions which might be used to police the system by using them to warn and punish cheats and exploiters. The fact that such moralistic aggression often seems out of all proportion to the offense discovered is explicable if, as Robert Trivers has suggested, selection may favor the final unmasking of deceptions which have been repeated many times in small quantities but might still nevertheless have exacted a real toll over a long period in terms of their cost to the exploited party.[12] Again, sham indignation and contrived moral outrage can be very effective adjuncts to the kinds of projection discussed in the paragraph immediately above and can sometimes be exploited to allow the moralists involved to do the very thing they are so indignant about. Examples might be anti-pornography campaigners who spend much time finding and studying the material they wish the public to be protected from or ascetics who claim to prove their immunity to the lusts of the flesh by inviting women to sleep with them naked!

By way of contrast, sincere feelings of gratitude might be selected to serve as a kind of moral payment-on-account in situations where the recipient of an act of altruism cannot reciprocate immediately or in full, but wants to ensure that the sacrificing party does not feel exploited or unappreciated. Feelings of guilt and a need to make reparation might also evolve for similar reasons, the former perhaps to inform an individual of the likely response to cheating of their own, the latter to motivate them to repair relationships purposely or accidentally threatened by defection.

Finally, a concern with one's own and other people's motives for their actions would tend to be selected if discrimination against cheats and protection against defectors were a vital element in human social behavior. Here may be the basis of the characteristic human tendency to judge altruism mainly in terms of motive and to think that motives matter. But this would not be because motives serve unproblematically to define altruism, as many seem to imply, for example, when they reject the use of the term in biology. On the contrary, the reason why motives matter is that they become contentious when real outcomes appear to diverge from subjective intention. Only when the intended recipients of some altruistic act fail to be satisfied do they begin to impugn the motives of their ostensible benefactors; and only then do the would-be altruists begin to appeal to their motives, by contrast to their acts, as vindication.

The biology of morality

Apart from claiming that it is our possession of free will and rational self-consciousness which distinguishes us from other animals, many have alleged that it is the existence of human morality which makes human beings different. In this respect morality is regarded as above nature – and very often seen as counter to it – and something which a theory of biological evolution cannot explain.

Nevertheless, the attempt has been made. An example with which we might begin is that of the distinguished evolutionist Richard Alexander in his book *The Biology of Moral Systems*.[13] His general conclusion is that most of the great problems which confront human beings have an ethical or moral dimension, rooted in conflicts of interest. Arguing from an evolutionary point of view, he concludes that human interests have been shaped primarily by evolution and reduce ultimately to reproductive self-interest, conscious or unconscious as the case may be. His primary conclusion is contained in his statement that "The function . . . of moral systems is evidently to provide the unity required *to enable the group to compete successfully with other human groups*," adding the dubious assertion that "Only in humans is the major hostile force of life composed of other groups of the same species."[14]

Although this seems a plausible theory, it is self-evidently a group-selectionist one, since, as the italicized words in the quotation above suggest, morality is being explained primarily in terms of its value *for the group*, rather than its value to the individual. The difficulty here is the perennial problem of altruism: even if morality benefits most members of human groups, why should free-riders not evolve who enjoy the benefit without paying the cost? What is to stop individuals behaving as if others, rather than they themselves, should conform for the good of the group? And what is to prevent the spread of genes for such defection if others are cooperating and thereby favoring them? After all, even if a few individuals defect, the force of Alexander's argument remains: if morality benefits the group in relation to other groups, it should still benefit it even if one or two members defect. Yet if those defectors gain the benefit without paying the cost, defection will be selected, and the defectors will increase as a proportion of the population, exactly as in our original thought-experiment. Indeed, we can see that this is a variation of the aggression-is-controlled-in-the-interests-of-the-group-or-species argument which we considered earlier (see above, pp. 30–1). Finally, it is worth pointing out that this is a theory which cannot explain the astonishing live-and-let-live cooperation which evolved on the basis of self-interest rather than group interest in World War I. On the contrary, this is precisely the argument which those who wished to destroy it used: killing the enemy is morally acceptable if it means that we win the war!

While we might be tempted to believe this in the absence of any other theory, it is worth wondering whether there is any alternative and in particular whether there is one which does not commit us to some form of group selection. Indeed there is. To see how morality can be explained on a wholly individual evolutionary basis, let us return to our free-riders.

One point often overlooked in considering the free-rider problem is that free-riders can exist only if there are others who are prepared to pay for the free rides. Obviously, if all those who rode on a public transport system refused to pay, the system could not operate, at least if nonriders could not be induced to pay. If they could, then the users of the system would all be free-riders, riding at the expense of the nonriders who did pay. But in either case, free-riders have a strong incentive to encourage *someone* to pay. If no one pays, they cannot ride at all. In other words, free-riders and defectors of all kinds have an incentive to "let George do it" – George being a cooperator who will pay. But if George does not oblige, they cannot go on free-riding or defecting in any other way at his expense.

But what is to stop George paying? According to his exploiters: nothing. But George himself might take a rather different view. Here his own self-interest will be the major factor in preventing him from doing it for others' benefit. If George, too, says, "Let someone else do it," with the consequence that no one does it, it will be because George, like his exploiters, is putting himself first. But his exploiters have a vested interest in preventing that. Therefore they castigate George's self-interest in not being exploited as "selfishness" and advocate that George should be an altruist *because they will benefit from his altruism.*

In general terms, self-interest must be the main factor opposing exploitation of some individuals by others. The inevitable consequence is that it is in the others' interest both to castigate such legitimate self-interest as "selfishness," "egoism," "greed," "individualism," or whatever and to advocate generalized, indiscriminate altruism for all. Of course, exploiters will inevitably want to exempt themselves from these generalized inducements to altruism on certain occasions; but in general terms they will probably find that, since others are almost always in a vast majority compared with themselves, advocating altruism in general, indiscriminate terms pays the self-interest of particular individuals. At the very least, generalized advocacy of altruism of the kind which attempts to attack others' proclivity to put their own self-interest first must be in the self-interest of anyone hoping to exploit them. As Nietzsche realized long ago, "One's 'neighbor' praises selflessness because *he derives advantage from it!*"[15] In other words, and reverting to our earlier discussion of the evolution of altruism for a moment, one does not need to imagine any group interest in the promotion of morality if one notices that what passes for it is in fact advocacy that others should in general play SUCKER. What could suit those wishing to play DEFECTOR better?

This effect would be much easier to see if the suckers were one group of people and the exploiting, moralizing defectors another, but human nature is not so simple. The previous discussion of human propensities to both cooperation *and* defection, to self-consciousness *and* unconsciousness, should have prepared us for the realization that, in the main, both the free-riders and those who pay are one and the same, with the tendency to free-ride or to pay being determined by the circumstances and the costs and benefits. Those who may be beneficiaries of effective free-riding in one context may find themselves having to pay for the free rides of others in other situations; and pratically everyone will manifest some form of one behavior *and* the other, sometimes at the same time. In short, human beings are not pure cooperators or defectors, but a mixture of both.

However, since individuals usually have an incentive to condone free-riding only in themselves (should they even be conscious of it), they normally have little incentive to advocate it in others. Precisely the reverse is true of advocating paying and opposing free-riding: here, everyone has a self-interest in someone else paying. From this point of view, morality does not seem to be something which benefits groups, but something which benefits individuals in groups where others may be tempted to put their self-interest first. Because individuals normally benefit much more from the altruism of others than they pay by being altruistic themselves, simply because there are so many others compared with themselves, individuals will have a strong incentive to advocate morality, even if their personal conformity to it often leaves much to be desired.

If we think back to the conclusion of the last chapter and the concept of induced altruism, we can now see the resemblance between my definition of that strange form of altruism and ostensibly "pure," "human," "ideal" altruism. There, I claimed that, looking at the matter in purely objective terms and ignoring subjective things like intentions or wishes, the altruism induced in other organisms by means of deceit, error, or coercion was just like ideal altruism in the human case, because the individual altruist did not benefit in the least from their self-sacrifice (see above, pp. 92–3). However, we can now see that, if this analysis is correct, morality is indeed a means whereby individual human beings attempt to induce altruism – or, at least, to discourage selfishness, which comes to the same thing – in others in their own self-interest. If we also notice that this self-interest is normally best kept completely unconscious for the reasons suggested earlier (see above, pp. 103–5), we can see that morality is likely to evolve as a characteristically human form of induced altruism.

Insofar as morality goes beyond nature or preaches against it, it seems to demand self-sacrifice beyond what identification and other cooperation-facilitating mechanisms like guilt or a sense of justice might dictate. Perhaps this is why guilt and justice loom large in moral systems. Again, my earlier observations regarding the pleasure principle (see above, pp. 97–9) would explain why moralists so often fulminate against it. If morality is sometimes altruism induced beyond the point at which it can pay for itself in terms of inclusive reproductive success, and if the pleasure principle is one of the main parameters set by evolution to safeguard such inclusive reproductive success, it follows that pleasure must be one of the prime obstacles which morality must overcome. Perhaps this is why altruism and asceticism so often go together in the theory and practice of moral systems and why some moralists seem to condemn any and all pleasure as intrinsically vicious, while they praise pain and privation as morally good.

In conclusion, it would seem that Alexander is right to this extent: that ethical and moral questions are rooted in conflicts of interest. If we add the qualification that the most critical conflicts of interest will always occur at the individual, rather than the group, level and will even occur within groups over the free-rider issue, we are left with the realization that morality is ultimately a question of cooperation with, or defection against, the actions and intentions of others. Moralists may have their own views about how such conflicts of interest should ultimately be resolved, but our recent insights into the evolution of cooperation leave little doubt about nature's answer to this fundamental problem. Indeed, some would argue that evolution has provided us with a natural morality far superior to the artificial, human kinds and one that is far simpler. *Cooperate with cooperation, but defect against defection.* Thus spoke natural selection, and thus, I suspect, speaks the natural morality within us all.

4

Male Behavior and Misbehavior

The fundamental factor

In many ways the revolution represented by recent evolutionary theory followed from new insights into animal behavior derived from numerous studies carried out in the years since World War II. For the best part of a century after the publication of *The Origin of Species* evolutionary thought was preoccupied with physical, rather than behavioral, evolution. Organisms were seen mainly as having evolved in terms of their structure and anatomy, and, of course, evidence of such evolution in the form of fossils was a major source of validation for evolutionary theory. Behavior was relatively neglected during this period, in part because behavior as such does not fossilize and in part because what studies of behavior were carried out tended either to be seemingly not relevant to evolution or actually to discount it. Nevertheless, modern field studies of wild animal populations in particular show that evolutionary considerations are not irrelevant to behavior, and today a vast literature of such studies exists which has been a major source of nurturance and inspiration to the revival of authentic Darwinism. For example, it was recent field studies in the main which provided the factual data which discredited the concept of group selection and which have validated much of the theory of social behavior outlined in the previous chapters.

But it is particularly in the context of sex that evolutionary considerations suggest that behavior must have evolved and must have been deeply influenced by selection. The reason for this is easy to see in the light of the earlier discussion of natural selection. If selection selects primarily and ultimately for reproductive success, as we have seen that indeed it does, then sexual behavior must be particularly pertinent to it, since sex and reproductive success are so closely allied. From the evolutionary point of view it seems highly unlikely that any aspect of behavior bearing on ultimate reproductive success – but sexual behavior especially – could have escaped the influence of selective forces and remained at the more or less arbitrary disposal of environmental conditioning in the way in which some influential psychological or sociological schools of thought have maintained. On the contrary, our modern insight into the true nature of natural selection predicts that behavior crucially bearing on reproductive success will be strongly and directly influenced by evolution and is most unlikely to be left open to chance influences.

One reason why reproductive success was not always given the prominence it deserved in Darwin's theory of evolution by natural selection may have been the result of nothing more than prudery. In the latter years of the nineteenth century and the early years of the twentieth in particular – in other words, at the very time when Darwin's theory first came to public attention – prudery about sexual matters was notorious; so it is perhaps not surprising that a theory of evolution which put reproductive success at the center should arouse some resistance. Another factor which may have been more important later and which certainly seems to have persisted right up to the 1950s may have been the tendency, already noted earlier, to conceive of selection as acting not on competing individuals as Darwin resolutely maintained, but on groups, populations, or even entire species: so-called group selection. To this, essentially non-Darwinian way of looking at things, the concept of sexual selection, with its open recognition of conflict and competition among organisms of the same species, population, or group, must have seemed an anomaly at best, and at worst must have seemed to call the whole concept of group selection into serious question. As we have seen, group selection made altruism too easy to explain and seemed to arouse few obvious contradictions, but when applied to sexual behavior, it encounters immediate and insuperable problems, despite the fact that reproduction seems self-evidently to serve the interests of the species, group, or family.

Reproductive success is perhaps far too close to the whole subject of sex and reproduction for it to have escaped the hypocrisy, euphemism, and sheer misrepresentation which normally surround the subject. When allied with considerations regarding cooperation or defection from the alleged shared interests of groups, the whole complex of ideas surrounding reproductive success must inevitably become highly contentious. There are probably very good evolutionary reasons why this should be so; but let us try to emancipate ourselves to some extent from our species' shortcomings where rational, objective discussion of this sensitive issue is concerned and try to begin by establishing whether there is any objective basis for a universal distinction made by human beings: that between male and female.

Indeed there is. Sex is not an arbitrary, human category attributed by analogy with subjective, human experience. On the contrary, in modern biology sex can be objectively and, in the vast majority of cases, unambiguously defined. Despite the fact that in the diploid case, which covers the vast majority of all sexually reproducing species, male and female donate exactly the same amount of genetic material to the nucleus of the sex cell, the sex cells which they produce are dramatically different. For instance, in the human case the largest cell found in the body is the ovum, which is almost visible to the naked eye. The smallest, by contrast, visible only with the most powerful microscopes, is the sperm. And this is typical. Throughout nature, in animals, plants, and fungi where sexes exist, there is almost always a massive, relatively immobile sex cell, the ovum or egg, always regarded as the distinctive attribute of the female, and a minute, relatively mobile sex cell, the sperm of the male. Furthermore, there is no question of one being only marginally larger or of the two being almost equal in size. Almost always, as in the human case, the disparity spans many orders of magnitude and is vast and unmistakable. In the few cases where no discernible difference is found, as in some fungi and algae, the sex cells appear to be indistinguishable and are arbitrarily labelled "plus" and "minus." But this is most exceptional; in the overwhelming majority of cases, the male is the sex with the tiny, highly mobile sex cell, the female that with the large, relatively nonmobile one.

Nevertheless, and as I mentioned above, it is not a question of any significant disparity in the quantity of genetic material contributed by each sex. This is equal, or at least it is so in the case of the nucleus of the fertilized cell. In fact, some genes occur outside it in subunits of the cell, such as the *mitochondria*, which play an important role in its internal economy. Since only the DNA of the sperm's nucleus becomes part of the fertilized egg and only the head of the sperm physically penetrates the ovum, leaving the rest behind, it follows that the nonnuclear parts of the resulting cell, such as its mitochondria, must be inherited solely from the mother. However, since the genes concerned constitute only a tiny minority of the total, the fundamental point remains the same: both sexes contribute an almost equal amount of genetic material.

Having said that, however, it is worth pointing out that the extra genes contributed by the female do have some significance, not so much in themselves but as a consequence of a deeper and more important disparity. This is related to the overall size of the sex cells. As we have already seen, the egg and sperm typically differ by orders of magnitude, but this difference in size still fails to reflect the true difference in organisms such as birds or mammals, where much more is at stake. In the case of a bird like a domestic hen, the true disparity in terms of what male and female contribute is not that between the sperm and ovum so much as that between the sperm and the hen's egg as it is laid, containing as it does, not merely the developing embryo, but all that it needs in the way of nutrients to bring it to a live birth sometime later. The disparity in size at this level is truly staggering. Sperm cells are so tiny that they are hard to visualize, especially in comparison to an everyday, easily visualized object like a hen's egg. So let us suppose that the roughly egg-shaped head of a typical cock's sperm is expanded to the size of an average hen's egg. Its whip-like tail will be about a meter long on the same scale, but how large would a typical hen's egg be if it were enlarged to the same degree? The answer is that, relative to a cock sperm with a head approximately the size of a normal hen's egg, the egg would be a massive object with a long axis a little less than a mile long, but more than a kilometer! In height it would dwarf the world's tallest buildings. What this astonishing contrast in size demonstrates is that, even though the amount of genetic material contributed by the sexes may differ by only a trivial amount, other factors contributed, such as nutrients, differ enormously.

But the nutrients stored in a hen's egg are not sufficient in themselves to bring about the birth of a live, fully formed chick. The egg must be incubated. Heat for incubation, as any poultry farmer knows, costs something. In nature it would be provided by one of the parents, but not necessarily always the mother. Body heat has to be produced from food and requires a digestion system and the metabolic processes of millions of cells to be released. But how can we visualize this addition to the egg? Furthermore, incubation is not just a question of heating the egg and keeping it at the critical temperature. It may also imply cooling, protection from predators, concealment, and so on.

The consequence of these observations is that even a hen's egg, massive as it is compared with a sperm, does not adequately represent the contribution of the parents who incubate it. In order to understand this clearly, we need a much more fundamental concept than size, one which includes not merely the provision an organism makes in the form of sex cells, but all the other factors involved in producing an offspring, such as warmth or shade, protection, instruction, transportation, food, and so on. The concept we need is that of *parental investment*, defined as *any benefit to an offspring's reproductive success at a cost to the remainder of the parent's reproductive success.*

Immediately we can rephrase our earlier definition of the difference btween the sexes in terms of this concept and say that, where sex cells differ in size, as they do in the overwhelming majority of cases, the female is the sex whose investment in the sex cell is larger, and the male is the sex whose investment is smaller. This establishes a fundamental distinction between the sexes based on the inequality of their respective investments in sex cells, but it says nothing necessarily about other forms of parental investment related to sex. Nor does it imply any value-judgments about which sex is "better" or "worse" or, indeed, any necessary assumption that one is more "valuable" to the purposes of procreation or natural selection than the other. On the contrary, as we shall see later, the fundamental inequality in size of the sex cells predicts that, ultimately, males should be worth exactly the same as females, at least if all other things are equal and if we take the sex ratio as our measure of nature's equal opportunities policy where the sexes are concerned (see below, pp. 197–8).

For reasons of convenience in the presentation of the relevant material, I shall now go on to concentrate mainly on male behavior in the remainder of this chapter. But I shall have cause to point out at the beginning of the next chapter that the fundamental concept of parental investment is one which is particularly relevant and sensitive to female interests (see below, pp. 158–60). Although these interests will be largely set aside for the moment, we shall see in due course that they are of no less consequence than those related to males, but that, on the contrary, they may claim to go to the root of the whole question of sex and the sexes when seen from an evolutionary point of view.

Four forms of the family

Let us continue with our discussion of the difference between the sexes and consider what, if any, behavioral considerations follow from it. A natural starting point might be supplied by the fundamental difference noted above relating to levels of parental investment in the sex cells. For instance, we could immediately predict that if one sex produces many more sex cells than the other, that sex ought, potentially at least, to be able to engender many more offspring than the other. In other words, males, with millions of sperm cells at their disposal, ought in principle to be able to have offspring numbered in the millions or, at least, ought to be able to father offspring orders of magnitude more numerous than can females.

Our confidence in the reliability of the basic theory is strongly vindicated by the realization that in practice this is almost always so. In the case of human beings, for example, it is clear that the lifetime reproductive success of a single woman is limited by the number of children she can bear (according to *The Guinness Book of Records*, the all-time record for one woman is sixty-nine offspring as a result of twenty-seven multiple-birth pregnancies). Nevertheless, a single man with enough wives in his harem could easily engender offspring by the hundred (one order of magnitude more) or even the thousand (two orders of magnitude more).

An example of the cumulative effect of male, as opposed to female, reproductive success is provided by the members of the modern Saudi Arabian royal family, who now number several thousand but are all descended from the man who founded the dynasty in 1932, Abdul Aziz Ibn Saud, and his 300 wives! But had the Saudi royal family been founded by a queen, even had she 300 husbands, the number of her direct descendants today would be minuscule by comparison. The Saudi example may, admittedly, be exceptional; but it is nevertheless a simple fact of arithmetic that where individual men number their wives in tens, their offspring may number hundreds by the end of their lives, and where they have wives by the hundred, there is nothing to stop them having offspring numbered in thousands. Indeed, in some of the smaller African kingdoms whose rulers aquired wives and concubines on a Saudi Arabian scale, a significant proportion of the entire population was eventually constituted by descendants of the ruling house.

The most important single behavioral consequence of all this as far as natural selection is concerned is that, thanks ultimately to their small and numerous sex cells, males can be vastly more reproductively successful than females. In the case of a species like elephant seals, for example, most offspring in any one breeding season are fathered by between 2 and 5 percent of the males. In the case of red deer, more than half the young were sired by 12 percent of the adult males in one closely studied population.[1] But these figures also reveal the inevitable corollary of the generalization above: if a male can have vastly greater reproductive success than a female can, thanks to his small and numerous sex cells, then equally he can have considerably less success than she. This is because the figures quoted above also show that in the case of the elephant seals 95 percent of the male population had little or no reproductive success and in that of the red deer that the other half of the offspring in the season in question had to have been fathered by the 88 percent of remaining males, many of whom fathered none at all. Facts such as these show that we must modify our assertion above and conclude that it is not safe to say that males have greater reproductive success than females do, but rather that males almost always show a greater *variance* of reproductive success than do females. By this we mean that whereas a male may be more reproductively successful than a female, he may also be much less successful, and that we must take note of both possibilities.

However, the actual degree of variance of male reproductive success is not entirely independent of other factors. One important variable in determining it will be the *mating strategy* characteristic of the species in question. Mating strategies can be classified in terms of the number and sex of the individuals concerned: we can have uni-female, multi-female, uni-male, and multi-male units combined in four possible ways (see figure 4.1). In a *multi-female* system, a number of females are mated to one or to a number of males. If it is the former, a number of females mated to one male, we have *polygyny*; if the latter, a number of females mated to a number of males, *polygamy* (or what, if there is little in the way of systematic contact among mating partners, we might call *promiscuity*). As far as uni-female systems are concerned, there are again two possibilities: one female may be mated to one male, what we know as *monogamy*, or one female may be mated to many males, what is termed *polyandry*.

The multiplicity of females available to each male in the cases of polygyny and polygamy results in males investing more in *mating success* than in offspring as such, and this produces the greatest variance in male reproductive success as

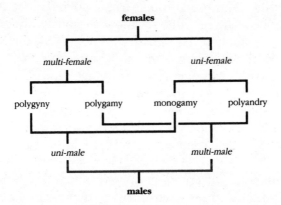

Figure 4.1 Male and female mating strategies.

a consequence. Clearly, where many females can be mated by a single male and where there is a rough equality in numbers of males and females, as there usually is, some males may be very successful, but others will not be. The cases of elephant seals and the Saudi royal family mentioned earlier illustrate this point well. But it would be a mistake to imagine that, where human beings are concerned, such enormous variance of male reproductive success is completely exceptional. In fact, the vast majority of human societies, approximately 84 percent of the total, are either generally polygynous or allow polygyny to those men wealthy or powerful enough to be able to practice it. Indeed, looked at from this point of view, one could argue persuasively that polygyny is *the* mating strategy characteristic of our species and that the remaining human societies which are mostly monogamous (with less than 1 percent polyandrous), represent a subordinate, minority trend in human mating systems.

This is despite the fact that there is no doubt that the vast majority of human *marriages* are monogamous: that is, they are marriages of one man to one woman. But this is largely because there are almost always many more men in a polygynous society who can manage only one wife as compared to those who can manage two or more. Because women are always in short supply in a mating system which allows men more than one each, it follows that there will usually be a large number of monogamously married men – as well as quite a few unmarried ones – in a society where some men have many wives. In asserting that polygyny characterizes the majority of human societies and may therefore claim to be the predominant mating strategy of our species, one must make the important distinction between men who are monogamists merely because they cannot manage to get a second wife and those who are monogamously married because polygyny is not an option under any circumstances. In presently known human societies overall, the former constitute the majority of monogamously married men, and many of them will later be counted as polygynists if, as is usually the case in such societies, a man's ability to acquire extra wives is directly related to his seniority. In other words, the overall majority of monogamous marriages comprises those of polygynists with only one wife, rather than those of monogamists as such.

Another important point to be borne in mind where estimations of the extent of polygyny in human societies, as compared to monogamy, are concerned is the realization that they often conceal a hidden, but real, masculine bias. Consider the following example. In the case of Miwuyt aborigines in Australia (sometimes called the Murngin), a representative population comprised 94 monogamously married men and only 58 who were polygynously married.[2] This appears to support the contention that polygyny is a minority matter and that monogamy is the dominant form of marriage, even in ostensibly polygynous societies. But this is true only if we count *husbands*; if we count *wives*, a different picture emerges. Now, 94 women are monogamously married, but 170 are polygynously married. In other words, what looks like a predominantly monogamous situation when looked at from a married man's point of view looks predominantly polygynous when regarded from that of a married woman. Indeed, simple logic demonstrates that, since every polygynously married man must have at least two wives, there will always be at least twice as many polygynously married women in a population than there will be polygynously married men. Furthermore, this is a minimum, because we can see that very often the actual proportion of polygynously married women will be greater, and in the example above is over half as great again as the number of monogamously married spouses of either sex. Evidently, then, estimations of the normality or otherwise of polygyny are affected by the relative weighting given to numbers of wives as opposed to numbers of husbands, with a marked bias in favor of underestimating the number of polygynously married women if only polygynously married men are counted. Where objective estimations are concerned, it seems that counting only husbands to the exclusion of wives is less defensible than counting wives rather than husbands.[3]

By contrast, uni-female systems represented by monogamy and polyandry often correlate with the opposite tendency to that found in multi-female ones. This is one in which males invest less in mating success and usually have much less chance of success because each male's number of mates is ostensibly limited to one in the case of monogamy and less than one in that of polyandry. As a consequence of this reduced variance of reproductive success in uni-female mating systems, males tend to invest more in offspring, with the result that male and female roles come to resemble one another much more than they normally do in multi-female systems. In the case of monogamy, both parents often contribute to raising the young as they do, for example, in the vast majority of birds. In large part this is because birds lay eggs which can in principle be incubated by either parent and because chicks are reliant from hatching on food which can usually be obtained by both parents.

Yet high levels of parental investment do not in themselves predict monogamy as a natural consequence. In mammals like ourselves for instance, only mothers can "incubate" the young by means of lengthy internal gestation and feeding via a placenta; and even after birth it is only the mother who produces the milk on which the newborn offspring is at first dependent. The consequence is that, although most mammals show levels of parental investment comparable to or even greater than those found in the predominantly monogamous birds, they are in general polygynous, probably because of the high degree of maternal role specialization in female mammals. Furthermore, we have already seen that this is a generalization which is also true of human beings in the sense that the majority of all human societies are polygynous.

Nearly all the remainder are monogamous, and, as we have also seen, very many men in otherwise polygynous societies are in fact monogamously married. Very often this is because a man just cannot afford another wife; but the striking relationship between wealth and the number of a man's wives is also reflected in the fact that in many societies both man and wife must work in order to support themselves and their children. The consequence is that, although a man, thanks to the extreme sex-role specialization of the order of mammals to which he belongs, cannot internally gestate his offspring and feed them in the way in which a woman can, he can nevertheless invest in them indirectly by undertaking activities which produce the means of parental investment and often requires the assistance of his wife in order to do so. This produces a situation at least analogous to that found in birds, if only in the cases of those men insufficiently wealthy or powerful to be able to sustain a plurality of wives.

The other uni-female system, polyandry – one female mated to many males – is rare in nature as it is in the human case, and presumably for the same reasons. Among these are the fact that only one male is needed to fertilize a female at any one time and that female reproductive success, unlike that of most males, is not directly linked to the number of her sexual partners. In other words, a woman with twenty husbands could not necessarily have any more offspring than one with a single husband. A man with twenty wives, however, almost certainly would have many more offspring than one who was monogamously married. Of course, where males contribute more than mere fertilizations, more of them may be useful to a female. For example, there are some birds who find that even two parents are barely enough to raise offspring, and so sometimes a second male is recruited by the female. If neither he nor the other male knows who is the father of the offspring, both may be induced to invest and support the female in raising young whom she knows are certainly hers.

Among mammals polyandry is unique to man, and in human societies it is normally found only where males are too poor to be able to afford a wife of their own and so club together with others to support one. The classic examples come from the Himalayan region, where high–altitude farming imposes exacting limits on both the minimum size of holding which is viable and the numbers of people needed to farm it. In order to prevent the breakup of farms, families with sons tend to contract only one marriage per generation, while those with a daughter ensure that by marrying a number of husbands she and her offspring will be adequately supported. For reasons which go back to our earlier discussion of kin altruism, it will not surprise us to learn that normally males who share a wife are brothers. In other words, even if a man married to the same wife as his brothers cannot know if he is the father of a particular child ($r = \frac{1}{2}$) because of the perennial uncertainty of paternity, he can at least know that he is an uncle ($r = \frac{1}{4}$). Although brothers might in theory have equal access to a shared wife, their age distribution almost always means that polyandry benefits older brothers more than younger ones and that for the latter monogamy is a better option where economically feasible. However, quantitative data show that completed polyandrous families have more children than monogamous ones and that marrying daughters polyandrously does indeed pay. Nevertheless, the fact that males typically do not invest as much as females in offspring and that selection will not reward those males who invest in the offspring of others to whom they are not related means that polyandry cannot be expected to be a common mating strategy and almost always reflects some degree of exceptional circumstances.[4]

An inevitable corollary of the principle that males show greater variance in reproductive success is the principle that females always invariably show less. The reason for this is easily seen. In all four mating strategies listed above, females are always mated. Whether it be a case of polygyny, polyandry, monogamy, or polygamy, a female will always find a mate. Because of their possession of relatively few, immobile sex cells, females will usually be a limiting resource for males and one for which they will compete, so that females will seldom go unmated. Their lower level of personal reproductive success will be reflected in a vastly greater certainty that they will indeed have some offspring. Furthermore, the number of offspring they have will tend to vary much less, thanks to their relatively fewer sex cells and their probable higher degree of parental investment. In this way, fundamental differences in parental investment at the level of the sex cells is reflected in basic behavioral differences between the sexes, crucially turning on their relative variance in reproductive success. This in turn creates four fundamental forms of the family, which exhaust the possible combinations of single and multiple mating groups for each sex throughout nature: monogamy, polygamy, polygyny, and polyandry.

Sex and violence

When examining the problem of altruism earlier, we noticed that the theory of group selection had effectively inhibited progress in real understanding of the evolution of cooperation, because it made self-sacrifice in the interests of the group seemingly self-evident. Altruism benefited others, groups were composed of others, and if selection selected at the level of the group, it would select self-sacrifice in the interests of others. It all seemed so easy. But it was too easy. Darwin's essential insight was into natural selection as a process of differential reproductive success of individuals *as individuals*, not as members of groups.

Much the same is true of sex. Here too, group selection had an easy answer. Sex was all about reproducing the species. If selection operated at the level of the species, then it had to select for sex in the interests of the species. Indeed, looked at from this point of view, sex seemed almost altruistic, as if individuals engaged in it for the good of the species rather than for any self-interest of their own. Of course, and as I observed earlier, sexual selection as a result of competition, for instance among males for females, sounded a discordant note in this rather complacent view; but even this could be accommodated by the observation that such competition ensured that only "the best" or "the fittest" bred in the interest of the future betterment or fitness of the species.

One effect of these group-selectionist views as applied to human beings was that sometimes sex – or, at least, reproduction – was portrayed as part of a person's public duty. Examples might be British politicians between the wars who fulminated against the practice of contraception by people at home, with dire warnings about the nation being swamped by the "black and yellow races" of the Empire. To what extent British couples went to bed motivated by their duty to king and country is wholly a matter of speculation, but my guess is that patriotism rates rather poorly as an aphrodisiac and that if anyone ever used this justification it was probably more in the nature of an excuse for something which they already wanted to do. Much more likely is it that decisions about family size were motivated by individuals' subjective feelings and their judgments about what was best for them and their families, rather than by what was best for nation, race, or the British Empire. Indeed, we know that when a recent Communist regime in Rumania tried to enforce a similar kind of policy by making the practice of contraception and abortion criminal offences, Rumanians – especially Rumanian women – went to extraordinary and often life-threatening lengths to avoid their "duty" to the state, usually by means of dangerous, back-street abortions. Considerations like these reveal the truth about sex and society and show that sex is something individual and potentially a source of conflict with the larger group, not something social and intrinsically an occasion for cooperation merely because it takes two to tango. Two it might take, but, as we have already seen, the two partners concerned will usually be of different sexes and will not necessarily have the same intrinsic self-interest in what they are doing.

One of the best examples of this that one can find relates to desertion and infidelity in birds. I choose birds here, rather than human beings, because birds are in many ways much closer to the model of ideal equality between the sexes which is often imagined to typify human beings – or, at least, 90 percent of them are. As we have seen, this means that the species in question have a type of breeding system in which one male is mated to one female, either for a season or for a lifetime. Unlike mammals such as human beings, who are typified by an extreme degree of female sex-role specialization represented by internal gestation of the young and reliance of infants on their mothers' milk, birds show much less sex-role specialization, at least once the eggs are laid. Evolutionary pressures for weight reduction in a flying animal have resulted in birds laying eggs which are much smaller and lighter than the final, fledged offspring will be. In order to compensate for this, both parents normally have to work extraordinarily hard to feed the hatchlings, once the incubation phase is over. This is probably why so many species are monogamous: it is simply that neither sex would have much reproductive success unless both cooperated to feed their rapidly growing chicks. The consequence is that in most monogamous species the sexes look practically identical, and both often appear to labor with equal dedication in raising the offspring. In short, it looks like an ideal, modern marriage, with both partners taking an equal share in nest-building, child-rearing, and bread-winning.

But even here there can be conflict. Consider the case of such an apparently harmonious set-up as this in which the breeding period for the birds in question is long enough to allow two families to be raised in one season. Furthermore, let us notice that as fledglings approach maturity, their food requirements decrease somewhat, and they can often be supplied by only one parent. The outcome is a Prisoner's Dilemma in which the pay-off for cooperation – remaining with the original partner – is nicely balanced by the reward for defection – leaving when only one parent's work is necessary to bring the existing offspring to maturity and setting up with another deserter to start a second family before the end of the season. If both desert or if either deserts before its offspring can survive on the ministrations of the remaining parent, both will be punished with the probable loss of their entire investment in the offspring in question. However, if either remains faithful regardless of temptation, the danger is that the other will defect and, by doing so, start a second family and thereby double its likely reproductive success in that season. Because natural selection selects for enhanced reproductive success, genes for successful defection must be selected, just as those for unsuccessful cooperation will be selected against. The consequence is a classical evolutionary Prisoner's Dilemma in which the outcome of what each partner does is inextricably involved with what the other decides to do.

Or, at least it is in the case of monogamous birds. In that of human beings one cannot help thinking that the male partner has an advantage when it comes to desertion. This is because a man's reproductive career can be much longer than a woman's, because of the menopause and the fact that human female fertility and offspring quality decline much earlier than do a male's. Furthermore, since command of resources is a vital factor in the mating success of human males and since such resources are very often progressively accumulated by a man as he matures, older men will normally be in a better position to benefit from desertion than will older women, whose prospects of remarriage and starting second families are not likely to be quite so good. Insights like these cast an interesting new light on modern divorce law and the question of its real beneficiaries (often portrayed as women), and they certainly blatantly contradict the supposition that, since it takes two to tango, sexual love and family life are predestined to be happy, equitable, and conflict-free.

Indeed, desertion might be regarded as merely the tip of the iceberg of infidelity, nicely illustrated by another bird example in which the male partners in monogamously mated pairs in a wild population were vasectomized but the vast majority of the eggs actually laid by the females turned out to have been fertile! Another ingenious experiment with a species of monogamous swallows suggests by whom they may have been fertilized. Male swallows possess two tail feathers which are about 10 cm long. The experimenters artificially manipulated the length of some of these by cutting 2 cm sections out of some birds' tails and gluing the cut pieces into the tails of others. Subsequent observation showed that males with lengthened tails were twice as likely to fertilize another male's female and attracted an official mate in a quarter of the time taken by those with shortened ones and about half that taken by standard, undoctored controls; finally, they were much more likely to father a second brood.[5]

Like desertion, infidelity is not unknown among human beings, not least in ostensibly monogamous cultures like our own. However, as fundamental biological principles would predict, although the actual degrees of infidelity measured by various researches vary with time and place, nearly all show a sex-specific difference, with men being more likely to have more extramarital affairs than women. While there seems little doubt that cultural factors play a role in determining the absolute level of overall infidelity in a society, it is difficult to escape the conclusion that the basic, biological facts of life are reflected in the practically universal relative difference in infidelity between the sexes. However we look at it, it is impossible to ignore the fact that whereas a female normally needs only a single male per fertilization, males can, in principle at least, fertilize as many females as may be available.

One possible consequence of the fact suggested by the last example is that males may compete among themselves for the privilege of mating with the largest possible number of females. One way in which this may come about is by means of direct conflict among the males in question. An extreme example of this is provided by elephant seals. These animals haul up on beaches to give birth to pups and to mate. Because breeding females are concentrated into dense groups in both time and space by this circumstance, individual males can and do succeed in monopolizing large harems. A measure of their success is provided by the statistic I quoted earlier which showed that in one particular case 80 percent of the pups born in one population had only three fathers, who accounted for less than 5 percent of the male population. As might be expected, conflict among males is intense and, indeed, bloody.

Elephant seals get their name from the enlarged nose of the male, who uses it to bellow and to warn off other males somewhat as a stag does. Presumably, as in the case of stags, the length, loudness, and frequency of the bellowing give an indication of the individual's health, size, and fighting ability. With the enlarged nose goes a set of elongated canine teeth which can inflict deep wounds. However, males have also evolved a covering of thick blubber around the neck, which, like the mane of a male lion, serves as a means of defense. When we notice that human males, too, have a mane of hair which covers their necks in the form of a beard at the front of the body and long head hair at the back, one cannot help wondering if these adornments – particularly the beard – may not have evolved for the same reason: namely, one of defense against bites to the neck from other males. There is certainly a precedent for this in some other primates (that is, the group that includes apes and monkeys as well as man), notably, gelada and hamadryas baboons. Like human beings, these two species are almost wholly ground-dwelling, and adult males of both species have impressive, lion-like capes of hair around the neck. Both species also show intense conflict among males for control of polygynous breeding groups of several females.

Characteristics such as these are regarded as examples of what is normally termed *sexual dimorphism*. This is just Greek for "two sexual forms" and means that in a sexually dimorphic species males and females differ from one another in a regular way. In the case of elephant seals, by far the greatest element of sexual dimorphism is in terms of body weight, with males being up to seven times heavier than females. Since elephant seals rear up and use their entire weight in attempting to knock over opponents, it is not surprising that natural selection has rewarded the largest and heaviest males with the greatest degree of reproductive success. Indeed, it is in general true that where size, muscularity, and sheer body weight are important factors in winning fights among males over females, such attributes will tend to become typical of males, simply because the males who best possessed those characteristics in the past left the largest number of descendants. Other adaptations such as enlarged teeth, horns, antlers, or claws may also be preferentially selected in males for the same reason, and the degree to which a species is sexually dimorphic in characteristics such as these will normally be a good guide as to the intensity of the sexual conflict among its males.

If, bearing these general principles in mind, we now look at the facts regarding human beings, we find that our species is indeed sexually dimorphic. This is true in the general sense that naked adult men and women are usually easily distinguished, regardless of culturally dependent factors such as hair length. Here human beings are unlike many birds, whose degree of sexual dimorphism is so slight that it sometimes takes an internal, post-mortem examination to determine their sex. The features which make men and women easily distinguishable in the vast majority of cases are female attributes such as breasts, rounded hips and generally fuller buttocks, more youthful complexion, and markedly less body hair. Males, by contrast, have broader shoulders, more muscle development and body hair, beards, and deepened voices. In terms of size and weight the differences are significant, with males standing on average between 5 and 12 percent taller than women, the figure being higher in traditionally polygynous cultures where, presumably, some degree of conflict or competition among men for women occurs. As far as weight is concerned, women are on average about 20 percent lighter than men. But this figure is more significant than it seems if one also takes note of the fact that the body weight of the sexes is not constituted in quite the same way. On the contrary, it seems to be independently dimorphic in the sense that whereas women have about one quarter of their body weight in the form of fat, men on average have only about half that amount. In other words, although women on average have about twice as much fat as men, they nevertheless weigh on average almost a quarter less than men. Clearly, the difference is explained not by how well fed the sexes may be but by the fact that males have larger skeletons on average, with heavier bones and considerably more muscle than do most females. When we observe that in women the degree of fat deposits is critical to reproductive success in primal conditions (see below, pp. 160–3), but that in men muscle, bone, and height are critical in aggressive encounters with other men, we are left in little doubt that in human beings, as in many other species, sexual dimorphism of this kind is an indicator of the fact that sex and conflict often go together.

In the case of human beings there is a considerable amount of evidence that this is so. According to Confucius, "Disorder does not come from heaven, but is brought about by women," and Darwin observed that among tribal peoples "women are the constant cause of war both between members of the same tribe and between distinct tribes." The most recent research summarized by Laura Betzig, bears out both authorities: "The evidence suggests that in virtually all societies women are a significant cause of male conflicts of interest."[6] Data on the proportion of male murders of other males as compared to female murders of other females from 35 different societies throughout the world show an immense contrast. On average, out of every 100 murders of a person of one sex by a member of the same sex, 95 will be murders of males by other males. Put another way, one could say on the basis of these figures that a man is twenty times more likely to be murdered by another man than a woman by another woman. Furthermore, since the figures just quoted ignore male deaths at the hands of other males in war and similar conflicts and include female murders which do not relate to conflict between mature women, such as female infanticides, they probably underestimate the true extent of homocidal violence among males as opposed to females. In the case of the polygynous Yanomamö Indians of South America, approximately 30 percent of deaths among adult males were attributable to violence, and almost half of all men aged twenty-five or more had participated in a killing, while nearly 70 percent of all adults over forty years of age had lost a close relative because of violence. Among the Mae Enga, Huli, and Dugum Dani of highland New Guinea the figures for violent death of adult males were 25 percent, 19.5 percent, and 28.5 percent respectively. That such violence can contribute significantly to the reproductive success of a man is suggested by the Yanomamö findings, which show that killers have on average two and a half times as many wives and three times as many children as nonkillers.[7] A recent study of the available data concluded that "There is no known human society in which the level of lethal violence among women even begins to approach that among men" and added that *"Intrasexual competition is far more violent among men than among women in every human society for which information exists."*[8]

However, male competition for reproductive success may not always be merely quantitative, with each male wanting to fertilize the largest number of females possible. It is also likely to be qualitative, with males competing for the most reproductively successful females. If such discrimination is possible, it is likely that selection will affect females as a secondary consequence of male competition. For example, a study of bridewealth payments by the Kipsigis people of Kenya gives an unambiguous insight into what males prefer by revealing what it is they are prepared to pay for in a bride. "Plump" girls were found to be more expensive than "skinny" ones because, as we shall see in more detail later, fatness is positively correlated with fertility (see below, pp. 160–3). General good health and physical well-being were also important, with two physically handicapped girls said to have been "almost free." Again, brides with existing offspring were significantly cheaper than women of comparable age who had no children. In general, youth was a major factor, and the study showed that women who reached menarche (the point at which a young woman begins to menstruate) earlier had, on average, three more surviving offspring than women who reached it later.[9]

The consequence is that in a polygynous species like human beings, females tend to mature earlier than males because their total lifetime reproductive success is critically dependent on the number of pregnancies they achieve in their reproductive lives, and therefore on its length. Since male reproductive success, by contrast, is dependent on how many females a male has access to in competition with other males, maturation may be slower if, as is usually the case, mature males compete better than younger ones, for example by virtue of being bigger or heavier. Although the growth rates of girls and boys are almost identical in infancy and childhood, a noticeable difference occurs at about age ten, when girls start to grow faster than boys, achieving the maximum rate by age twelve and completing their growth by age fifteen. Boys, by contrast, do not start their growth spurt until two years later than girls and do not achieve full growth until approximately seventeen to eighteen. Four-fifths of the mean height difference of 10 cm between adult men and women is accounted for by the delayed onset of the growth spurt in boys, which allows them a longer growing time, and only one-fifth by the increased magnitude of that growth.[10]

However, sexual dimorphism, although important, is not the only indicator of inter-male competition in a species and thereby, indirectly, of its characteristic mating strategy. Another, only recently appreciated indicator is the size of the male's testes. A glance at figure 4.2 shows that the size of the testes relative to the body of men, gorillas, and chimpanzees

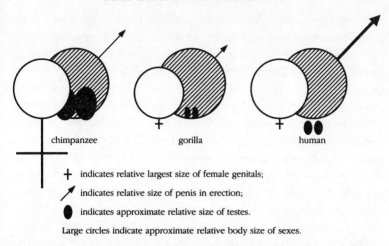

Figure 4.2 Sexual dimorphism, testis and genital size in three primate species.
(Modified and redrawn from R. V. Short, "Sexual Selection and its Component Parts: Somatic and Genital Selection as Illustrated by Man and the Great Apes," *Advances in the Study of Behavior*, 9 (1979), pp. 152–3.)

reveals some interesting similarities and differences. It also indicates the average degree of sexual dimorphism in each species. As one might expect, gorillas, which are highly polygynous, show the highest degree of sexual dimorphism but the smallest relative testis size. Chimpanzees, by contrast, who are markedly less sexually dimorphic than gorillas, have testes which are proportionately much larger (and, like those of gorillas, but unlike those of men, are largely retained within the body). From the evidence of reduced sexual dimorphism, we might conclude – correctly as it happens – that chimpanzees are nothing like so polygynous as gorillas. This is indeed the case, because, although dominant adult males will pair off with females during their period of *estrus* (that is, when the female advertises that she is about to ovulate by means of the large sexual swelling characteristic of the species), the generally much more fluid and variable nature of chimpanzee groups means that single males cannot monopolize entire harems of females as do gorillas. The consequence of this is that, because any one chimpanzee male cannot effectively exclude all others from a female, as can a gorilla, male chimpanzees must carry on the fight by other means than merely physical aggression and social dominance. This they do by means of *sperm competition*: letting their sex cells continue the struggle for greater reproductive success within the female's reproductive tract. Here, obviously, the male who deposits the largest quantity of sperm at the same time as others is likely to win, and so natural selection appears to have rewarded males with large testes. Similar effects have been found in a number of other species, such as gray whales and one or two to be mentioned later, where males cannot exclude others from copulation with a female but can compete by means of their sperm.

In short, if sexual dimorphism indicates the likelihood of a multi-female breeding group (whether polygynous or poly-gamous/promiscuous as the case may be) because it indicates conflict among males for females, testis size indicates the likelihood of there being a multi-male breeding group, since it is only the regular presence of sperm from other males which is likely to cause large testes to be selected. However, relatively small testes *and* marked sexual dimorphism, as we find in the gorilla, for example, indicate both a multi-female breeding group and the absence of a multi-male one, meaning that the mating system in question must normally be polygyny. This is clearly so in the case of gorillas, and a glance at figure 4.2 shows that it is also likely to be true of human beings. Although we are not quite as sexually dimorphic as gorillas, we are evidently somewhat more dimorphic than chimpanzees and certainly have much smaller testes, despite the fact that men have far larger penises than chimps. Although some evidence has recently been found that a man produces less sperm when he has only a single sexual partner than when he has more than one, the mechanism involved remains unknown and clearly has not resulted in human males evolving testes which are of comparable relative size to those found in male chimpanzees. Evidently, sperm competition is a relative matter, and while men may turn out to have the ability to increase sperm production to meet the needs of multiple partners, there is no way in which they could increase it to compare with the relative level of sperm production found in chimpanzees. On the contrary, human testis size falls right in the middle of the range for ground-dwelling polygynous primates such as gelada and hamadryas baboons, which suggests that, like them and like gorillas, human males are not as adapted for easygoing promiscuity as some earlier enthusiasts for the chimpanzee model of human adaptations may have wished.

Cryptic conflict

In the wider field of animal behavior, sperm competition as an alternative to open conflict among males has some interesting effects. For example, in some species males mimic females in appearance and certain aspects of behavior but do not invest any more in offspring than do other males. One of the best examples is the bluegill sunfish. In this species sexually dimorphic males who are larger than females command nesting sites to which females are attracted. However, some males do not develop in this way and instead become female mimics, or *transvestites*. Such males are never the first to enter a regular male's nest but will do so once a genuine female has done. As she lays her eggs and the resident, normal male fertilizes them, the transvestite enters and, welcomed by the resident male as a second female, adds his sperm, rather than more eggs, to those already there. Comparable cases are reported in sticklebacks, scorpion flies, and Canadian garter snakes. In the case of the bluegill sunfish, transvestites begin their deceptive careers as "little sneakers," small, fast-moving fish who dart in and out of a male's nest in quite literally a fraction of a second and instantly ejaculate.

In other words, bluegill sunfish feature three distinct types of male: a regular, dimorphic one which builds nests and defends them; a female mimic, or transvestite, who parasitizes the female sex role while actually being male; and a diminutive, sneak male who relies on an amazing turn of speed to intrude into a regular male's nest and fertilize some of the eggs. The little sneaks and the transvestites clearly do not represent true cases of sex-role reversal. On the contrary, the "deviant" males in question play a quintessentially male role in the sense that they do not resemble females in terms of parental investment in offspring but simply mimic them in order to deceive other males. Indeed, one could even see them as exaggeratedly masculine in certain respects, such as the fact that they contribute even less to offspring care than do normal males and have vastly larger testes in proportion to total body weight than the latter.

This last aspect is worth dwelling on for a moment. How paradoxical it seems that a male who is feminized in appearance to the point of being mistaken for the real thing by other males can nevertheless produce semen in vastly greater quantities than normal, unambiguous males! However, the paradox vanishes once we recall that such sperm competition is only another kind of inter-male conflict, something which we have come to expect of males, with their characteristic tendency to invest in mating effort rather than offspring as such. Indeed, sperm competition seems to be only love and war carried on by other means. Both little sneak and transvestite bluegill sunfish need more sperm because they have so little time to fertilize the eggs. Whereas a regular, resident male can take his time and make his available sperm go further, intruders, whether they be female mimics or fast-moving instant ejaculators, have got to hurry and get it all in first time. No wonder selection has favored deviant males with large testes!

If male "deviants" like these are not true instances of sex-role reversal, they might instead be seen as examples of what we might call *cryptic sexuality*. By this term I mean *behavior or appearance which serves to hide, disguise, or confuse sexual activity or identity to the benefit of the deceiver.* We have long been familiar with cryptic appearance as it is found in camouflage, for instance in protecting an organism from predators. It does not seem paradoxical that an insect should come to resemble a twig or a leaf in order to escape the attention of birds or other animals who might want to eat it. It should seem no more paradoxical, then, to suppose that sexual conflict, particularly between males, should result in comparable kinds of camouflage in both appearance and behavior and that some individuals might go so far in pursuing their personal sexual aims as to appear to be members of the opposite sex.

But this is not the only option for males, as the case of the little sneaker bluegill sunfish has already shown. Another possible expression of cryptic sexuality, particularly in species in which there is considerable sexual dimorphism, is for some males to remain apparently permanently immature, or at least, less mature than the norm: something which is often called *paedomorphosis*. Clearly, this is the case with the sunfish sneaks, who are small, immature forms who will subsequently mature, as it happens, as female mimics. But this is not something confined to fish. In populations of red deer, some males, so-called hummels, never reach the size of normal bucks and do not grow antlers. As a consequence, they resemble young male or even female deer to some extent. These apparently retarded, paedomorphic deviants live out a life on the fringes of the harem groups of regular males and attempt what hurried mountings of unguarded females they can manage. Among mountain sheep, young males resemble females so closely that they are routinely mounted by dominant males and mimic females behaviorally as well as in appearance when they perform *lordosis*, the characteristic presentation posture of females, in response. Such young, nondimorphic males have to tolerate the sexual attentions of older ones because sheep need to congregate in groups led by dominant males for protection against predators.

However, young rams also take what opportunities they can with yews, but, like the bluegill sunfish sneaks, find that they must hurry and ejaculate quickly, before the dominant ram can intervene. Finally, and closer to home, some dimorphic primates like orang utans also feature paedomorphic males who appear to avoid conflict with dominant, territorial males by seeming not to be fully mature and, as a consequence, less of a threat.

In considering the relevance of these examples to human behavior, it is worth recalling that even though there are only two sexes physically speaking, there are at least four as far as psychology is concerned: along with masculine males and feminine females one finds masculine females and feminine males. In the past, what we might call the third and fourth sexes have been assumed to be largely nonreproductive by evolutionary theory. Here the idea is that genes for maiden aunts and unmarried uncles could be selected in exactly the same way as genes for worker sterility seem to have been selected among the social insects (see above, pp. 73–5). In other words, although such unmated individuals might have no reproductive success of their own, they might contribute more to that of the genes which they share in common with close relatives than they would to their own genes were they to reproduce themselves.

As an explanation of the existence of nonreproductive individuals in human populations, this may be true, but as a theory of homosexuality it clearly raises some difficulties. First, it seems to assume that homosexuality and a non-reproductive status are one and the same thing. Yet studies show that in modern societies many homosexuals of both sexes have children. Second, it would lead us to predict that if homosexuality is selected the way worker sterility in social insects is selected, it should be a largely female phenomenon, since females – especially female mammals – are role-specialized for much greater parental investment than males. Yet the evidence seems to be the exact contrary of this, with male homosexual behavior being much more common than lesbianism in all known cultures, past and present, without exception. Third, such a theory would find it hard to explain the astonishing level of sexual activity, measured in terms of both number of partners and number and variety of different sexual acts, reported of male homosexuals (and demonstrated in the early, explosive growth of the AIDS epidemic among them). This hardly seems to be the behavior one would predict of "sterile" "nonreproductives." Finally, evidence from depth psychology shows that homosexuality is not an all-or-nothing phenomenon, with some individuals being homosexual and some not. Although some exclusive homosexuals are found, by far the most common pattern is a co-existence of both tendencies in the same individual, often with a fluctuating balance between them, so that in-depth analysis of predominant homosexuals often reveals hetero-sexual undercurrents, and vice versa.

An alternative view would be that, whereas lesbianism and maiden aunts might be explicable as either reciprocal (in the lesbian case) or kin altruistic (in that of the maiden aunt) helper-in-the-nest behavior (see below, pp. 183–5), male homosexuality might not be. On the contrary, it should perhaps be seen as comparable to the examples of male cryptic sexuality given earlier, in which a male deceives other males by appearing to be less-than-male in appearance or behavior. Although the three different types of male bluegill sunfish referred to above do not have a *physical* parallel among human males, it is conceivable that they may well have one in purely behavioral or *psychological* terms. Indeed, my use of the term "transvestite" earlier to describe the pseudo-female cryptic male bluegill sunfish suggests that there is indeed an analogy to be seen between the third and fourth sexes above and homosexual behavior. Perhaps natural selection would favor pseudo-feminine behavior in a man or quasi-masculine behavior in a woman if the result was to promote their individual reproductive success by means of deceit or deception of some kind. For instance, it is not very difficult to believe that a man who could not compete for females with other males directly and openly might achieve more by giving the impression that he was just not interested in the opposite sex, but preferred his own sex (homosexuality) or even his own person (narcissism). Again, a male who seemed boyish and immature (paedomorphic) or feminine and unmale ("transvestite") in appearance might encounter much less sexual conflict with other males than would otherwise be the case. Indeed, if his immature or unmasculine behavior or appearance also served to deceive women, he might succeed in catching some of them off their guard also, perhaps with ultimate benefit to his reproductive success. (For example, some modern women report feeling "more relaxed" or "less guarded" with homosexual than with heterosexual males. If such lowering of normal defenses against male sexual adventurism sometimes results in easier seduction, genes for such behavior could pay for themselves in the only currency evolution accepts: reproductive success.)

Indeed, if male reproductive and hunting success were originally strongly linked during the one or two million-odd years of hominid evolution, it is possible that homosexual tendencies evolved to facilitate it. For instance, a male whose hunting prowess was not up to that of some others in his band might find that he had to tolerate some degree of sharing of his sexual partners with the more competent hunters. Although his heterosexual instincts might balk at this and make him deeply resentful and openly antagonistic, the circumstance that the best hunters might also be likely to be the best fighters might tend to select for more passive, less obviously masculine behavior. Indeed, as Robert Trivers has pointed out, it is well known that males are often aroused sexually when other males appear interested in their mates and that some males even seek the sight of another male copulating with their mate in order to achieve sexual arousal.[11] As Trivers also points out, this has long been known to be an aspect of homosexual behavior, but it is one which makes good evolutionary sense in terms of sperm competition, since a female who has just been inseminated by another male might be prevented from conceiving by him if more, competing sperm is immediately placed in her reproductive tract. If, as we have already seen, such sperm competition is an alternative to more direct competition among males, it could certainly evolve in the human case in accordance with behaviors which also appear to avoid open confrontation with other men by means of the appearance of being nonmasculine or even feminine. But since the composition of hunting bands would often be fluid, one would not expect such homosexual tolerance of other males' heterosexuality to be fixed or permanent, but correspondingly fluid and variable as it is often observed to be. If this were indeed the case, homosexuality – at least in males – would be seen, not as an "aberration" or "monstrosity of nature," but as a flexible sexual response in the individual, motivated by considerations ultimately bearing on the individual's reproductive success.

Indeed, the fundamental principle which says that a man's reproductive success varies much more than that of a woman may apply in a qualitative sense as well as in a purely quantitative one and may explain why the overwhelming majority, not merely of homosexuals, but of sexual perverts in general has always been male. (I use the term "pervert" here in the enlightened Freudian sense of someone whose sexual satisfaction is derived from something other than the genitals of the opposite sex and intend no other, pejorative or prejudicial meaning, which clearly has no place in a scientific discussion.) Crime statistics, services offered by prostitutes, and psychotherapists' case records – not to mention common experience of life – leave little doubt that this is so.

But if we see sexual perversion as a product of a lack of discrimination regarding appropriate sex-object on the part of males (something which the scientific, Freudian concept of perversion clearly implies), it seems much more likely to have a natural foundation in the minuscule degree of parental investment represented by a sperm. After all, if a male has millions of sperm and if they cost him very little, why should he worry about what happens to them? Such a lack of discrimination on the part of males is very common throughout nature. In the case of invertebrates such as insects, males commonly attempt to mate with anything that vaguely resembles a female, a fact exploited by one species of orchid whose flower looks and smells somewhat like the female of a species of wasp whose males pollinate it in their unsuccessful, but frantic attempts at copulation with it. Male guppies – who, unusually among fish, have to copulate with the female in order to fertilize her internally and are indefatigable in doing so – will mate with anything that vaguely resembles the usually larger female of the species, including other, larger males! If one is tempted to conclude from these examples that similar generalizations could not apply to mammals, it is worth recalling that modern beef and dairy breeding is wholly dependent on the circumstance that bulls can be induced to mount heifers (sometimes, even vaulting horses) and to ejaculate into artificial vaginas and that dominant male mountain sheep mount anything that looks like a female, younger males included. When male chimpanzees and baboons are seen to engage in mutual masturbation with other males and, under captive conditions, to adopt rubber boots as fetishes, one cannot any longer sustain the illusion that sexual aberration is unique to human beings any more than one can credit the theory that most sexual perverts are male because of some effect of purely cultural conditioning. On the contrary, the conclusion seems inescapable that it is the very fact of being male which predisposes men to perversion and that such sexual aberrations as result are likely to be qualitative expressions of the fact that male demand for sex-objects will always vastly outstrip the supply, thanks to the fact that, fundamentally, a male is what he is because his sex cells are sperm.

5

Sex and Female Interests

Abortion, fat, and fertility

The last chapter was devoted mainly to a consideration of
sex from a male point of view. It concentrated on mating
because this is characteristic of male behavior, thanks to the
fact that, as we saw at the beginning, sex is defined in terms
of the size of the sex cells, and males, by definition, have sex
cells which are small, highly mobile and, in terms of the key
concept of parental investment, cheap. The consequence, as
we saw, was that males tend to concentrate on mating
success – in other words, on gaining access to females and
fertilizing them – rather than on investment in offspring as
such. But now the time has come to redress the balance
somewhat and consider the female point of view.

The first thing which might be said is that the concept of
parental investment is one which is much more sensitive to
female interests than is a concept which narrowly defines sex
in terms of chromosomes. According to the latter, sex is
determined by the sex chromosome, something which, in
the case of mammals at least, defines the male, not the
female. This is because a mammalian female has two so-
called X chromosomes, whereas a male has one X and one Y
(a terminology which vaguely recalls the shapes of the
chromosomes in question). Recent research has shown that,
as one might have expected, the genetic determinants of
masculinity are found on the male's Y chromosome. Indeed,

we know today that masculinity is determined by a single gene on that chromosome which acts as a biochemical switch, or trigger. This gene turns on other genes (not all necessarily on the Y chromosome), which in their turn initiate a cascade of biochemical activity, transforming an embryo that would otherwise develop as a female into one that will become a male.

According to this way of looking at things, sex is a question of chromosomes, and masculinity a case of having a chromosome which females lack. Indeed, sex itself seems essentially masculine in the sense than an asexual species is one lacking a sex chromosome. However, it is by no means an invariable rule that the sex chromosome, if it exists, defines the male. In the case of birds, for example, the situation is the reverse, and it is the female who possesses the sex-defining chromosome analogous to the Y chromosome in mammals, and it is as a male that a bird embryo would develop in the absence of this chromosome. Indeed, in some cases, such as alligators, crocodiles, and turtles, there is no sex chromosome of any kind, despite the fact that adults are unambiguously male or female. By contrast, the distinction of the sexes on the basis of parental investment in the sex cells is a universal one where sex cells are distinguishable and one, furthermore, which takes account of what is distinctively female in sexuality, as well as what may or may not be distinctively male.

As we have already seen, what is distinctively female is a greater degree of parental investment, something which recalls our attention to the fundamental reality of sex: that it is basically concerned, like all evolved adaptations, with reproductive success, but that, unlike many, it is intimately involved with the process of reproduction itself. Here parental investment is an essential factor, not merely genetic transmission; and here the female, with her greater commitment to parental investment – at least in the sex cells and often in many other ways as well – represents a reality which males, with their minimal degree of parental investment, have reasons of their own to discount. Nowhere is this more clearly seen than in mammals like ourselves, where an extreme form of sex-role specialization has occurred whereby females retain the developing young within their own bodies and continue to invest in them heavily after their birth by producing a specialized food in the form of breast milk. If sex chromosomes are taken to be the essential factor in sex, male and female appear to contribute equally because, in a diploid species with sex-defining chromosomes like human beings, the male contributes one sex chromosome and the female the other. But in terms of the more general and abstract concept of parental investment, females invariably contribute much more in the case of most organisms and, in that of mammals like human beings, unmistakably so. A view of sex which ignores this fundamental fact is likely not merely to be superficial, but to be particularly insensitive to the characteristically female aspect of sex, especially in an organism like a mammal where female parental investment is great, unequivocal, and essential to a female's reproductive success. Modern human beings especially, with cheap and efficient means of contraception, are particularly likely to want to divorce the idea of sex from that of reproduction, and many of these may in fact be women. But, as we can now see, sex divorced from reproduction and fertilization isolated from further parental investment are characteristically male ways of looking at things and can hardly be regarded as free from subjective bias.

But if a narrowly genetic or superficially anatomical or behavioral view of sex does violence to female interests, so too does group selection, with its implicit assumption that sex exists for the benefit of reproducing not the individual but the species. If this were the case, then females, with their usually much greater commitment to parental investment, would be seen as doing their duty for the species. So too, of course, would males. But the fact that females are obliged to contribute so much more in terms of investment in their offspring means that while the benefit is regarded as accruing to all members of the species equally, the highly unequal cost born by females is largely ignored. In a way typical of group-benefit thinking, there is a tendency to neglect the individual's point of view and to ride roughshod over the fact that some invariably pay much more for the presumed mutual benefit than do others. While males have fun indulging in sex and violence "for the benefit of reproducing the species," females stay at home doing their rather more exacting duty also for the species' benefit. But such a view seldom questions why females should put up with an unequal share of the costs of reproduction of the species. On the contrary, it tends to assume that all this is right and proper and that the sexual division of labor is unproblematic, fixed, and much more equitable than it ever is. An individualistic view, however, immediately reveals the violence done to female interests in this tendentious, collectivistic way of thinking. It reminds us that the costs of reproduction do not fall equitably on all and that female interests are seldom identical to male ones and never the same as some vague, abstract "good of the species." With these general considerations in mind, let us now turn to a consideration of the whole question of sex from the point of view of the theory of parental investment and its unique insights into individual – and particularly female – interests.

Looking at sex in the broader terms of parental investment rather than the narrow terms of genetics has prepared us for the realization that in mammals especially, where the offspring is retained within the mother's body for the duration of its early development, the mother ought to be sensitive to the enormous costs involved in bringing a pregnancy to term and should be selective, both about the embryos implanted in her and about their subsequent development. Indeed, in certain circumstances she should be sensitive to the desirability of ovulating at all. Since maternal investment in the developing fetus is principally in the form of nutrients, it is not surprising that recent research has shown that it is the level of such nutrients stored in the mother's body – fat, in other words – which is critical to fertility. This finding explains why the age of menarche (the point at which a young woman beings to menstruate) has dropped progressively with rises in living standards in general and nutrition in particular, from an average of 15.5 years a century ago in the USA to one of 12.6 years today. It also explains why body weight, rather than other indicators such as height, appears to be the critical factor. Body fat increases prior to menarche by a factor of 120 percent and in so doing reaches a critical level of 24 percent by weight at the onset of sexual cycling. However, early sexual cycles tend to be infertile and irregular, and a further increase in body fat proportion to a typical 28 percent is achieved by age eighteen, at which point full fertility is normally achieved. So sensitive is the female body to body weight variations that some women athletes can turn their sexual cycles on and off at will with just a three-pound change in weight.[1]

In the case of the Ache hunter-gatherers mentioned earlier (see above, pp. 86–7), the mean age at which women first gave birth was found to be the same as that at which they first reached mean weight for adult females in the population. It was also found that heavier women had more children, had them more closely spaced, and had children who survived better than did the offspring of lighter women.[2] If twinning can be seen as a comparable effect, it is worth pointing out that sheep have long been known to be much more likely to give birth to twins if ewes are fed a high-calorie diet for a week or two prior to mating. In what seems to be a close human parallel, the rate of fraternal twinning was found to decline during the wartime food shortages in a number of Western European countries but returned to normal levels afterwards. The fact that the rate of identical twinning remained the same suggests that, since fraternal twins develop from two eggs but identical twins from one, it was an increase in the number of eggs released during the cycle which accounted for the change. The fact that both menstruation and ovulation appear to be inhibited by weight loss and restored by gains in weight can be explained by the observation that the vascularization of the uterus which precedes menstruation in women can be seen as a form of parental investment in anticipation of conception and implantation and consequently represents a real cost which can be saved (for example, to the extent that menstrual bleeding can increase the risk of anaemia).

Again, the finding that emotional stress can interrupt or disturb the sexual cycle is also explicable if we make the not unreasonable assumption that such stress would normally indicate unfavorable social or psychological circumstances for starting a pregnancy.[3] Indeed, according to a recently proposed model, anorexia nervosa, an eating disorder found predominantly in young women and involving severe loss of weight with the resulting suppression of the sexual cycle, may be explicable as an extreme example of this. Its occurrence at the beginning of a woman's reproductive life and often after her first sexual experiences, along with its effect of suppressing her fertility, suggests it may be seen as a means whereby young women who are not yet ready to begin their reproductive lives bring about a postponement. If this were true, we would expect anorexia to be more common where the costs of delaying reproduction were lower thanks to increased life expectancy, decreased child mortality, and generally high standards of health and welfare. The fact that it is indeed found in the affluent societies of the West but hardly at all in the Third World bears out the prediction that anorexia is to be expected predominantly where life is most secure and a woman's reproductive life is the longest. Again, anorexics often come from family backgrounds with above average social, economic, or psychological stress or have dominating manipulative parents who wish them to postpone their reproductive lives in the interests of educational, social, or career achievement. This finding too argues for seeing anorexia as motivated by stresses of various kinds which a young woman might implicitly interpret as evidence of the undesirability of embarking on her reproductive life at that particular time. The finding that weight loss plays a central role in the illness only underlines the force of the realization that fatness is a critical factor in fertility.[4]

The circumstance that the maximum number of fertile cycles does not usually occur until a woman is between twenty-six and thirty years of age suggests that disorders like anorexia, although largely confined to the affluent societies of the West and therefore presumably to the modern world, nevertheless rest on a deeper evolutionary foundation: one which discounts early sterility as less costly than it would be later. However, the incidence of infertile and irregular cycles rises again sharply after age forty, to be followed within five to fifteen years by a complete cessation (menopause). This shows that as a woman ages, a point may be reached when her ultimate reproductive success is better served by terminating her own reproductive life and instead investing in her existing children and grandchildren. (That a comparable effect is not seen in men to anything like the same extent presumably results from the fact that while a man of sixty might easily manage the exertions involved in fertilizing a woman, a woman of sixty would face a much more daunting task in carrying his offspring to term and caring for it afterwards.)

But even if a woman is cycling normally, not all her eggs will become fertilized by any particular individual male's sperm. Indeed, approximately 25 percent of all cases of female infertility involve an immune response to sperm, which are treated as if they were invading micro-organisms, and even among normally fertile women 8 percent have antibodies against some sperm. Of those eggs which are fertilized, 10–15 percent will fail to implant, and only 42 percent will be sufficiently viable to halt the menstrual cycle. Even then, the probability of a spontaneous abortion before term is approximately 28 percent, which means that only about one-third of all eggs susceptible to fertilization result in a live birth. Here too, age is a factor, with the number of potentially effective copulations per pregnancy rising from

176 for women under twenty years of age to 290 for those in their thirties and 1,434 for those over forty.[5] Such findings are corroborated by recent experience with *in vitro* fertilization (that is, fertilization of a woman's eggs outside her own body), which suggests that the mother's reproductive tract actively discriminates against fertilized eggs which are abnormal or imperfect. Indeed, if we recall the basic principles of parental investment theory set out earlier, we will see that mammalian mothers in particular ought to be selected to be especially discriminating about starting out on the enormously long and costly process of gestating an embryo and bringing it to a live birth.

. Furthermore, exactly the same argument should apply to spontaneous abortion (or miscarriage), and indeed a great deal of evidence suggests that it does. In human beings overall about a fifth of all pregnancies do indeed end in spontaneous abortion. As far as age is concerned, the number of miscarriages per pregnancy is approximately 4 percent for teenage mothers and rises to 18 percent for women over forty. However, the fact that older women abort only about 3 percent of normal fetuses, whereas mothers at the peak reproductive age of twenty-five abort 30 percent, suggests that older women are more selective in the fetuses which they do retain, despite their higher overall rate of spontaneous abortion. The same picture is conveyed by the finding that when age is held constant, mothers with existing offspring have twice the rate of spontaneous abortion as compared with mothers who are pregnant for the first time. Mothers in England and Wales with unusually large families for their age also tend to have high rates of miscarriage, and even if we were tempted to put this down to the general wear and tear of having a large family, the fact remains that this is a further example of the critical role which maternal health plays in the likelihood of conception.

In more than 60 percent of miscarriages some abnormality is found in the rejected fetus, and at least 30 percent of spontaneous abortions in the first three months of pregnancy show gross chromosomal anomalies. But perhaps the most telling evidence for maternal discrimination against defective fetuses in spontaneous abortion comes from a study of 268 female prison inmates who collectively had 373 live children and of whom 136 had had at least one termination of pregnancy. On average, 27 of the children would normally be expected to have been born with birth defects, whereas in fact there was none – a finding which suggests that the unfavorable environmental conditions of these women's lives had led to increased discrimination against fetuses which were in any way unfit. Finally, the fact that at least 78 percent of all fetuses spontaneously aborted in the first three months of pregnancy are male suggests that, since spontaneous abortion is correlated with maternal condition and abnormality in the fetus, maternal investment discriminates against males in such unfavorable circumstances for reasons which will be explained later (see below, pp. 197–207).

Again, parental investment theory would predict that the earlier the pregnancy was terminated, the better, since further investment in a failing project is seldom justifiable. In fact, 30 percent of spontaneous abortions occur within eight weeks, 60 percent between nine and sixteen weeks, and only 10 percent thereafter. As we would also predict, miscarriage, although most always fatal for the fetus, seldom kills the mother, with an overall rate of between five and ten maternal fatalities as a result of spontaneous abortion for every 10,000 live births.[6] Furthermore, it is worth pointing out that, contrary to myths circulated by anti-abortion pressure groups, the same is true of induced abortions which are competently carried out. Statistical data show that legal abortion is distinctly safer than giving birth, with women undergoing therapeutic abortions being one hundred times less likely to have complications requiring surgery than women bearing children.[7]

Again, as theory would predict, a study of the reproductive lives of 300 white, middle-class American women in the Los Angeles area aged thirty-five to forty-five years of age found that the pregnancies were much more likely to be ended by voluntary induced abortion if the mother was unmarried, older, or, if married, uncertain that her husband was the father of the child. By contrast, greater reproductive success was found to be associated with being married, having confidence of paternity, being less promiscuous, coming from a larger family, and having better mental health. Since coming from a larger family seemed to mean having more relatives to invest in one's own offspring, and being less promiscuous served to heighten confidence in the husband's paternity and therefore his presumed readiness to invest in offspring, it seems that every one of these factors reflects the single most important underlying factor in mammalian reproductive success: the degree of parental investment.[8]

Finally, it is worth mentioning the possibility that postnatal depression (sometimes called "baby blues"), a very common affliction among women who have just given birth, may also have an evolutionary explanation along these lines. Here, the idea is that birth is the first opportunity a mother has of testing the ability of her offspring to survive unaided. A child who is not going to make it to reproductive age would normally not justify further investment, because it could not be expected to contribute to the mother's ultimate reproductive success. The fact that human babies are born with unusually large deposits of subcutaneous fat (for a primate) suggests the possibility that they have evolved this trait to enable them to survive the week or so of comparative maternal neglect which postnatal depression seems to produce in mothers. The Mexico City earthquake a few years ago showed that, long after their mothers were dead, newborn babies could still be retrieved alive, in a few cases up to fourteen days after they had first been incarcerated by the collapse of a maternity clinic. As far as mothers are concerned, postnatal depression may simply be a kind of hormonally induced psychological brake on their readiness to accept a child and invest in it until, by surviving a few days of relative neglect, it has proved that it has the right stuff to justify the enormous investment that will still be necessary if it is to reach reproductive age. From before ovulation to after birth – and, as we shall see later, well beyond that – parental investment appears to be the critical factor underlying numerous characteristic female adaptations.

Sex and female choice

Where a sexual species has become asexual, as is the case in some lizards and fish, we could regard all individuals as "female," and all their offspring – the occasional mutant aside – would be exact genetic copies of their "mothers": so-called clones. One consequence of this is that the population could grow much more quickly because its members would not need to "waste" resources producing males who cannot directly produce offspring of their own, not to mention benefit from the savings gained from not having to bother with courtship, finding a suitable mate, and dealing with problems like the desertion dilemmas or other conflicts outlined in the previous chapter. Since sexual reproduction always demands two cooperating individuals of different sexes, and since the self-interest of the sexes will seldom be identical in every respect, the cost of such a social dimension to reproduction must almost always be significant, and its avoidance by means of asexual cloning seemingly worth-while. Insofar as males contribute little or nothing to investment in offspring – and it is important to remember that this is the rule in sexual species overall (not least in mammals) – it seems especially paradoxical that females who do invest in offspring should both produce such males themselves and be dependent on them for fertilization. To the extent that every organism in an asexual species is a female, one might rephrase the problem in the form: why should females bother with males who at best might abandon them completely after mating and who at worst are nothing but a continuing source of trouble? More pertinently for human beings, we might ask: why should women put up with men at all?

Since men do indeed exist, we can presume that, unlike the extinct males of some species of lizard which have become uni-sexual and exclusively female in this sense, men continue to exist because they benefit individual women in some way or other. This in its turn suggests that women specifically, but females in general, might have some kind of choice, with regard to both the very existence of males and perhaps the choice of particular attributes of the males they have. This, in its turn, casts a new and surprising light on the question of the relation between the sexes in evolution. Indeed, it suggests that females are far from being the passive victims of male domination which evolutionary biology allegedly makes them. On the contrary, it raises the possibility that the existence of males in general and men in particular may be ultimately the outcome of female interests and that Darwin's widely ridiculed concept of *female choice* may be the key to understanding why at least some males are the way they are – possibly even human ones.

Much of the contempt with which the concept of female choice was met at the time it was first put forward and some of the skepticism which still greets it today may be accounted for by the fact that females often appear to submit passively to male advances and to be victims, either of male size and force or of male propaganda and advertising. In the former case, admittedly, it looks as if females are physically coerced by males, who are usually larger and more aggressive than they. Nevertheless, appearances can be misleading, because even where, as in the vast majority of quadrupedal mammals, males mount females in what seems to be a dominating posture, it only takes a little movement by the female in question for all the male's efforts to penetrate her to come to nothing. For instance, she can always walk away. If the male has his front legs upon her back and his two back legs on the ground, there is absolutely no way that he can succeed if she does not at least stand still! And even if she does not walk away, an uncooperative posture can often make penetration difficult or impossible for a quadrupedal male. In the case of camels, for example, the female must first sit down before the male can mount her, and the subsequent copulation takes some considerable time. In very many animals the female must perform lordosis, a characteristic arching of the back, if successful mounting by the male is to occur.

So important is female cooperation in mammalian mating that some males have evolved a subtle trick in the form of neck-biting to calm and coax the female. Mothers in many quadrupedal mammalian species pick up their younger offspring between their jaws to carry them and natural selection has long since disposed of those who squirmed and tried to escape and were bitten deeply as a result. Today a reflex triggered by being grasped by the scruff of the neck induces relaxation and immobility in the infants of many mammals such as cats and dogs. Evidently something of this reflex survives into adult life, because males sometimes appear to exploit it in mounting females, who often become noticeably quieter as a result. Again, even fiercely armed males, like wild sheep or deer, court their females gently and affectionately, rather than aggressively, because they too need the cooperation of their female partner if successful mounting and impregnation are to occur.

Darwin himself based the idea of female choice on the fact that not all sexually dimorphic males appear to be so as a result of the inter-male conflict that so often accompanies sex, especially among mammals. The tails of peacocks and the plumage of birds of paradise suggest that ostentatious male displays can also be an aspect of sexual dimorphism and that sheer beauty, as well as naked violence, can be a product of sexual selection. This also suggests that an ability to appreciate beauty, so often jealously claimed by human beings as distinctive of themselves and evidence of some intrinsic superiority, cannot in reality be limited to them alone. On the contrary, an aesthetic sense must be fundamentally common to all animals where displays of these kinds have evolved, because it is a fact that what impresses females of the species in question often impresses human aesthetic sensibilities as well. Furthermore, this is an observation which would have to include, not merely peahens and birds of paradise but also the female guppy, whose discerning eye evidently sees much that many human keepers of guppies do in the gorgeous tails of the males of this species of small, freshwater fish.

The vivid plumage of "bright birds" such as parrots represents something of a paradox, because it hardly makes them less visible to predators. Indeed, the greatly elongated and no less colorful tails of peacocks cannot possibly help in this respect either, and studies of guppies – the peacocks of the fish world – indicate that they do indeed pay a price in increased vulnerability to predators for their greatly enlarged, gorgeously iridescent tails. However, other studies of guppies have shown that males with larger and brighter tails are preferred by females, who, as in many other species, have some choice in which male mates with them, since fertilization is internal and cannot be achieved without at least the tacit compliance of the female in not swimming away. Evidently, the cost of a brightly colored tail to male survival is balanced by its benefit to a male's ultimate reproductive success in a natural equivalent of what one might call the "too-fast-to-live-too-young-to-die" syndrome.

In the case of male guppies, tail and body coloration are exquisitely sensitive to the health and well-being of the individual in question, so that even a purely psychological stress like being moved from one aquarium to another usually registers as a distinct fading of coloration which often persists for as much as a day or two. The phrase "off-colour" applies to them much more than it does to females, in whom the first signs of illness are more often the appearance of actual fungal growths, visible wasting, or other direct manifestations of attack by disease or parasites, rather than any loss of what dull coloration they have.

According to a recent theory, much the same is true of

bright plumage in many birds, which "advertises," so to speak, the healthy status of the male in question and, by implication, the superior, disease-resistant nature of his genes.[9] Like harmony in human aesthetics, which may reveal an absence of deception and inner contradiction in a symbolic message, the appearance of bright birds may please because it reveals the essential integrity of the individual's health and well-being. If, as seems likely, sex itself evolved as a means of genetic recombination in an uncertain, changeable world in which large, long-lived organisms were constantly under attack by diseases and parasites, it follows that genes for disease-resistance may be especially important if, as in the case of birds like parrots and fish like guppies, the advertising organism has a much longer generation time than the parasites which attack it. If endemic infestation by parasites which cause chronic, debilitating illnesses is present, natural selection might favor females who chose males with the best genes for resisting such attack. Yet genes cannot be seen, so bright plumage or some other external show which can be vividly and unmistakably recognized evolves in order to advertise the superior disease-resistance of its bearers. If the advertisement is truthful in the sense that it does indeed take excellent health and good disease-resistance to stay "in the pink" rather than "off-color," then selection could favor it, despite its inevitable cost in also advertising the existence of the male in question to predators or other dangerous adversaries.

If female choice results in distinctive forms of sexual dimorphism like the colorful tails of peacocks and guppies or the plumage of parrots, it follows that males who currently possess those attributes must be descended disproportionately from those males in the past who first acquired them. Obviously, for female choice to have any meaning, it must result in certain, preferred males having a great deal of reproductive success and other, less preferred ones having much less. Furthermore, since female choice implies a scale of preferences for females, it follows that even if all males do come to possess the preferred attribute, such as a colorful tail, some males are likely to possess it to a greater extent than others, so that female choice for the attribute in question tends to drive sexual selection to an extreme. Such is evidently the explanation of the glorious tails of peacocks and guppies, which probably represent the extreme degree of selection possible – that is, the point at which the cost of the decoration begins to outweigh its benefit to the individual male's ultimate reproductive success.

Such competition among females for the genes of the choicest males implies multi-female breeding of some kind: either classic polygyny, with a number of females choosing a single, preferred mate; polygamy, with a number of females mated to a number of preferred males; or, at the very least, some highly compromised form of monogamy in which some males account for many more actual fertilizations than do others (for example, by cuckolding the other males as the swallows with the elongated tails did in my earlier example: see above, pp. 140–1). In the case of birds of paradise, sexual dimorphism appears to be largely the result of female choice of bright, ostentatious plumage in males whose degree of dimorphism reaches an extreme in the most polygynous species and a minimum in the most monogamous.[10]

But to what extent does human polygyny – evidently the predominate mating strategy of human societies overall as we have already seen – relate to the foregoing arguments about female choice and selection for signs of disease-resistant genes? A recent study tried to answer this question by considering the degree of polygyny and exposure to disease in ninety-three distinct societies chosen from a larger standard cross-cultural sample. It found that there was a significant relationship between the total seriousness of the risk of disease and the degree of polygyny, no matter how it was measured. Nor could this finding be explained by some other connection, such as one between the size of groups and the degree of polygyny, because the former is not correlated with the prevalence of disease and the latter does not correlate with group size.[11]

Nevertheless, these findings raise a number of difficulties. One of these is establishing the reality of female choice in recent polygynous cultures. As the study acknowledges, it is very doubtful whether women do have a great deal of freedom to decide whom they will marry in most of the polygynous societies sampled. Another difficulty is that men do not appear to possess any obvious display comparable to the plumage of parrots or birds of paradise. As we have already seen (above, pp. 143–5), what sexual dimorphism they do show seems to be largely related to conflict between males rather than to female choice as such. Even if beards, for example, are taken as such displays rather than as protective manes, they are hardly colorful enough or sufficiently appealing aesthetically to suggest that they were produced by the same mechanism that gave the peacock its fabulous tail or birds of paradise their plumage. Furthermore, the fact that males of some primate species display gaudily colored patches on the face suggests that such adaptations are not confined to birds and can be found in a few cases at least in our own order. Again, the study from which I quoted above found that even if culturally augmented sexual signals were considered (such as personal dress and ornament), only a very marginal correlation was found with risk of disease.[12] Indeed, in modern societies one cannot help noticing that it is women, rather than men, who collectively spend billions of dollars on cosmetics and that female attire is usually considerably more colorful and ostentatious than that of males. Admittedly, this does not seem to be quite so true in polygynous societies such as those of the modern Muslim world, in which women, by contrast to men, dress drably and self-effacingly, often to the literal extent of veiling themselves in the black cloak of purdah. Yet even here it would be very hard to show that what males advertise in their rather more ostentatious appearance is directly and immediately related to their resistance to disease.

However, such complications are by no means limited to the human case. In that of bowerbirds, males are not so much decorated themselves as decorators of elaborate constructions to which females come, often to be shown the most prized pieces of the resident male's collection of flowers, shells, and other brightly colored objects. Some even paint their bowers with the juices of berries, and others decorate structures which resemble maypoles or Christmas trees. One bower-bird no larger than a robin constructs a thatched, rain-proof bower 1.5 m high by 2.5 m wide. If such bowers were used as nests, there would be little difficulty in saying just what it is that females are choosing. Obviously, if males provide investment in the form of a nest or food or some such item, females will choose the males who are the best providers, and often do. Indeed, we shall see in a moment that this may be the key to some of the secrets of the human female sexual cycle. In the case of birds who build bowers, however, no such practical purpose is normally fulfilled, and females who visit and are sufficiently impressed to allow a male to mate with them will not be seen by him again. However, experimental manipulation of the bowers and decorations of the satin bowerbird in Australia showed that the best-built, best-decorated, and best-maintained bowers were indeed those of males who showed the greatest mating success. Observation also revealed that males had competed among themselves, both for scarce resources in the form of sites, building materials, and decorations and in defending their bowers from theft, hijacking, and vandalism by other males.

From this it seems to follow that females were making choices based not merely on a male's bower-building skill (which is related to his age and experience, since younger males take time to learn the art) but also on his status in relation to other males where competition for scarce resources was concerned. This is something which happens more or less automatically where males compete directly with one another for mating success, and it is not implausible to suppose that success in competition with other males is just as good a guide to the quality of a male's genes, including those for disease-resistance, as is the maintenance of bright and elaborate plumage. The finding that male bowerbirds' coloration tends to be less vivid and ostentatious the more colorful and elaborate their bowers suggests that they have effected some kind of transfer of their display from their own plumage to the decorations of their bowers. Indeed, it is noteworthy in this respect that the trophies which satin bowerbirds appear to value most highly of all are blue feathers so rare that they are stolen much more frequently than any other decoration.[13]

Such a transfer from bird to bower would make evolutionary sense if males benefited by reduced vulnerability to predation thanks to a reduction in the brightness of their plumage. Perhaps females who went along with this transfer were also implicitly choosing males who could not merely resist disease and other males better, but those who also faired better with regard to predators. However, the weakness in this chain of reasoning lies in explaining how females could have started on such a transfer in the first place. Probably we shall never know, but one possibility is that bower-building may have begun as a form of nest-construction and that females choose males partly for what they were able to contribute in terms of parental investment and not merely for their bright coloration or elaborate displays. If, at a later time, circumstances changed so that females did not need male assistance in nest-building, then the purely ornamental bower might have evolved purely by female choice of matings with the most desirable males.

Female choice for male parental investment in one form or another is certainly much easier to explain than the mysteries of bower-building, and the human equivalent of the latter in no sense strains credulity. For example, to claim that men may compete the way bowerbirds do for scarce resources in order to attract desirable mates makes perfect sense if the women attracted see males' potential for holding scarce resources such as homes, land, provisions, and wealth in general as indicative of his capacity to invest in offspring. The excellent evidence now available from computer dating agencies shows that while both sexes rate an attractive personality, intelligence, and good health highly, women put a higher valuation on a man's general earning and wealth-holding ability than do men on comparable qualities in a woman. Since women have traditionally been reliant on men for important aspects of parental investment in their offspring, this finding is not in the least surprising. Indeed, and as we shall go on to see, it is possible that one or two peculiar adaptations of human females fit in with this picture.

Secrets of the sexual cycle

Earlier, when considering male sexual adaptations, we saw that testis size is a surprisingly significant indicator of sexual behavior, albeit one which was largely overlooked until very recently (see above, pp. 147–9). A parallel case where female adaptations are concerned is what we might term *cryptic estrus*. Estrus is that part of a female's sexual cycle when fertilization is likely to occur. Figure 4.2 (p. 147) illustrates how much bigger a female chimpanzee's external genitalia get at this point in her cycle as compared to those of a woman. The reason for this massive genital engorgement in female chimpanzees is that it serves to advertise the time at which they are most likely to conceive and to motivate males to mate with them then. Indeed, the multi-male breeding group to which female chimpanzees normally have access may mean that females benefit as a result of the ensuing competition among males for sexual access. This would not be female choice so much as feminine incitement to encourage the most successful males to make sure it is they who sire the greatest number of offspring. But it would also be to the ultimate benefit of a female's reproductive success, because the sons of males who succeed in fathering the greatest number of offspring would presumably inherit the secret of their fathers' reproductive success in many cases, thereby providing a female with many more grandchildren than she might otherwise have. Yet although closely related to chimpanzees in terms of evolutionary descent, modern women are totally unlike their chimpanzee sisters, not merely in not advertising the time at which they are going to ovulate and conceive, but in actually hiding it so effectively that it was not until the 1930s that medical science definitely established when it occurred. This is why we are justified in calling human estrus "cryptic," a term defined by *The Concise Oxford English Dictionary* as meaning, among other things, "secret," "mysterious," "enigmatic," and "serving for concealment."

According to an influential theory first put forward by Richard Alexander and Katharine Noonan, cryptic estrus evolved in humans because it enabled females to force desirable males into "consort relationships" with them – this by virtue of the fact that a male who lacked any indication of when a female was about to ovulate would have to have intercourse with her over a considerable span of the sexual cycle if he was to make her pregnant with his own offspring. This, in turn, they argue, would heighten a male's confidence that his female consort's offspring were indeed his, because "only a male who tended her more or less continuously could be sure of the paternity of her offspring."[14] This is important because natural selection will obviously not reward males who invest in other male's children and because Alexander and Noonan are probably right in regarding increased male parental investment as the key to human evolution. The enormous expansion of the brain is obviously an important factor and seems to have gone along with a trend towards the birth of bigger-brained, but more helpless and slower-maturing offspring, who would presumably be more dependent on parental investment from *both* parents. They also apply a similar argument to try to explain female orgasm, suggesting that a dramatic release of sexual tension by a woman may help to persuade her mate that she is truly satisfied and that she is unlikely to seek further matings elsewhere (thereby arousing inevitable doubts about paternity of any offspring conceived).

Although this story is probably correct in its general outline, it may have defects in its details. For example, many divorced and deserted wives – not to mention the odd husband – will wonder why a "consort relationship" (presumably modeled on monogamy) excludes the possibility of philandering (some would argue it does the exact opposite!) Again, one could turn the argument about certainty of paternity on its head and argue that advertisement of ovulation would increase it, since a male who consorted with a female at the critical time (as some chimpanzees do, for example) could be much more certain that the offspring were his. This way of looking at the matter is suggested by studies of polyandrously mated hedge sparrows, which seem to show that males allocate their investment in relation to the likelihood of offspring being theirs as a result of having had access to the female during the mating period – which DNA fingerprinting confirms as a good predictor of paternity.[15]

As far as orgasm is concerned, the fact that human females, by contrast to males, are capable of multiple orgasms might be explained by arguing that they were adapted to want as many orgasms as a male could give in order to prevent him going elsewhere. But, to the extent that this suggests sexual insatiability, it tends to contradict the argument about female orgasm signaling complete satisfaction. Rather than the female orgasm evolving to mimic the male's, as Alexander and Noonan suppose, it may instead have been a question of females choosing males who could not conceal – or fake – the moment of ejaculation as preferable to those who could. Satisfied that a male had truly ejaculated and able to provide as many opportunities as he might wish to repeat the experience, his female partner's confidence in his commitment to her might also be enhanced. A woman's orgasm would then be an adaptation making it difficult for her to let go of the man until she was fully satisfied and he had ejaculated, with her satisfaction tending to take longer than his, as it evidently often does. Finally, the terms "parental care" and "parental investment" are vague in Alexander and Noonan's theory and could probably be made more specific, perhaps in the following way.

For approximately 98 percent of the time that the genus *Homo* has existed, we have been hunter-gatherers and are probably predominantly adapted for a way of life like that pursued by the Australian aborigines and a number of other groups such as the Ache of Paraguay mentioned earlier. As we have already seen when discussing reciprocal altruism, primal hunting was almost certainly a cooperative venture and, in the case of present-day hunters of small game in forest habitats like the Ache, kills are widely shared among the whole hunting group. As we also saw earlier, a study of the latter showed that the men provided 87 percent of the calorific intake of the group from hunting, with the women providing the rest from their largely vegetarian collecting activities. However, although food was usually shared out by someone other than the one who had killed it, better hunters (understood as those who acquired more meat per hour spent hunting) had higher survivorship of their reported offspring and more sexual success measured in terms of extramarital relationships (see above, pp. 86–7).[16] If such findings are typical – and there is every reason to think that they should be, since natural selection would indeed reward hunters whose success could be measured in ultimate reproductive terms – it follows that, since time immemorial, male hunters may have bargained their meat for matings. (Indeed, if we come to think about it, even today it is not unknown for a man to establish his place in a lady's affections by first providing her with presents and a meal at an expensive restaurant.)

If this is so, it follows that females who advertised their period of estrus as chimpanzees do could not have expected much in the way of meat when they were not in estrus. This is because natural selection would reward males who tended to part with meat only for a mating with an estrous female –

in other words, with one who was likely to conceive. Meat given to non-ovulating females would have been "wasted" in the sense that it would have secured fewer offspring than that exchanged for matings with females in estrus. Since meat is a highly nutritious and very concentrated form of sustenance, and since food is a major resource needed by human females (so much so that, as we have just seen, they will stop cycling altogether if their weight drops below a critical value), it is not inconceivable that estrus-concealing females became selected merely because they could obtain much more meat from males than could their estrus-advertising sisters.

But here a problem arises (as Alexander and Noonan recognized in their original, rather more generalized version of the theory). It is this. If males were sexually aroused by signs of estrus in ancestral human females in much the same way as male chimpanzees are aroused by the genital swellings of female chimpanzees, there is no reason to think that females who suppressed an estrus signal would benefit at all. Rather than provide them with meat because they could not know when such females were about to ovulate, males would have been more likely to ignore them altogether and to become aroused only by estrus-advertising females. Obviously, natural selection would not favor permanently non-advertising females; but it probably would favor permanently advertising ones. In other words, hominid females who retained the estrus advertisement throughout their sexual cycle would indeed have succeeded in mystifying males about when they were actually going to ovulate and at the same time would have succeeded in making it necessary for those males to provision them – as well as to mate with them – throughout the sexual cycle. If such continuous provisioning played a part in promoting the reproductive success of such seemingly permanently estrous females, as it almost certainly would have done, then cryptic estrus could have been a major adaptation of hominid females in response to hunting by hominid males.

But, if this is the case, where is the permanent estrus

signal? Figure 4.2 (p. 147) shows that it is not of the kind found in female chimpanzees. Admittedly, pubic hair seems an obvious permanent signal, easily visible in a naked biped, and does indeed develop at puberty and fade after menopause. But its possession by men weakens the argument and suggests that in both sexes it probably serves more to indicate reproductive status in general than to suggest permanent estrus in particular. Nevertheless, the adult women of some African hunter-gatherers exhibit *steatopygia*, a permanent enlargement of the buttocks, and all women exhibit some degree of rounding-out of this part of their bodies. Furthermore, if men's magazines are taken as the reliable indicator of male tastes that they probably are, it is evident that some men find this part of the female anatomy especially interesting (with the human version of lordosis one of the most popular poses). Equally, if not more, interesting is another feature which women do not share with chimpanzees but do reveal in men's magazines: their prominent breasts. Human beings overall show numerous adaptive parallels with the gelada baboon, one of which is that we are the only two primate species whose females carry a secondary sexual display on the chest. In the case of female geladas this is a hairless area hung with small polyps which enlarge and redden during estrus. However, young female geladas also show a notable swelling of the chest patch during estrus, and it is tempting to speculate that the permanent chest swelling which we call the female breasts may indeed have evolved from a once periodic sexual signal which has become permanent in the way which I have suggested. If this is so, then estrus would have become cryptic in the human case not so much by hiding the ovulation signal, as by permanently exhibiting it in the form of the female breast.

Mysteries of menstruation

If correct, this line of reasoning may also explain another peculiarity of human female adaptations: *menstrual synchron-*

ization. By this I mean the tendency for women who live in close domestic intimacy to have their periods at more or less the same time. Modern research has shown that the synchronization comes about through chemical contact; experimenters were able to synchronize the cycles of women who did not come into contact via armpit dabs from one being applied to another's top upper lip. Nor does the effect take long to make itself felt. The last time I held a class on this subject a student remarked that she had been living in a residence with a group of other female students for only four months, yet already their cycles were more or less completely synchronized.

A possible explanation for this relates to the foregoing argument about cryptic estrus. One cyclic symptom which women cannot conceal is menstrual bleeding. Presumably this is because the benefit of parental investment in anticipation in the form of a richly vasculated lining to the womb is worth more to the ultimate reproductive success of a woman than its concealment would be. Yet there is nothing to stop males with meat avoiding mating with menstruating females to the males' advantage. Indeed, we know that in many cultures, both modern and traditional, men tend to avoid intercourse with menstruating women. If the result of this was that a woman lost potential parental investment in her offspring, either born or unborn, thanks to the fact that she was menstruating when another potential partner of her mate or mates was not, selection might favor synchronizing menstruation so that, even if menstruating women were not provisioned, no individual woman lost out, and all did equally well – or badly – as the case may be.

Some have argued that synchronized menstruation should be interpreted as Alexander and Noonan interpret cryptic estrus, as a means of "increasing the stability of an existing consortship."[17] However, the fact that it is found in hamadryas baboons, a highly polygynous species, argues that the "consortship" need be neither monogamous nor involve a degree of male parental investment which even remotely approaches human levels. On the contrary, the fact that it is not reported for the otherwise comparably polygynous gelada baboon suggests that menstrual synchrony has evolved among hamadryas baboons thanks to the fact that, unlike geladas, females in the harem group are not likely to be related. The consequence may be that, lacking any kind of kin-altruistic cooperation with other females in the breeding group, hamadryas females compete with each other for the attentions of the male by means of synchronizing their period of estrus, just as I am suggesting that hominid females may have done with regard to provisioning of meat by males. If this interpretation is correct, then menstrual synchronization, so apparently expressive of sisterly solidarity, would turn out to be the exact opposite: a symptom of sexual conflict among women.

This way of looking at things may also throw some light on another kind of female behavior which looks even more sisterly and cooperative: lesbianism. Earlier, when discussing cryptic sexuality, I touched on the subject of homosexuality among males, but neglected at that point to say anything about females (see above, pp. 152–6). The time has now come to remedy that omission. Although cryptic sexuality appears to be largely confined to males, we have already encountered one important aspect of it in the form of cryptic estrus in women, and the fact that female spotted hyenas possess a fully erectable cryptic penis every bit as large as that of a male as well as a cryptic scrotum suggests that sexual mimicry is not wholly confined to males. But neither is lesbianism confined to human beings. It is known among birds and has been reported in four species of gull, one species of tern, and one of geese. The birds in question are usually monogamous, but pairs of females sometimes form a lesbian relationship, which occasionally lasts many breeding seasons, often using the same nest. Homosexual female pairs of Western gulls court one another and display the same territorial behavior as do heterosexual pairs, although the characteristically male behaviors of courtship feeding and copulation are rare. Such lesbian couples usually lay more eggs than conventional male–female pairs, and genetic analysis of the contents of one such nest showed that both females had laid eggs, fathered by three different males (which meant that they could not have been co-widows of one polygynous male). However, because of the absence of courtship feeding of the female by the male, lesbian couples' eggs tended to be lighter than those of heterosexuals and hatchling survival rates were lower. The explanation of these findings (confirmed by experimental removal of males at one colony) appears to be that normally monogamous females will form lesbian relationships with other females if there is a shortage of males. A single female has no chance of raising her offspring alone, because other gulls kill chicks left at an unguarded nest. However, two females can take turns at guarding their joint progeny in a nest when the other goes off to feed, and, once fertilized, two female birds can rear young almost as well as a mixed-sex couple.[18]

Inevitably, these findings suggest an evolutionary background to human lesbianism, and it is a fact that many lesbian couples are quasi-monogamous in the sense that the partners exhibit long-term association with one another in a home that is otherwise very much like that of a mixed-sex couple, even to the extent of one tending to play the masculine, the other the feminine role. If both women have children, the analogy becomes complete and suggests that, once again, it is the concept of parental investment which is the key, not merely to sexual behavior in general, but to female behavior in particular.

But however that may be, there seems to be a case for regarding a number of characteristic adaptations of human females, such as cryptic estrus, menstrual synchronization, and, possibly lesbianism too, as indicators of a generally increased reliance on male parental investment of some kind or another. If this is the case, it suggests that our hominid ancestresses may have had a greater effective degree of choice, at least over the long span of evolutionary time, than do some of their female descendants in recent polygynous cultures. This is because selection *for* such paternal investment–acquiring adaptations as cryptic estrus and menstrual synchronization implies some kind of selection *of* males who could provide it. Furthermore, some degree of transfer of choice could have occurred in the human case as it may have done in that of bowerbirds so that features which might generally have indicated a male's capacity to provide in competition with other males could also have attested to the superior quality of his genes in general – the disease-resistant ones no less. It may be that although human male sexual dimorphism appears to be the result of inter-male conflict, which rewarded increased height, weight, and strength, such features may also have been critical in hunting success and, as a consequence, also the outcome of female choice for hunters who could deliver the goods.

However, one possible objection to such a view is that, if it were simply a question of female choice for hunting skills in males reinforcing selection for sexual dimorphism as a result of inter-male conflict, we might expect much more sexual dimorphism in the human case than we actually see. This creates problems, because there is a considerable amount of evidence that one notable feature in human evolution has been what is sometimes termed *paedomorphosis*, that is, a tendency for human beings of both sexes to become more child-like, or immature, in appearance by comparison with their ancestors. Symptoms of paedomorphic tendencies in recent human evolution are loss of body hair, reduction in the thickness of bones, flattening of the plan of the face and general rounding-out of the skull, absence of a penis-bone in males, relatively late closing of cranial sutures, and more generalized, undifferentiated form in general – all features which are also seen in fetal apes. Although, as we have already seen, the external genitals of women are dramatically different from those of adult female chimpanzees, they do bear a striking resemblance to those of sexually immature female chimpanzees, and people of both sexes retain adult teeth which are more like the milk teeth of apes than their mature dentition. Underlying this paedomorphic pattern is a tendency to reduced sexual dimorphism, since, obviously, the sexes resemble each other more the more immature the form of the organism is.

But such a paedomorphic trend could be explained if we could somehow show that it was part and parcel of the overall process of female choice for hunting skills. In fact, this is easier than it seems, because there are good reasons for believing that it would have been young, rather than mature, male hominids who first began to hunt. Experiments in which a colony of monkeys living near a beach were fed first with potatoes and then with rice left on the sand showed that it was a young member of the group who first discovered how to wash the food (as it happens, a female) and that the readiness to adopt this practice varied directly with age, younger individuals being more ready to take it up than older ones. In the second place, it seems likely that younger, unmated males, probably associating in loose "all-male groups," would have been much better placed to undertake what must have been cooperative hunts than were older males encumbered with females and young who could not be left unguarded while their "owner" ran off chasing game. If hominid females with a taste for meat were prepared to reward younger, meat-giving hunters with matings, the reproductive success of such younger males would rise relative to that of older ones. This in itself could favor paedomorphosis by way of selection for youth, but it would also have set the scene for the other inevitable consequence of a meat-eating economy, in which greatly increased male parental investment could enable the gradual evolution of more retarded, paedomorphic infants.

If we now ask what possible adaptive advantage such a general trend of paedomorphosis could have for human beings, the answer is obvious. It is simply that one, universal feature of paedomorphosis among vertebrates generally is that more immature forms tend to have larger brains relative to the rest of the body than more mature ones. Selection *of* young hunters by females would thereby have enabled selection *for* larger brains to come about as an inevitable, but unintended consequence. If the possession of larger brains benefited the offspring of such selected females, as it evidently seems to have done, the vexed question of how and why human hunting and brain growth could go together would have been largely solved. It would have come about, like many of the other adaptations discussed in this section, as a result of female choice. Modern man, it seems, may not have been made so much in the image of God as to the specification of primeval woman.[19]

6

Family, Sex, Conflict, and Cooperation

Parent–child conflict

One of the major methodological innovations represented by recent evolutionary biology is a concern with the individual as a valid unit of description and analysis. In large part, this was a by-product of the fall of group selection and disillusionment with the too-easy explanations of the approach which maintains that behavior evolves for the benefit of the group or species. The practical effect of this, for example in field studies of animal behavior, was to make observers label and track individual animals, rather than follow previous practice and make do with observations regarding the "herd," "family," or whatever other group was regarded as important. Once this was done, observational data bearing on the real costs and benefits to individuals of membership of groups like families, herds, or local populations began to accumulate and dramatically to document the principle that, while groups may tend to draw attention to the benefits of membership, only the study of distinct, identifiable individuals can reveal the frequently hidden and sometimes surprising costs of such membership.

Theoretically, the effect of this was to focus attention on individuals who were previously ignored, because they were not seen as playing key or dominant roles in the groups which were assumed to be the important units in the earlier view. Two types of individuals in particular benefited from this change of focus: females and the young. The reason is probably to be found in the fact that these two categories seemed little more than a convenience for family or larger groups in the older, group-selectionist view. Females existed for the benefit of reproducing the species, and Darwin's belief that they could sometimes exercise an important and determining choice in evolution was openly ridiculed. The young were nothing more than adults in the process of formation and were seldom, if ever, considered to have any independent or important interests of their own, distinct from those of adults.

After all, even if one takes the modern view that evolution is ultimately about reproductive success, rather than personal health or fitness or "advancement of the species," offspring *are* the reproductive success of their parents. This suggests that there can be no conflict of interest between parents and offspring, because both ultimately share the same evolutionary interest in the offsprings' success. Indeed, one could argue that, not only should an absence of conflict be predictable in the circumstances of family groups, but that, since family members are kin, kin altruism should dominate their interactions, both in making members of the family kin group avoid selfish behavior and in bringing about genuine altruism. Because the degree of relatedness between siblings and parents and offspring is the same ($r = \frac{1}{2}$), one might expect that both parents in regard to their offspring and offspring in regard to one another and to their parents should have the same interests in cooperation and that harmony, peace, and mutual self-sacrifice should prevail.

Unfortunately, things are not so simple. To see why not, let us return to our earlier discussion of kin altruism and parental investment. From the point of view of a parent, all its offspring are equally related to it, so where parental investment is at stake, such sacrifices will be made wherever their benefit exceeds their cost to the parent's reproductive success. This is because we have already defined parental investment as *anything contributed by a parent which enhances the reproductive success of an offspring at a cost to the remainder of the parent's reproductive success* (see above, p. 128). However, we should not conclude from this that all offspring will necessarily be treated equally. On the contrary, even though a parent is equally related to all its offspring, both the benefit and the cost of particular offspring may differ, sometimes dramatically. One of the best examples of this is provided by birds which usually lay two eggs but normally fledge only one chick. Almost always, one hatches before the other, and this is the one which is preferentially reared by the parents, who will even tolerate attacks on the younger by the senior. Evidently, although equally related to both offspring, parents have reasons of their own for preferring the elder and investing in it to the detriment of its younger sibling. The reason is that these are species which can normally raise only one offspring per season, but start a second as a "back-up," should the first one fail. Evidently, being able to fledge only one chick per season makes it very important to have one to fledge, and so the parents normally start with two.

If we now look at things from the neglected point of view of the individual offspring, we notice that the discriminated-against, younger offspring in this example is not in the same position as its parents. For them, it may only be a back-up copy of their genes, but for itself, it is the only one! Admittedly, its full siblings share half its genes, but the important point is that such an offspring is identically related to itself ($r = 1$), which is twice as closely as it is related to such siblings ($r = \frac{1}{2}$). The consequence is that the principles of kin altruism which we reviewed earlier should apply in interactions between such siblings. We will recall that selection might favor a gene for altruism if it conferred benefits on identical copies of itself in near kin which exceeded the cost to itself of the self-sacrifice in question. (We saw that such altruism can be selected if $Br > C$, where B is the benefit to the gene for altruism in the recipient, C is the cost to the gene in the altruist, and r is the degree of relatedness between them (see above, pp. 70–1).) The consequence of this is that a fundamental and unavoidable difference of interest must exist between parents and offspring where the altruistic behavior of the offspring is concerned.

Even if we neglect intrinsic differences in benefit and cost of individual offspring to their parents and assume that costs and benefits of all offspring are equalized, it is clear that parents will favor an altruistic act favoring a full sibling among their offspring wherever the benefit exceeds the cost. This is because we are assuming that all offspring are equally valuable, and all are equally related to the parents. However, since altruistic acts towards full siblings will be selected only where the benefit to the recipient sibling is more than twice the cost to a sacrificing one, it follows that parents will be selected to want twice as much altruism – or only half as much selfishness – from their offspring towards one another than the offspring themselves will be selected to want.

If this still seems confusing, consider a simple, illustrative case. Let us suppose that parents have two offspring, A and B, each of equal value to them. Let us ascribe ten arbitrary units of reproductive success to each. Clearly, if A does something to reduce B's ten units without correspondingly increasing its own values, the parents should be selected to intervene and prevent this waste of their reproductive future. If B does something which merely transfers a unit of reproductive success to A, the parents should be unconcerned, since, if all other things are equal, the greater reproductive success of A will completely compensate them for the loss to B. However, if A does something which increases B's reproductive success, perhaps by increasing it from ten points to fifteen, but only sacrifices three points of its own reproductive success (for example, by foregoing investment in itself which would benefit its sibling more), the overall reproductive success of the parents invested in both offspring will have risen from twenty units to twenty-two – a net gain which selection must favor. In other words, *parents will be selected to encourage any behavior whose benefit is greater than its cost to the siblings in question.*

However, sibling *A* will take a different view. Any sacrifice on its part can be selected only if the gene for the sacrificial behavior is going to find its reproductive success promoted in its sibling. Since its sibling has only a one-half chance of sharing an identical copy of such a gene by common descent, *A* can be selected to favor such an act only where its benefit is at least twice its cost. This is because half the time any sibling, such as *B*, will not be likely to be carrying the copy of the gene for altruism in question. As far as *A* is concerned, the benefit to *B* would have to be at least an extra six, rather than a mere five, points to justify the sacrifice on its part. Thus, selection favors not only the parents wanting the sacrifice, but also the sacrificing offspring resisting their wish. In this way conflict between what parents wish of their offspring and what their offspring themselves want becomes absolutely fundamental and unavoidable.

Where other relatives are concerned, the resulting conflict can be even greater. Consider the case of an altruistic act directed towards a maternal cousin by the offspring. The cousin's degree of relatedness to the offspring will be one eighth, because the cousin, the mother's sibling's offspring, shares half his or her genes with the mother's sibling, who in turn shares half his or her genes with the mother, who in her turn shares half her genes with her offspring ($r = \frac{1}{2} \times \frac{1}{2} \times \frac{1}{2} = \frac{1}{8}$). Consequently, the offspring will be selected to perform an altruistic act towards a maternal cousin wherever the benefit is greater than eight times the cost. However, the mother is selected to calculate the sum differently. She, as we have already seen, prefers an altruistic act in her offspring wherever the benefit exceeds the cost. Where her sibling's offspring are concerned, this will be reduced by the degree of relatedness between herself and her sibling – one-half. Thus she will be selected to want such an act wherever the benefit is only twice the cost. In other words, if all other things are equal and if we concentrate only on the critical degree of relatedness, parents will tend to want between twice and four times as much altruism (or one-half to one-quarter as much selfishness) in their offspring's behavior towards mutual kin than the individual offspring will want. Yet even parents will not agree, since it is clear that the father, who may not be related to his wife's siblings at all and cannot be anything as closely related to them as she is, will not favor kin altruism of any kind towards them, because he may not be related to them or is related to them much more distantly.

However, these considerations apply mainly to acts of kin altruism which are performed by offspring. Reciprocal altruism is to some extent a different matter. This is because acts of reciprocal altruism, as opposed to those of kin altruism, need only confer a net benefit to be selected. As we saw earlier when considering this type of altruism, genetic relatedness need not be a factor at all (even though kin groupings may often provide a stable context in which reciprocity can evolve). The consequence is that parents and offspring will tend to agree about the desirability of reciprocal altruism, because both favor acts of altruism whose benefit exceeds their cost. Nevertheless, a parent faced with a choice of a reciprocal interaction which benefits two of its offspring as opposed to one which favors only one of them prefers the former and should be selected to encourage such interactions wherever possible. (To see why this is so, imagine that *A*'s and *B*'s parents have a choice in the example above between *A* entering into a reciprocal interaction with *B* which benefits both one unit of reproductive success more than it costs and a similar interaction of *A* with a third, unrelated party. In the former, *A*–*B* interaction, two units of reproductive success are added to the offspring, whereas in the second case of *A* interacting with a stranger only one is added.)

Offspring, by contrast, will not necessarily take genetic relatedness into acount to anything like the same extent if reciprocal, rather than kin, altruism is at issue. In short, not only will parents favor more kin altruism than will offspring, they will also tend to favor more altruism between kin as opposed to nonkin than will their offspring. Furthermore, in the human case at least, the parents will probably be more concerned with relatedness as a condition of cooperation than will their children – a prediction which seems to be broadly in agreement with experience.

If offspring conform to parental wishes in directing cooperation preferentially towards kin, or, indeed, if they perform acts of altruism towards their kin which go beyond the extent of their personal self-interest in doing so, we may be tempted to see such acts as archetypical instances of kin altruism. Looked at from the point of view of the parents, they have indeed performed acts of simple kin altruism, because we assume that the benefit of the act exceeds the cost and that the recipient is a relative. But what of the viewpoint of the offspring? Why are we justified in neglecting that? Although twentieth-century socialization theory and behaviorist psychology have routinely ignored the offsprings' point of view, the modern, evolutionary approach is not prejudiced in favor of one point of view or one set of actors at the expense of another.

If we look at an act of supererogatory altruism – one that satisfies parental demands, rather than the demands of the offspring – we must conclude that, from the offspring's point of view, what he or she has done which goes beyond its own altruistic self-interest in its kin must constitute an act of *induced* altruism if it is not reciprocated in any way. This is because in the absence of reciprocation it could not qualify as reciprocal altruism and, to the extent that the cost of the act of altruism might exceed the benefit discounted by the recipient's degree of relatedness to the altruist, it represents more kin altruism than the altruist would have been selected to favor. If the extra amount of altruism cannot be accounted for by reference to the altruist, it must be accounted for by reference to some other agency, who, whether by means of deceit, coercion, or error on the altruist's part, has succeeded in *inducing* more altruism than would have occurred otherwise.

That this is not a purely abstract point is provided by the

readiness shown by many human parents to resort to various forms of deceit and coercion in the course of dealing with their children. It is not unknown for children to be beaten, threatened with various forms of deprivation, and coerced by many other means besides crude violence. They are sometimes told blatant lies (often in the form of "This hurts me more than it hurts you" or "I am doing this for your benefit, not mine") or more often are not told the whole truth or are told a highly edited and selective version of the truth which portrays the situation as the parent sees it or believes the child should see it. Finally, a child's tendency to make errors in relation to facts or their interpretation is often exploited by parents in the almost always erroneous belief that their offspring's best interests are served by ignorance of the facts rather than knowledge of them. Such prejudicial treatment of the young by powerful and manipulative adults will very often be defended as serving some family, group, or public interest which transcends that of the individual child. But however we look at it, self-sacrifices which exceed those which serve the interests of the individual will always be at the individual's cost and will always tend to be induced, rather than reciprocated or paid for in the currency of inclusive reproductive success.

In other words, the concept of induced altruism not only generally describes selfishness from the point of view of its victim, as suggested earlier, it specifically describes parental self-interest in manipulating offsprings' altruism from the point of view of the offsprings' self-interest. Since these interests are seldom the same and often in conflict (if not with regard to the degree of cooperation to be shown, at least with regard to whom it should be directed), we must conclude that, once again, the concept of induced altruism is an unavoidable one if we want a complete description of forms of cooperation which is not prejudiced in favor of any privileged viewpoint or interest. Finally, the fact that we can indeed account for the discrepant interests of offspring and parents regarding altruism with only the three categories discussed earlier argues the case that our theory of cooperation is complete and that no further fundamental forms of altruism remain to be found.

If we now stand back from the detail of the theory of parent–offspring conflict and look at the general effect, we immediately notice that this is something familiar. As human beings, we are habituated to finding that parents demand better behavior – or less bad behavior, which comes to the same thing – from their offspring than their offspring often wish. We take it as an obvious fact of life that parents will need to discipline and socialize children and that children will not always be as cooperative about this as they might be. Furthermore, conflict among parents over their children's behavior towards relatives is also far from unknown, as is the fact that parents often put much greater emphasis on obligations towards relatives than do their children. What is surprising about this is that such a conclusion should have been reached purely by means of our basic, biological argument about altruism and parental investment. This has some very important consequences, because it suggests that we may have been mistaken when in the past we assumed that parent–offspring conflict in the human case was purely a question of conflict between the biological self-interest of the child on the one hand and the cultural responsibilities of the parent on the other. On the contrary, we now realize that such conflicts can be seen as arising from the biological self-interest of both parties and that

> one is not permitted to assume that parents who attempt to impart such virtues as responsibility, decency, honesty, trustworthiness, generosity, and self-denial are merely providing the offspring with useful information on the appropriate behavior in the local culture; for all such virtues are likely to affect the amount of altruistic and egoistic behavior impinging on the parent's kin, and the parent and offspring are expected to view such behavior differently.[1]

As so often seems to be the case, conflicts which might otherwise have struck us as peculiarly human turn out, with the benefit of deeper insights into the basic biological principles involved, to have an evolutionary basis, unappreciated until quite recently.

Conflicts that kill

Fundamental evolutionary considerations suggest that if an individual's sex is important to his or her reproductive success, it must also be important to the reproductive success of his or her parents, whose only direct reproductive success that individual is. If parents could metaphorically "know" which sex would have the greatest reproductive success and in which it would therefore be best for them to invest, their own reproductive success would obviously be enhanced. However, the fact that parents usually do not "know" anything in this regard means that in the vast majority of cases parents are selected to invest equally in both sexes if the cost of raising each is equal in terms of parental investment – which it often is. Because every future individual in a sexually reproducing species must have one mother and one father, it follows that if parents do not know who those mothers and fathers are likely to be, production of equal numbers of male and female offspring is the best strategy. Furthermore, this will be true even if the mating arrangements are not monogamous. Even in a highly polygynous species in which, for example, only one in ten males may mate, each male who does mate is worth exactly ten times more to its parents' ultimate reproductive success than the nine who do not. As long as the parents have no way of "knowing" which particular males are likely to be particularly reproductively successful, they ought to invest in equal numbers of males and females irrespective of the actual outcome, and this appears to be the evolutionary explanation for the common finding that most diploid, sexually reproducing species produce males and females in roughly equal numbers.

However, if parents could predict the likely future reproductive success of individual offspring, the situation would be quite different. All that would be necessary is that mutations which favored the correct choice of sex allocation would be reproductively successful, irrespective of what the exact mechanism might be. As we shall see in a moment, here we touch on one of the most surprising and disturbing insights of recent evolutionary studies when applied to human beings; but, for the time being, let us restrict ourselves to other, simpler cases.

One of the best ways to begin is with the phenomenon of so-called *environmental sex determination*. This is a situation in which sex is not determined by chromosomes. In lizards, alligators, and turtles, for example, sex is environmentally determined – specifically, by ambient temperature during incubation. In the case of lizards, crocodiles, alligators, and the snapping turtle, all eggs will hatch as males above a certain critical temperature, while at temperatures below this they will all be female. In the case of most other turtles, the reverse is true: a higher incubation temperature produces females, a lower one, males. Given that sex allocation is such a critical factor in future reproductive success, it is highly unlikely that environmental sex determination of this kind would evolve purely haphazardly. On the contrary, the best recent evidence suggests that ambient incubation temperature is indeed a reliable guide to future reproductive success, since higher temperature produces faster body growth and greater final body size. We should therefore predict that, where larger body size favors males, males should be determined by the higher temperature, and that where females are favored by greater body size, the situation should be the reverse. And indeed, this appears to be what we find. In the case of alligators and certainly in that of crocodiles, greater body size favors males, who compete with other males for females; and this is also true of the snapping turtle. However, in the case of most other turtles, larger body size favors females and their egg-producing capacity, and so we find that higher temperature produces females, just as we would predict.

More surprising is the finding that the effect can be found even in organisms whose sex appears to be determined by chromosome inheritance at conception. A careful study of an isolated population of red deer on the Scottish island of Rhum showed that the social status of mothers was strongly reflected in the sex ratio of their offspring: the highest ranking females produced about 70 percent males as compared to the lowest ranking females' 30 percent. Yet lower ranking females nevertheless managed a higher survival rate for their female offspring than did those at the top. Although the exact physiological mechanism involved is not known (and could conceivably entail some kind of active discrimination by the mother's reproductive system with regard to the two different kinds of sperm), the evolutionary basis for such a finding turns out to be the same as in the case of environmental sex determination. We have seen already that red deer are a highly polygynous species, with stark differences in the reproductive success of males, as well as that of males compared to females (see above, p. 130). In the population in question, for example, half the offspring were sired by only 12 percent of the males. The consequence is that a female's ultimate reproductive success is likely to be greater if she invests preferentially in males who are going to enjoy high reproductive success themselves. Females who have high social status also command the best resources for parental investment in terms of access to food and are themselves likely to be relatively more able to bear the additional costs which male offspring impose. Low-status females, by contrast, ought to do the exact opposite and invest preferentially in female offspring since, unlike males, all females in a polygynous mating system will tend to be mated, and most will enjoy some degree of reproductive success, albeit usually more modest than that of the most successful males.[2]

In the case of organisms with a haplo-diploid system of sex determination, we have already seen that the sex of the offspring is determined by whether the egg is fertilized or not: if it is, the offspring is female; if not, male (see above, pp. 73–4). Such a circumstance provides another very telling test of this idea, since we might expect that selection could produce situations in which a haplo-diploid mother could manipulate the sex of her offspring if reliable indicators of their likely future reproductive success existed. The fact that the females usually store sperm for long periods of time and then use it to fertilize eggs as they are laid means that such a method of sex determination could be very simple in principle and reduce to what is effectively a method of self-fertilization, once the male's sperm has been obtained.

In fact, a number of insects do seem to act in conformity with theory in this respect. In the case of many bees and wasps, females are the larger sex, because larger size means increased capacity to produce eggs. Larger adult body size is a function of feeding during development, and often the mother provides this in the form of a food supply immured with the eggs in a burrow or brood cell or provided as a dead or immobilized host in which the parasite's eggs are laid. In the latter case it is the size of the host which usually correlates with the sex ratio, and in that of some parasitic wasps, females will lay eggs with a strong male sex bias if the host in question has already been parasitized, but a marked female bias if it has not. Such cases as these leave little doubt that where the sex of offspring can be manipulated, selection will produce parents able to do so in accordance with their ultimate reproductive self-interest.

Differential parental investment according to offspring sex is a consequence, then, of the fundamental inequality of the sexes, which stems ultimately from the differences in size of their sex cells. Because male reproductive success usually varies more than does that of females, parents who have some way of reliably predicting likely offspring reproductive success should be selected to invest in males if the prospects are good, but in females if they are poor. One of the most striking experimental confirmations of this prediction comes from studies of zebra finches, a desert-living species ideal for laboratory work because they will breed whenever sufficient food is available. An observant experimenter noticed that the colored leg tags used to identify individual birds seemed to affect their mating success. Red leg tags promoted the attractiveness of males to females, whereas green reduced it. In the case of females, by contrast, black tags were preferred to red by males. But experiment showed that if either parent had had its attractiveness to the opposite sex artificially enhanced in this way, the sex ratio of that pair's offspring was biased towards males. Correspondingly, a female bias among offspring was found when one of the pair had had its attractiveness artificially reduced. Comparable effects have been reported of guppies fed a high-protein diet and of wild populations of American possums whose food supply was experimentally manipulated. Female wood rats fed a sub-standard diet preferentially nurse daughters, bringing about death by starvation in their sons. In human beings too, this effect can be found. In the United States, for example, people at the top of the socio-economic scale have an 8 percent higher chance of producing a male than those at the bottom. A likely explanation is that since the sex ratio at conception for Americans may be as high as 120 males to every 100 females, but the sex ratio at birth is only 106 males to 100 females, any spontaneously aborted fetus will be more likely to be male than female. Indeed, we saw earlier when considering the whole question of spontaneous abortion that there is indeed evidence that male fetuses are preferentially aborted (see above, p. 165) and now we begin to see why. Presumably the American figures are explained by the fact that women at the top of the social scale, who enjoy good health care, living conditions, and general welfare, may be less prone to spontaneous abortion than those at the bottom and so may retain more male fetuses.

If offspring are not naturally or artificially aborted prior to birth, their chances of survival after birth may be strongly influenced by parental interests of one kind and another. In human beings in particular, the unprecedented length of childhood dependency on parental investment and the high degree of that investment may well result in parents manipulating both their children's survival in general and the survival of children of a particular sex. Earlier, in discussing step-parenthood and child mortality, we saw that such is indeed the case where clashes of interest among parents, their new spouses, and their existing children are concerned (see above, pp. 67–8).

As to the way in which sex may effect child survival, one of the most extreme examples is provided by the practice of female infanticide in nineteenth-century India. A classic study by Mildred Dickemann showed that in some Rajput castes almost all newborn females perished. For example, early in the nineteenth century and in spite of public renunciations of female infanticide by chiefs, public meetings, and cash awards to fathers of daughters, only twenty females could be identified in one subcaste census. A few years later only sixty-three females (of whom all but three had been born after the initiation of the anti-infanticide campaign) could be found in an area whose population at the time must have been at least 4,000–5,000. And even as late as 1840 and with the inclusion of new districts in the census, a sex ratio of 420 males to every 100 females was reported. That such an enormous preponderance of males was not natural is proved by the fact that although the ratio for children under one year of age was still 225 males to 100 females, at birth there was parity. Nor were these figures exceptional. Subsequent inquiries uncovered the practice in numerous castes in northern India, including Brahmins, Rajputs, Khatris, Jats, Gujars, Ahirs, Sikhs, and Muslims, as well as some tribal groups.[3]

How are such extraordinary facts as these to be explained? Two factors in particular seem to be important. First, these were societies in which subcastes were both ranked in terms of social stratification and were *exogamous*. In other words, women had to marry out of their natal subcaste into one of different status. Second, women were meant to marry into a *higher* status group (*hypergyny*) and were expected to provide a payment (or *dowry*) to their husband for the privilege of doing so. As a consequence, female infanticide was positively correlated with social status, so that those at the bottom of the status hierarchy practiced little or no female infanticide, while those at the top often destroyed all their females at birth. With less incentive to export females to superior groups and to pay dowries for the privilege of doing so but much more incentive to acquire dowry-bringing daughters-in-law from lower castes, higher castes did the obvious thing and reduced their production of daughters, evidently sometimes to very near zero. The fact that these infanticidal castes were primarily dominant military elites in a feudal structure who had imposed their rule through conquest perhaps explains a great deal about how the system got going and how it was maintained, at least until the British set out to eradicate it.

However, female infanticide was by no means confined to the nineteenth century. Data collected in an Indian hospital quite recently show, for instance, that of ninety-two pregnant women who had their amniotic fluid tested to determine the sex of the fetus, all chose to abort the fetus if female and to retain it if male, even when the test also showed that there was a chance of a genetic defect in the male child. In another hospital, 430 out of 450 women who were informed that they were carrying a daughter (95.5 percent) had the fetus aborted, and every single one of 250 women who were diagnosed as carrying a son took the pregnancy to term, despite advice in some cases that the child was probably suffering a genetic defect.[4] Furthermore, female infanticide has not been confined to India or to the Indian subcontinent. Dickemann quotes figures from traditional China showing childhood sex ratios of 430 males to 100 females and adult ratios of two males to one female as late as the 1870s. She adds that infanticide is now known to have been practiced in Europe from ancient times down to the late nineteenth century and that medieval British data show adult sex ratios as high as 133 males to 100 females.[5]

At first sight, a purely economic motive might seem to explain these astonishing findings. For example, in the case of Rajput India, one might argue for such an economic motive in higher-caste families accepting the daughters of lower-caste groups in exchange for dowries. Others have interpreted such strikingly male-biased sex ratios as evidence of population control for the benefit of the society or species (but without explaining why higher-status, more powerful groups should make such an altruistic sacrifice for the good of the lower-status, oppressed majority).

At the beginning of this section we saw that natural selection could favor preferential parental investment in one sex or the other depending on the quality of the offspring or the resources available for investment in it. Since males usually have much greater reproductive success than females when successful and much less success otherwise, parents ought to be selected to invest in sons when prospects for their reproductive careers are good and in daughters when they are not. In the light of these predictions it is interesting that the sex of the half-orphan in the data from seventeenth- to nineteenth-century Ostfriesland mentioned earlier in connection with step-parenthood was also found to be relevant to his or her survival (see above, pp. 67–8). Although no sex difference in survival was found for children who had lost mothers, sons who had lost fathers were found to be significantly more likely not to survive their first year of life than were daughters who had lost fathers. The author of the study suggests that this may have been because a surviving husband would be less likely to encounter economic difficulties than would a surviving wife, because men were the main subsistence providers. Such considerations may also explain why the study found that men were twice as likely as women to remarry. Economically distressed mothers, by contrast, may well have been unable to raise successful sons and so may have invested preferentially in daughters, just as theory would predict.[6]

Similar historical data from a parish in Schleswig-Holstein suggest that preferential parental investment in both males *and* females can sometimes be discovered. The parish in question was nothing like so highly stratified as the Indian castes but did show a status gradient from wealthier farmers at the top to unpropertied farm laborers and tradesmen at the bottom. As evolutionary theory would predict, the lowest rate of male infant mortality *and* the highest rate of female infant mortality occurred among the highest social class, the farmers. However, purely economic factors could not explain why daughters of the lowest social class survived better than those at the top, whereas sons survived worse. This is because if child survival were purely an effect of affluence, one would expect children of both sexes to fair better at the top of the social scale and both to do worse at the bottom. The fact that the data in question show that they did not, but that a sex-specific effect of differential valuation appeared to apply in both cases, strongly argues that parental care or neglect may have been the operative factor. This is the most likely explanation of the discrepancy in rates of survival when deaths during the first twenty-seven days of life were ignored. Figures for survival between day 28 and day 180 of an infant's life showed that just under 7 percent of both girls at the top and boys at the bottom of the social scale died during this period, whereas the corresponding figures for their siblings in each case was almost exactly 4 percent.[7]

Comparable findings are provided by a study of 3,700 members of the Portuguese nobility born between 1380 and 1580 for whom remarkably detailed information regarding birth, death, marriage, fecundity, inheritance, and even illegitimacy and concubinage has been preserved and recently analyzed. Our basic theory would lead us to predict that the effect of differential parental investment according to sex and social status found among the relatively lowly farmers of the

German parish just discussed would be amplified among the nobility of a highly stratified society like fifteenth- and sixteenth-century Portugal. We would expect wealth and social standing to be important factors in promoting the reproductive success of the sons of noble families, and this is precisely what we do find. But it is also interesting to note that a difference in total reproductive success could be found even between the higher and lower nobles, accounted for by the addition of illegitimate offspring. For titled males as a whole, the number of serial marriages was a major factor in their overall reproductive success, and the probability of marrying more than once increased considerably with status.

As far as women were concerned, marriage to higher-status males enhanced their reproductive success, and although, as basic theory would lead us to predict, the range of reproductive success was less for females overall, low-status females nevertheless out-reproduced low-status males. Clear evidence was found that parental investment in girls was greater among the lower nobility than the higher, with daughters of the lower nobility being more likely to marry than their brothers. It was also found that the probability of daughters of the lower nobility ever marrying exceeded that of women of the higher nobility ever marrying. Since brides had to provide a dowry, enhanced parental investment in daughters was both significant and obvious among the lesser nobility as a result.

If women married more than men at the lower end of the social scale, despite having to provide dowries, then men married more than women at the top, with surplus daughters tending to be sent to convents, rather as surplus sons were sent off to the wars or to the church in the case of the lower nobility. Parental investment was concentrated in males at the top of the social scale by the means of inheritance through the male line and also by the practice of primogeniture, which gave priority to the eldest son (with excess sons always being a valuable back-up in an age of high infant and child mortality). Whereas dowries tended to represent modest, movable wealth (often also preferentially invested in the eldest daughter), male inheritances of the upper nobility tended to be much more substantial and to be in the form of landed estates and feudal rights. This meant that the more modest wealth of the lower nobility could be invested in marrying a daughter into a higher status. Indeed, it may actually have had a higher reproductive value than the estate inherited by the son, again making preferential parental investment in daughters the natural choice among the lower nobility.[8]

Problems of paternity

Another peculiarity of human behavior which is illuminated by insights into parent–child conflict is the social institution known as the *avunculate*. This is a term derived from the Latin for "uncle" and refers to an especially important, socially institutionalized tie between a man and his sister's children often involving his exercising some degree of authority over them and making some provision for them in terms of inheritance.

The institution of the avunculate is important, in part because it has been widely touted as something which contradicts biological views of the family and illustrates the pre-eminent role of culture in the social, rather than genetic, definition of kinship. According to this view, the "natural" family comprises the father, mother, and children. This is often also termed the "nuclear" family, allegedly more typical of modern, Western societies. The avunculate, however, introduces another figure, the mother's brother, to the existing "nuclear" group. This is the core of the so-called extended family, supposedly more typical of traditional, non-Western and nonindustrial societies and includes in the person of the children's maternal uncle a purely socially defined, culturally significant figure, one in no way explicable by biological considerations. After all, no corresponding socially significant role is known for the father's sister (who appears to be biologically equivalent to the mother's brother), and, to the extent that the mother's brother could be seen as a substitute for the father, appeared not to have a genetic relationship with his sister's children in any way comparable to that of the biological father. In short, the avunculate seemed to be a cultural creation, not a biological one; a social construction, not the product of nature.

By far the best known example of the avunculate is found in the works of Bronislaw Malinowski (1884–1942), and specifically in his writings devoted to the principal culture which he studied, the Trobriand Islands of Melanesia (off the north-eastern coast of Australia and to the south and west of New Guinea). Malinowski conceived his account of the Trobriand avunculate in terms of an ostensible refutation of the Freudian theory of the family, and especially of the notorious idea of the "Oedipus complex." According to Malinowski, the allegedly "natural," biologically based, oedipal eternal triangle of father, son, and mother was not found in the Trobriand Islands. There, according to his account, relations between the father and son were not strained and full of conflict, but relaxed and friendly. It was the mother's brother, not the father, who, according to Malinowski, "represents the principle of discipline, authority and executive power within the family."[9] The conclusion seemed obvious: that the Oedipus complex was a cultural artifact of the Western "bourgeois" culture so widely despised by the intellectuals of his day, and the "natural," "biological" basis of the nuclear family merely a social contingency. In particular, it was the role of the father which was shown to be contingent, so that however indissoluble the child's tie with the mother might be, that with the father was not. When Malinowski combined this with a caricature of the typical Western father as brutal, overbearing, and authoritarian, his recommendation of the Trobriand situation seemed to dethrone the father from his place as head of the family, consigning him instead to a subordinate, culturally contingent one.

In doing so, Malinowski implicitly followed a lead given him by the Trobriand Islanders, who deny that men play any role in conception (while also being fully aware that a virgin cannot conceive). This is an idea which strongly supports the institution of the avunculate by denying any very significant role to the father while emphasizing that of the mother. Perhaps not surprisingly, descent is traced in this society through the female line (what is known as *matriliny*), and every man is obliged to contribute some food to his brother-in-law – that is, his sister's husband – and her children. Inheritance also runs through the female line, so that a man's wealth ideally passes to his sister's children, rather than his own, and, as we have already seen, it is the mother's brother, and not the father, who exercises moral authority in the family. Here indeed seems to be a society without fathers, one in which culture, rather than biology, reigns!

But however that may be, closer inspection shows this example to be far from perfect. If there were a social institution whereby men supported their wife's siblings' children and passed on their wealth to them, there might be a case for such a view, but no such society is known. Unlike the avunculate, a situation such as this would be one in which there was no necessary genetic relationship whatsoever between the parties since, clearly, a man is not normally related to his wife's kin by close ties of blood. However, he is indeed closely related to his sister's offspring, who, assuming that he and his sister share the same father, possess on average one-quarter of his genes (that is, one-half of his sister's genes, with whom the brother shares half). Admittedly, this is still only half the degree of relatedness which we would expect between a man and his own children, so curiously neglected by the conventions of the avunculate. But here we must examine our assumptions more closely and ask ourselves if there is any factor which might alter this situation and make us reconsider our conclusion. Indeed there is, and it is a wholly biological and genetic one. In order to understand it, let us leave the Trobriand Islands for a moment and consider an apparently quite unrelated case: piracy among peacock wrasse.

The peacock wrasse is a common Mediterranean fish whose females mostly lay their eggs in nests excavated and guarded by males.. Nest-building and maintenance are costly, with nesting males losing up to a fifth of their body weight in a month of breeding activity. Such expenditure by males is a classic instance of male parental investment and obviously pays, because a male can normally insure that eggs deposited by females in his nest are fertilized by him, with all that means for his ultimate reproductive success. Clearly, if parental investment after egg-laying can pay a female, it can also sometimes pay a male.

Yet not all males, as we might have predicted, behave so well. Some who are larger and more aggressive than others become so-called pirates and hijack the nests so laboriously built by others, who are driven out after a short fight. But now comes the surprising part: the evicted nest-builder usually stays on and, after the pirate has finished fertilizing the eggs of as many females as are likely to spawn in the nest, returns to it and continues to look after it until all the eggs have hatched!

At first sight, this looks like a classic example of group-selected altruism, because one could argue that the nest-builder is doing more for the reproductive success of the pirate than for himself and that it must be the species, rather than the individual, which gains as a result of his self-sacrifice for a higher cause, peacock wrasse survival in general, not individual peacock wrasse's personal reproductive success. But there is another possibility. This is that what attracts the ousted male back to guard the eggs is the fact that at least some of them must be his and that total abandonment by him at this stage might well result in his ultimate reproductive success being less than it could be if he returns. This interpretation is strengthened by the finding that, as one would predict if it were true, ousted males are much less likely to return to a nest with very few eggs fertilized by themselves in it and much more likely to do so immediately after the most active period of the spawning season, when a sufficient number of their own eggs are likely to survive. Indeed, even pirates are affected by comparable considerations, since it appears that while they readily eat fertilized eggs in the nest on take-over, they are less likely to do so after a period of residence, when some proportion of the eggs present must have been fertilized by themselves.[10]

Far from being evidence of altruism in the service of the species, the surprising tolerance of the ousted male reflects his purely individual self-interest in his own offspring. The fact that he cares for both these *and* those of the pirate is simply that there is no way in which he can discriminate between eggs which he has fertilized himself and those fertilized by the pirate. He must care equally for all of them if any which are his are to prosper and thereby to contribute to his own reproductive success. In this example it is the fact of *uncertainty of paternity* which explains the apparently altruistic commitment of males to eggs fertilized by other males who have abused them.

If we now return to the Trobriand Islands with this example in mind, we might begin by noticing something similar. In that case too, paternity was uncertain in the sense that, as we have seen, Trobriand Islanders denied that fathers contributed in any way to children, who were seen wholly as the offspring of the mother. Furthermore, this ideology of nonpaternity reflected the truth, because the Trobriand Islands, like many matrilineal societies with an institution of the avunculate, was a society characterized by high degrees of premarital and extramarital sex, divorce, and adultery. Unlike many, usually much more patrilineal societies (that is, those where descent is traced through the male line), in which women are often guarded and restricted and in which girls have to be intact virgins at marriage and adultery is severely punished, matrilineal societies like the Trobriand

Islands are often notably relaxed about such things. Obviously, the restrictions imposed in the patrilineal case all serve to promote certainty of paternity, since if a woman is a virgin at the time of marriage, unable to divorce and remarry, and prevented from carrying on extramarital liaisons, the chances of her conceiving offspring except by her official husband are much less than they would be in the absence of these restrictions.

The consequence of all this is that if a man's certainty that his wife's offspring are indeed his own drops below a certain, critical value, his ultimate reproductive success may be promoted by some degree of investment on his part, not in his wife's offspring – who may or may not be his – but in his sister's. This is because maternity, as opposed to paternity, is always certain in the sense that a child is physically part of its mother and issues from her in an unmistakable way. But paternity is always more a matter of probability, since no one – outside the exceptional circumstance of laboratory fertilization – is ever in a position to track the sperm of an individual man and observe its union with the ovum. There is a fundamental sense in which it could always have been the mailman! But where a man's sister's offspring are concerned, maternity, rather than paternity, guarantees that he is related to them and that investment made in them is not misdirected to children to whom he is not related at all and who are in reality the progeny of other men. Indeed, nothing can be so self-destructive of a man's parental investment in evolutionary terms than to invest in other men's reproductive success through having been cuckolded. In such circumstances natural selection favors the adulterer, not the cuckold.

Of course, uncertainty of paternity will also affect the likelihood of a man and his sister being full, as opposed to half, siblings. Nevertheless, and taking such factors into account, it is possible to calculate what the critical degree of certainty of paternity is likely to be, and it turns out to be a little more than one-quarter (actually, 0.268), or odds of better than one to three.[11] In other words, more than a quarter of the children whom a man shares with his wife must be his if his investment in them is to promote his inclusive reproductive success more than it would be promoted by diverting the investment in question to his sister's offspring.

At first sight this sounds like quite a low figure, but in practice it is more significant than might be imagined. If promiscuity is high and marriage is short-lived, it is likely that remarriage will be common and that men may well find themselves living with women with whom they do indeed share less than a quarter of their joint offspring, since the woman in question may have existing offspring from a previous marriage or marriages. Again, a man's parental investment, for instance in the form of agricultural labor or hunting, may not be easy to subdivide in the sense that he can control which children in his household get what share of it. The consequence might be that provision of investments to his sister, all of whose offspring are certain to be related to him by at least one-eighth, may be more worthwhile where the ultimate reproductive success of genes which he shares with her is concerned. Nor are such calculations purely abstract, because common observation of our own societies shows that where divorce and remarriage are common, it is links with maternal kin which tend to be preserved, and it is often the child–mother and brother–sister ties in particular which are most important.

Far from vindicating theories which make culture control behavior, the avunculate appears to be an exquisite example of how inclusive reproductive success, the key concept of modern, evolutionary biology, affects the patterns of parental investment found in human societies. Certainty – or, rather, uncertainty – of paternity may promote otherwise inexplicable cooperation on the part of nest-builders with pirates in the peacock wrasse; but in human societies it seems that it may have the effect of rewarding investment in sisters' offspring if a man's certainty of paternity of his own offspring falls below the critical 0.268 level.

These findings also explain the role of the mother's brother as an authority figure alluded to earlier. In our consideration of another aspect of human behaviour ignored by traditional social science, we saw that parent–child conflict is an inevitable and unavoidable factor in all situations in which parents and offspring have an opportunity independently to rate the value of performing an altruistic act towards kin or avoiding a selfish one. As we saw, parents will favor an altruistic interaction among their offspring wherever its benefit exceeds its cost $(B > C)$, but offspring will apply the standard criterion involved in acts of kin altruism and discount the benefit to the recipient by the degree of relatedness $(Br > C)$. We noted that a fundamental clash of interests results from the fact that parents will normally be selected to want at least twice as much altruism as offspring themselves are selected to want (see above, pp. 190–1).

Where interactions between a man's own children are concerned, he and his wife's brother will be in agreement if they are indeed his own; both will favor sacrifice wherever benefit exceeds cost. However, if his paternity is uncertain, his degree of agreement with his wife's brother will decline in direct proportion to the degree of uncertainty involved, and will fall towards that which the offspring themselves will favor when uncertainty of paternity reaches the critical, approximately one-quarter level at which mother's brothers should begin to become significant figures. (This is because uncertainty of paternity will tend to mean that siblings are related only through their mothers, and therefore r, the degree of relatedness, will fall from ½ to ¼.) Since the father in such a situation is normally unrelated to any of his wife's relatives, such as her brother and his offspring, he will have no evolutionary incentive whatsoever to encourage kin altruism towards them on the part of his offspring. His wife's brother, by contrast, being his wife's nearest male relative in a culturally important kin group, the matrilineage, will be selected to encourage altruistic interactions between his sister's offspring and his own at levels at least four times higher than the man's own offspring will (see above, pp. 192–3). No wonder, then, that Malinowski found that the relationship between a father and his children in such a matrilineal society as that of the Trobriand Islands was markedly more relaxed, more affectionate, and less ambivalent than that between the same children and their mother's brother. It seems that facts held to "prove" the culturally created character of family relationships vindicate predictions of evolutionary biology, in this case that of parent–offspring conflict theory. Even authority relations, apparently so much a matter of culture and convention, are found, on closer analysis, to reflect evolutionary, biological considerations when they are set within their proper context and related to the key factors: the degree of certainty of paternity and the inevitability of parent–child conflict on the question of altruism towards relatives.

The infant strikes back

One of the best examples of parent–offspring conflict is provided by so-called weaning conflicts: that is, conflicts relating to the termination of a period of investment in the offspring. In mammals, females show an extreme form of sex-role specialization by means of which they – and only they, never the male – provide the young with a specially produced food resource in the form of milk. At first, the young are totally dependent on it and can take nothing else; but later, milk is a supplement to the diet, so that offspring can be weaned. This is the point at which conflict can occur, especially since persistent nipple-stimulation inhibits the sexual cycles of female mammals. The consequence is that the mammalian mother faces a very real conflict between the interest of her existing offspring to consume more milk (with a presumed benefit to her ultimate reproductive success) and the alternative reproductive success open to her in the form of new offspring. However, the fact that she cannot expect to conceive as long as her existing offspring is suckling results in an inevitable conflict, since almost always, existing offspring will rate the benefit to themselves of more of their mother's milk above that represented by the birth of further siblings.

Nowhere is this conflict more extreme and unmistakable than in the case of human beings. Human mothers, too, will not cycle for up to two years or so if their nipples are stimulated by frequent suckling and, in the primal hunter-gatherer societies in which our ancestors evolved, faced a similar conflict with their offspring. (For reasons which we have already seen, the mother's weight is also likely to be a factor in determining the duration of infertility induced by breast-feeding, which, by contrast to the norm in the West, is carried on practically continuously, day and night.) Data on child survival in comparable conditions in the Third World and in hunter-gatherers still existing until recently show that the greatest single threat to the life of an existing offspring is the birth of another within the first four years or so of its life, with the threat greater the earlier the second birth occurs.[12] In the case of the !Kung San, hunter-gatherers until recently in the Kalahari Desert, an increase in inter-birth interval from two to four years reduced infant mortality from over 70 percent to about 10 percent. In circumstances such as these the benefit to copies of a gene for tolerating the birth of siblings within approximately four years or so of the beginning of the life of an existing offspring could not exceed its cost in most cases, and so it is not surprising that human infants appear to be particularly demanding where their mother's nipples are concerned.

Moreover, it is not surprising that under conditions such as these mothers themselves take a similar view and will sometimes terminate the life of a sibling born too close to an existing child if they feel that the new baby will be a threat to the survival of the existing one. Whether this comes about by an intentional act of infanticide, by merely not intervening when the elder sibling contests for the breast and excludes the younger, or by unintentional neglect, the outcome often makes sense in terms of the mother's reproductive success. This is because an existing child has already received a considerable amount of her parental investment and, assuming it to be fit and normal, is further down the road towards a successful beginning of its own reproductive life, where natural selection will pay the mother's genes the dividend on her original investment. Favoring the younger offspring, by contrast, will merely threaten the mother's existing investment in the older child and needlessly postpone the point at which the ultimate reward for all her sacrifices can be won. Indeed, a mother who consistently gave birth to babies too closely spaced to allow for two to be supported, but constantly sacrificed the elder for the younger, would raise only one to maturity and be most unlikely to find her behavior favored by selection.

I said just now that human babies appear to be particularly demanding where their mother's *nipples* are concerned, rather than being especially demanding of their mother's *milk* because, as I observed above, it is known to be the neurological stimulation of the nipples which actually inhibits the mother's sexual cycling, not the production of milk as such. Nor would milk be quite such a vital resource for a child of three or four years of age as it would have been earlier. Consequently, our insight into the threat to the life of existing offspring would lead us to predict a specific instance of weaning conflict in human beings: one concerned not so much with the existing offspring's demand for milk as with its desire to postpone its mother's conception of competing siblings. Furthermore, this is exactly what we find, and nowhere more visibly than in modern, industrial societies, where, thanks to unprecedented affluence, mothers can afford to space children much more closely without paying the heavy price that would be exacted in primal conditions or in the Third World. On their side, children up to three years of age or older are found to suck compulsively, independent of hunger. This is because they are intent, evidently, on keeping up the stimulation of their mother's nipples for as long as possible and are carrying out a behavioral program which originally evolved in quite different, primal conditions, where failure to do so would have resulted in one of the most life-threatening eventualities possible: the birth of a sibling within the first four years of the existing infant's life. Mothers, on their side, outwit the modern child in its primeval concern with their fertility by early termination of breast-feeding, hiding their nipples under clothing (and it is the *nipples*, not the breasts, which are hidden), the use of substitute foods, and the provision of artificial nipples in the form of pacifiers and teething toys.

Looking at things from this point of view casts a very different light on mother–child relations in early childhood from that found in most twentieth-century literature on the subject, where nurture, rather than nature, reigns supreme and the child is little more than the passive recipient of parental care. What is different about it is that the child is regarded as an independent, active protagonist in the relationship, one with his or her own interests and motives, not all of which will overlap completely with those of the mother. Of course, the child is at a disadvantage. He or she cannot physically dominate the parents in the way in which they can dominate the child. Nor has the child the benefit of the parents' experience of life or fully developed, adult skills. Yet, for all that, the infant does have weapons of his or her own in battles with the parents. Because of the child's physical inferiority in size and maturity, these will tend to be psychological and behavioral, rather than physical and social, but they will be real nevertheless.

One good example of this is *crying*. According to the traditional, children exist for the benefit of the family or society view, crying is *functional*: that is, it is a means of communication by which an infant signals his or her needs and distress to an adult. But, as Robert Trivers pointed out in his original, landmark paper on parent–offspring conflict, once evolved, infants can use the crying signal out of context or can amplify it to get more attention, care, or whatever than the parent might think appropriate. In this way a signal originally evolved to indicate real hunger, for example, can be used to try to elicit just a little more feeding, even when the baby is largely satiated. Since it is precisely in these marginal areas of parental investment that conflict is most likely to occur, infants have an incentive to exploit distress signals like crying.to secure any additional investment which they might favor but the parent might not.

But if selection favors offsprings' amplification of signals like crying, it will also favor parents' ability to respond accordingly. One obvious way in which this occurs is by means of *recalibration* of their responses – in other words, by adults developing two different standards of sensitivity to signals like crying, one for children and one for others. The result is that most adults will tend to ignore children screaming in the street if those children are not obviously abandoned and alone, but will pay close attention to even slight signs of distress in an adult. The reason for this is obvious: tears are common and expected in children, who tend to resort to them easily, but much less common in adults, who do not normally exploit such signals of distress to anything like the same extent. The result is a double standard of adult sensitivity to crying.

Another psychological tactic open to the offspring is *regression*. What this means is behaving or appearing younger than one really is. Because the need for parental care tends to be greater the younger an offspring is, the quantity which adults are selected to provide will tend to reflect the offspring's age and developmental status, as judged by the parents. However, an offspring intent on a little more investment might solicit it successfully by misleading its parents about its actual developmental progress and appearing to be less advanced than it really is, thereby indicating to the parents the need for somewhat greater investment. Once again, we find much evidence of this in the case of human beings, among whom regression has long been a familiar finding to psychologists, especially in children.

Parents, by contrast, can exploit an exactly contrary tactic by exaggerating their greater age, competence, and experience of life to give the impression that they are much better informed and much more capable of knowing and taking care of their offspring's interests than is the offspring. Since these assurances of greater knowledge and experience are likely to be partly true, the offspring is placed in a very difficult position with regard to them, since selection will not tend to favor offspring who fail to take advantage of parental guidance where it is valid and overlaps with the offspring's self-interest. Yet neither will selection favor offspring who are easily misled by their parents' greater apparent knowledge or experience to the point that their own reproductive success benefits less than that of the parents. The result is that offspring will be selected to be critical and even skeptical of parental claims to greater wisdom and will tend to want to test each and every piece of information imparted in the course of parental guidance against some independent, or at least different, standard, such as their own experience, that of others apart from the parents, or wholly unrelated authorities, if they are available. Such criticism of parental efforts at socialization and education of the young will not stop short at the mere content of the information imparted. It will extend to the motives of the parents and to their assurances that they are in the best position to judge and decide what is best for their offspring. Offspring will be selected to be critical of these claims too and to evaluate parental motives to discern instances where the latter's self-interest does not overlap that of the offspring themselves. Furthermore, these are conflicts which are likely to become much more apparent as the offspring grows older and approaches the beginning of its own reproductive life. With their own reproductive life about to begin, human offspring in particular may find that conflict with parents becomes intense if the latter take a different view to the adolescents in question regarding the desirability of potential partners; the timing of the onset of reproduction; attitudes to other kin, or whatever. In this way the conflicts characteristic of adolescence in most societies, but most especially our own, can be seen to be rooted in the general theory of parent–offspring conflict and to have deep evolutionary roots going far beyond merely human behavior. Neither in infancy, childhood, or adolescence are human offspring likely to be the passive, accepting, and uncomplaining recipients of socialization or conditioning that the dominant schools of twentieth-century sociological and psychological thought seem to have believed they were.

7

Freudian Findings

Parental investment and oedipal behavior

To say that Freud has never been popular with most twentieth-century behavioral and social scientists is an understatement; their reaction to him has been more phobic than anything. Furthermore, those who did take notice of Freud – social scientists in particular – almost without exception misconstrued his work to be just another theory of socialization. The irony of this is that although Freud began believing in the determining influence of parental figures and thought for a while that all neurotics had been childhood victims of seductions and assaults by adults, his disillusionment with this so-called seduction theory resulted in his views turning into the exact opposite. The discovery of infantile sexuality which followed the fall of the seduction theory and which was to cause him so much trouble with public opinion and academic psychology was, effectively, a realization that children are not passive victims of parental conditioning, but active protagonists. Indeed, the compulsive sucking which we touched on in the last chapter in our consideration of parent–child conflict was first brought to the notice of behavioral science by Freud's observations of what he termed the "oral phase," or infantile sexuality.

One might imagine that he arrived at his insights into oral behavior by means of direct observation of children, but this is not so. On the contrary, Freud discovered the oral phase through the psychoanalysis of adults and through the retrospective insights into his patients' childhoods provided by the analysis of dreams, free associations, and symptoms. Only much later did the psychoanalysis of children as such become possible, and direct observation of infants was not included in the formal training of psychoanalysts until very recent times. Freud interpreted what today we would call *oral behavior* as something to do with sex because he correctly recognized its essential nature: what we may define as *compulsive sucking independent of immediate hunger*. When he related this to the fact that intrinsic pleasure is felt in oral activities such as kissing, licking, and sucking in adult sexual behavior and to the finding that in some cases such activities completely supplant the normal genital aim of adult sexuality, he felt justified in concluding that sucking for its own sake probably has a sexual dimension in infancy also. It certainly seems to serve the "pleasure principle," to which we referred before (see above, pp. 97–9).

What Freud did not know, but we know now, is that, as explained earlier, oral behavior understood as compulsive sucking independent of hunger seems to have evolved as a factor in parent–child conflict over the mother's fertility. To this extent it appears to have more to do with the mother's sexuality than with that of the child. Indeed, one might point out that the situation seems to be the exact reverse of that portrayed by Freud's early instinct theory. This theory was one which proposed that there were two sets of instincts: so-called ego instincts concerned with self-preservation and "libido" concerned with reproduction. By speaking of "oral libido" in the context of infantile sexuality, Freud obviously regarded oral behavior as more concerned with sex than with self-preservation. In fact, we can now see that the opposite seems to be the case and that oral behavior is mainly concerned with the preservation of the life of the infant (what Freud would have called an ego instinct in his early theory), rather than with its reproduction as such.

Nevertheless, looked at from the point of view of our

modern understanding of evolution, Freud's characterization of oral behavior as "sexual" looks a lot closer to the truth than other recent theories, also inspired by now outmoded group-selectionist biology, which saw it in terms of "attachment" and assumed an unproblematic harmony of interests between offspring and parent. If we interpret Freud's emphasis on the libido as the driving force in human psychology to be a psychological equivalent of the modern Darwinian emphasis on reproductive success as the driving force of selection, then Freud's interpretation of oral behavior in terms of infantile sexuality makes a great deal of sense. This is because it is indeed concerned with the ultimate reproductive success of the infant and because Freud's approach, unlike just about every other approach in twentieth-century psychology, ethology, and sociology, emphasizes conflict, rather than concord, between the infant and its parents. Admittedly, he may have expressed this conflict of basic, biological self-interest in outdated biological terminology, but he seems to have correctly concluded that fundamental to parent–child relations in early childhood are deep and ineradicable clashes between the needs of the child and the interest of the parents. Furthermore, if this is true of oral behavior, might not Freud's notorious idea of oedipal behavior have a similar explanation? Indeed, might it not be a natural development of it?

As far as the oedipal stage of childhood development is concerned, one further fact regarding human mothers and their sensitivity to nipple-stimulation as a means of inducing sterility may be pertinent. This is that, as basic parent–offspring conflict theory would predict, a mother's self-interest in remaining sterile and her existing child's self-interest in her not conceiving again will not coincide exactly at the margin. In particular, they will diverge as the existing child becomes more independent and consequently less threatened by the conception of a sibling. But whereas, in accordance with the principles explained earlier, the existing child will be selected to make sacrifices for a sibling where the benefit to the sibling is twice the cost to his or her self, the mother will take the view that the existing offspring ought to make a sacrifice where the benefit exceeds the cost by any amount (see above, pp. 189–97). The consequence is that by the time the existing child is about twenty-five months old, the mother's sensitivity to nipple-stimulation as a means of inhibiting her sexual cycles begins to wane and eventually vanishes completely, so that conception is likely to occur, no matter how much an existing child stimulates her nipples. Thus it is probably no coincidence that Freud found age two to three to mark both the end of the oral phase and the beginning of the oedipal one. But if this is so, then oedipal behavior would seem to be "sexual" in the same sense that oral behavior is, and as more concerned with securing parental investment than with incest or parricide.

Perhaps what Freud really discovered was that, as the child finds oral behavior becoming a less and less effective means of securing continued parental investment in it on the part of its mother, evidently the chief provider at this early stage of life, the child takes advantage of increasing maturity and psychological sophistication to try to induce the mother to invest in it by purely psychological means. The best way of achieving this, given that what the child wants is general commitment to its well-being, is likely to be strong feelings of love and affection directed towards the mother for no other reason than that she is the mother. A child who loves, values, and appreciates its mother is much more likely to be loved, valued, and appreciated in return as compared to one who seems indifferent or lukewarm towards her. Indeed, one might predict that competing siblings might vie with one another *for* the love of their mother by means *of* the love of their mother, and that selection would favor the most successful if, as does not seem unlikely, success in procuring preferential parental investment in childhood tends to be reflected in the lifetime reproductive success of such children. In other words, oedipal behavior understood as love and devotion to mothers *as* mothers might be selected by classical evolutionary means if the result were enhanced parental investment in such offspring to the benefit of the ultimate reproductive success of the genes for such oedipal behavior in those offspring.

This might account for what we could regard as the positive aspects of oedipal behavior: those concerned with securing parental investment. In the case of the earlier, oral phase, the behavior which solicits the investment – sucking milk from the mother's breasts – also functions to prevent her from cycling and thereby fulfills a negative function of inducing sterility. However, passionate love and devotion directed towards the mother during the oedipal phase will not have any such negative effect on her reproductive activity. Yet children of three, four, or five are still threatened by the birth of siblings, even if the consequences of one actually being conceived by the mother become less dire as time goes by. Perhaps this is why Freud, and psychoanalysts generally, have reported another aspect of oedipal behavior which in the context of modern living conditions looks unmistakably and precociously sexual by any understanding of the term.

This is so-called primal scene experiences: the finding that adults regularly report having seen, heard, or otherwise having intuited episodes of parental sexual activity which occurred when they were young children and which often figure prominently in the repressed, unconscious residues of childhood. Whether these residues are regarded as actual memories (and in some cases where they can be independently checked, they have indeed been proved to be), as fantasies, or as a mixture of both, they have a number of regular features: first, the young child shows evidence of curiosity about the parental sexual activities; second, it usually interprets what it sees and/or hears as evidence of violence, usually done to the mother by the father; and third, it often seems to want to intervene or even participate in what is going on, feeling both "left out" and very anxious. At face value, these findings, which are extremely common in psychoanalysis, give much credence to Freud's belief that they are evidence of precocious, infantile sexuality.

But however that may be, it is worth wondering whether the real reason for the curiosity, anxiety, and desire to intervene might not be an existing child's self-interest in sabotaging parental sexual activities which might result in the birth of a sibling. In primal conditions, such as those found until recently among the Australian aborigines, families bedded down for the night in the open around camp fires. Significantly, the one restriction on children's sexual activities reported of such people in central Australia was that they may not witness parental sexual intercourse. Such taboos obviously represent parental self-interest in situations of parent–offspring conflict. They suggest that parents and young children are at odds on this issue and that the parents feel the need to protect themselves from the attentions of their existing offspring where engendering more is concerned. Young children witnessing parental intercourse, for their part, have every reason to be apprehensive in such conditions and to feel fear and anxiety at the prospect of the birth of rivals while they themselves are still very young. Even active intervention might be selected if young children who were both wakeful, curious, anxious, and successful in putting the parents off succeeded in postponing the birth of offspring often enough to promote their own reproductive success at the expense of others who might not take such an active, interventionist role. In short, behavior which may look biologically absurd because of its apparent purposelessness, incestuous overtones, and generally bizarre character could very easily be quite the reverse and could have paid for itself in the hard currency of reproductive success.

If this were true, we could immediately make two testable predictions. First, we could predict that if oedipal behavior is in large part designed to solicit parental investment, then, where parental investment is provided in excess of what the child wants, oedipal behavior should be muted or absent altogether. Here it is worth reporting the researches of

Robert Stoller into the childhoods of so-called transsexuals. These are individuals who regard themselves as members of the opposite sex, and we must leave on one side for the moment what this might have to do with the matter in hand. For our present purposes the important thing to note is that his studies show that, as children, transsexuals are normally overwhelmed and smothered by parental investment on the part of the opposite-sex parent. He also comments in passing that he found no evidence of oedipal conflict in them, and this would appear to confirm a prediction which would certainly have surprised Freud, who regarded oedipal behavior as both universal and unavoidable. [1]

Second, we would have to predict that, since children of both sexes are equally at risk from the birth of siblings, oedipal behavior as described so far should be found in both sexes. This is important, because some of Freud's followers and imitators, such as Carl Jung, insisted that the sexes should be completely symmetrical and that if boys have an Oedipus complex, then girls should have a so-called Electra complex. Clearly, this cannot be so if the interpretation advanced here is correct, and it is significant that Freud himself maintained that, initially at least, both sexes regarded the mother as their first love-object and that both directed oedipal feelings towards her. Later, and by direct observation and analysis of children themselves, Anna Freud and others confirmed her father's findings that, in the earlier part of the oedipal period (sometimes confusingly called the "pre-oedipal" phase in the case of girls), both boys and girls show similar behavior.

Nevertheless, observation also shows that at a later stage girls do indeed adopt a position symmetrically opposed to their brothers and target their fathers for oedipal feelings, feeling some rivalry with their mothers. Two considerations in particular may explain why this is so. First, we can predict – and specific studies confirm – that, in a mammal like a human being, parental investment by the father as opposed to the mother will become more important the older the offspring is, thereby making the father an important source of parental investment for a girl later in her childhood. Second, it follows that if oedipal behavior exploits loving, amorous feelings in the parents for the children, a child of the opposite sex to that of the parent is most likely to succeed in awakening these, particularly as she or he grows older. For boys, this poses no problems because the mother is retained as the target of oedipal feelings; but for girls it introduces a complication and necessitates a switch in their oedipal behavior from one parent to the other, perhaps motivated in part by the realization that it is unlikely to be as effective with the mother if she has sons who can exploit oedipal behavior directed towards her so much more than can her daughters. The consequence of this would be the classic Oedipus complex in both sexes as described by Freud: a finding which, thanks to the modern theory of parental investment, may at last be beginning to make some biological sense.

Penis envy and parental preference

Freudian findings leave little doubt that, although oedipal behavior is certainly found in both sexes, it is heightened, exaggerated, and prolonged in males. Two important considerations may explain why this is so. First, we might observe that human beings are pre-eminent both in the total amount of parental investment which is made after birth of the offspring and in its duration. Second, we should recall that natural selection will favor discriminating parental investment if there is some way in which parents can reliably choose between different strategies of investment, for example in relation to offspring sex, age, birth order, or whatever. We have already seen that various types of evidence cumulatively point towards our species being a predominantly polygynous one. We have also seen that an inevitable consequence of polygyny is increased variance of male reproductive success: where only a few males are mated to all the females, a few males have a great many offspring, some will have a few, and many will have none at all (see above, pp. 129–31). Where there is a greater variance in male reproductive success, there is also a greater variance in the reproductive success of parental investment in males as opposed to females in general and in successful males as opposed to unsuccessful ones in particular. If there were some way in which reproductively successful males could attract preferential parental investment to themselves, and if there were also some way in which parents could discriminate in favor of such males, selection would favor the resulting preferential investment in them if, as is almost certain to be the case, it enhanced their eventual, adult reproductive success.

Perhaps what Freud described as oedipal behavior in males is what we are looking for. After all, it consists in precocious sexuality directed towards the mother and sisters, along with aggressive, rivalrous behavior directed towards the father and brothers. Perhaps what seems on the surface to be biologically unacceptable incest and parricide is, on closer inspection, not so biologically absurd after all. If sons who behave in a sexually precocious way towards the women of the family and in a sexually rivalrous one towards the males are indeed more likely to mature into men whose reproductive success is above average, then preferential parental investment in them on the part of the parents could pay. If such behavior begins in infancy when the mother is still the main provider of investment, it might be especially successful if directed towards her by sons.

An important consideration here is the fact that, thanks to the fundamental disparity in the size of the sex cells, a woman's personal lifetime reproductive success can easily be much less than the corresponding lifetime reproductive success of her sons, each one of whom could in principle father many more offspring than she could bear herself, especially in a polygynous mating system. Admittedly, grandchildren are only half as valuable as a woman's own offspring in terms of their degree of relatedness to her, but it is by no means impossible for a son's reproductive success to be much more than twice that of his mother, should he indeed be successful. The consequence is that mothers in particular, who are in any case the chief providers of parental investment in early childhood, have special reasons for preferring to invest in sons who show signs during childhood of above-average reproductive success in adult life.

Here, essentially, may lie the true biological rationale for oedipal behavior in boys. It is one which, paradoxically, hinges on its ultimate evolutionary value to their mothers, who, by means of preferential parental investment in oedipal sons, secure for themselves a degree of indirect reproductive success which would otherwise be possible only if they were males themselves. Where reproductive success in a polygynous mating system is concerned, the next best thing to being a successful male yourself is to be the mother of one, particularly if, as a mother, you can promote your son's ultimate success by preferential investment in him. This means that if you are to be such a son, you must impress your mother that you are indeed potentially one by starting your career of sexual conquests with her, as well as proving that you are not going to let other men – like your father – stand in your way.

As far as girls are concerned, the fact that their fathers are never likely to be such important investors in them as their mothers are inevitably means that oedipal behavior on their part is unlikely to be as prominent as it is in the case of boys. Furthermore, the fact that their father's personal lifetime reproductive success will always be in principle much greater than theirs and can be directly procured by their fathers themselves, rather than being indirectly realized through offspring, must result in oedipal behavior being much less critical to a girl's future reproductive success.

But what is a little girl to do if the foregoing arguments about the male Oedipus complex are correct? Basic theory predicts one or two possibilities. First, even if there is only a possibility that parents might discriminate investment on the basis of sex, a little girl ought to be selected to form her own, independent judgment on the matter. We would certainly not expect evolution to leave her at the mercy of what her parents told her. As we have already seen, fundamental and ineradicable conflicts of interest between parents and offspring mean that parents will in general be selected to want at least twice as much self-sacrifice from a girl on behalf of her brothers than the girl herself will be selected to want, and tolerating preferential parental investment in brothers is indeed a form of self-sacrifice for the daughter who has to go without as a result of it (see above, pp. 189–91). No doubt much of the scandal which Freud caused by his discovery of infantile sexuality arose from the self-interest which parents may have in denying and hiding sexual discrimination with regard to their allocation of parental investment. By bringing infantile awareness of sexual differences to light, Freud was implicitly siding with the child and perhaps with the female child in particular, who, if she is indeed being discriminated against in favor of her brothers, has every reason to take serious note of sexual differences between children and to base her awareness of them on an unimpeachable authority: the evidence of her own eyes.

A million-odd years of hunter-gatherer prehistory in which our ancestors, like the Australian aborigines of recent times, almost certainly wore no clothes of any significance would have meant that a little girl's eyes could indeed give her reliable information about her own sex and that of others. But the individuals concerned, being children, would not show adult, dimorphic sexual differences – which, in any case, are notoriously variable. Consequently, natural selection may well have had a hand in fashioning what Freud found in the unconscious of both sexes: the unshakable conviction that the penis, and only the penis, is what defines a male, and that a female is indicated by its absence. Since the presence or absence of a penis is indeed the only really reliable indicator of sex in infancy, Freudian findings on this point make perfect sense – but once again, only if we set them in an evolutionary context and relate them not to sex as such, but to its wider implications centering on parental investment. Indeed, seen in this context, a desire on the part of young children to inspect one another's genitals seems much less evidence of precocious sexuality than it does a classic evolutionary adaptation aimed at equipping a child to deal with conflict over.the allocation of its parents' investment.

Furthermore, we might predict that if preferential parental investment is at stake, a little girl should also be primed by evolution to expect that those with a penis may well get things which she, who lacks one, may not get. She may even have been primed to feel envy at what the penis-possessors get and to feel that not having a penis is tantamount to being discriminated against – which, essentially, it may be if her brothers are indeed receiving preferential parental investment merely by virtue of being male. What Freud called "penis envy" may be the natural, compulsive awareness of this possibility. Consciously wanting things which others have is simply envy; unconsciously wanting parental investment which boys get is penis envy and again, contrary to first appearances, makes good evolutionary sense once it is placed in the context of our modern understanding of sex and parental investment.

In this respect it is worth drawing attention to a reproach which, according to Freud's findings, often accompanied the expression of penis envy in his woman patients, which he calls "rather a surprising one," although it could not seem more natural here. It "is that her mother did not give her enough milk, did not suckle her long enough . . . did not feed her sufficiently."[2] But what may have sounded to Freud like a largely subjective and delusional idea would have been the literal truth in many parts of the world where it is indeed a fact that boys are habitually breastfed longer than girls. It seems that findings which surprised even Freud, let alone his readers, seem much less surprising when set in the new perspective of recent evolutionary theory.

Like the Electra complex, "womb envy" on the part of

males was discounted by Freud, is seldom reported, and is definitely not predicted by this line of argument, despite seeming plausible at first glance. Its initial plausibility seems to derive from the consideration that if preferential parental investment in males pays if the outlook for their reproductive performance is good, corresponding preferential investment in girls is the selected strategy if the outlook is bad, making envy of them by males as likely as envy of males by females. In fact this is not so. To see why the sexes are not symmetrical in this respect, we must recall the more fundamental asymmetry relating to variance of reproductive success. We know that in general, but in polygynous species like human beings in particular, males are usually much more or much less reproductively successful than females. This means that presently existing males are likely to be descended disproportionately from the most reproductively successful males of the past. Such males would have had no reason to envy females if the line of reasoning being pursued here is correct, because they were the successful ones who presumably solicited and got preferential parental investment. This means that whereas most females will have descendants and will pass on genes for penis envy, most males will be descended from previous generations of males who had no need to envy females anything, because they were the recipients of what the majority of females envied them for. Only the sex enjoying limited but reliable reproductive success is likely to evolve adaptations to a form of parent–offspring conflict over high-risk investment of the kind involved in precociously sexual, male-antagonistic, oedipal sons.

Yet the fact that insight into early childhood could be obtained by Freud only after laborious analysis involving the overcoming of considerable resistances in his patients suggests another finding, perhaps fully appreciated only now that it can be set in the context of the modern theory of parent–child conflict. This is the fact that memories of early childhood are universally forgotten. So habituated are we to this completely normal finding that we fail to see how extraordinary it is. In what other recording medium are the first impressions the least likely to register and be retained? Why is it that, in later life, the first experience of something is likely to be recalled, often vividly, whereas later ones tend to be more easily forgotten? How could a totally novel and astounding experience like birth pass without any lasting recollection being registered in the memory, when completely trivial sensations obtained at later ages are minutely recorded and readily recalled? These questions are especially pertinent, since experiment shows that memory does indeed function in early childhood and that, for example, children of only a week or so old can learn and recall the characteristic taste and smell of their mothers. Again, experience of slightly older children reveals that they can indeed recall familiar faces, recognize voices, and give every appearance of having accurate memories of things like toys, clothing, people, and places. And if we suggest that linguistic ability is critical (and there is little reason to think that it is, since animals who cannot speak seem able to remember perfectly well), it is worth pointing out that considerable skill in using simple words and phrases is usually found at ages before which continuous and voluntary recall of childhood will later be possible.

Finally, it is worth pointing out that if general amnesia does indeed seem to affect everyone's recollection of early childhood, it should nevertheless still be possible to overcome it occasionally, for example by means of recollection of previously forgotten incidents from infancy. This would suggest that even if complete recall cannot prove that extensive memory of early childhood exists, intermittent memory might at least indicate its probability. In this respect it is important to note that Freud found that memory of early childhood is not merely forgotten but actively *repressed*. In other words, he found that such memories are forcibly excluded from consciousness by an active process of repression. But to the extent that his psychoanalytic method could overcome and undo such repressions, he also found that it was sometimes possible to retrieve previously forgotten material – a feat that is especially impressive when, as has occasionally happened, it has also proved possible to check the validity of the recollections by objective means or independent corroboration. Again, his findings regarding so-called *screen memories* – that is, manifest memories of one thing which allude to lost, latent memories of another – further argue the case that even in quite early childhood the human brain is fully able to record continuous memories and, under the special conditions which apply in psycho-analysis at least, to recall them much later in life.[3]

We saw earlier (see above, p. 104) that recent evolutionary theory has rediscovered the true Freudian meaning of repression in its insights into self-deceit as a means of deceiving others by way of deceiving oneself. In that discussion we saw that reciprocal altruism is critical, because it is there, rather than in kin-altruistic interactions, that deception really does pay. However, we saw earlier that the situation seems to be reversed where parents and offspring are concerned, because there will be more agreement about reciprocal altruism than about kin altruism, with regard to which a serious clash of interest is likely to occur. We also noticed that in the human case parents will tend to try to induce more kin altruism in their children than the children themselves would wish and that coercion, manipulation, and deceit – the classic instruments of induced altruism – are likely to be exploited by parents (see above, pp. 190–7). Insofar as deceiving children and encouraging their errors serves this interest, parents could be seen as promoting self-deception in their offspring. However, modern evolutionary theory and classical Freudianism differ from popularized psychoanalysis and socialization theory in understanding "repression" to be an autonomous process, carried out by the individual concerned in order to avoid conflict and to reduce psychological stress, not one which can be directly imposed by others, no matter how powerful and manipulative they may be.[4]

This means that while parents can certainly attempt to bring about repression in their offspring to their parental advantage, they cannot cause it directly and must usually encounter the child's resistance in any attempt to induce self-deception. But where they themselves are concerned, self-deception by means of classical Freudian repression is an ever-open option. and can be expected to occur. Blanket forgetting of early childhood by anyone old enough to be a parent seems to be a universal instance of this and suggests that it is a form of repression brought about as a specifically evolved adaptation.

The reason that repression of memories of early childhood may have become a prime human adaptation is probably to be found in the realization that parents who could easily and vividly recall how they felt themselves as young children when being dealt with by their parents would find it much harder to play a parental role with regard to their own children when the time came to do so. They would experience many of the problems of ambivalence and self-doubt which afflict many modern parents in their dealings with adolescents and which probably arise mainly from the fact that such parents can recall all too easily how they felt at a similar age. Because adolescence is much less prolonged in primal societies, evolution has not taken a hand to ease the plight of the parents by making it impossible for them to recall their own adolescence, which, in the protracted form in which we know it, is a very recent development in evolutionary terms.

But extended childhood is a much more long-standing fact of human life, and is a fully developed adaptation, not merely a psychosocial effect of modern affluence like protracted adolescence. The result is that natural selection has had time to produce a specific adaptation in adults to counter adaptations concurrently evolved in offspring. The main effect of this parental adaptation seems to be to blank out nearly all memory of the first four to five years of life. This is the very time during which the most crucial parent–child conflicts are likely to occur, and the principal effect of such repression is likely to be to leave parents singlemindedly aware of their own self-interest. Fundamentally, it serves to counter the distraction and ambivalence which voluntary recall of how they themselves felt as children would cause parents in their never easy task of dealing with their children. It seems that parents have good reasons for wanting to forget how they felt as infants in conflict with their parents. Specifically, they may need to forget their infantile interest in sex because of potential conflicts with their own children over the question of differential parental investment in relation to sex and will need to see it from their own, rather than from the child's, point of view – a psychological maneuver which Freud found to be typical and which he described as repression of infantile sexuality. To the extent that psychoanalysis is essentially based on the return of repressed memories from early childhood, one cannot help wondering whether this is the true, evolutionary reason for the widespread resistance to the findings of Freud and whether his real offence was nothing more than voicing the self-interest of the child, so seldom heard in the world of adults and so contrary in many respects to the self-interests of parents.

The prime role of the father

Although the blanket forgetting of early childhood may indeed serve the evolutionary function which I have just suggested, what Freud actually found was that it largely took place not at puberty, as we might at first expect, but immediately following the oedipal phase, at the beginning of the so-called latency period. This extended until puberty, running approximately between seven or eight years of age to the early teens. Latency was marked by a notable reduction in the precocious "sexual" behavior of the oedipal period, a tendency to identify with parents and their values, especially the parent of the same sex, and an altogether more "grown-up," sensible, and tractable attitude on the part of children which appeared to be largely the result of repression of earlier childhood.

It seems a reasonable assumption that parent–offspring conflict of the kind that I have suggested may underlie oral and oedipal behavior should begin to attenuate once a child is old enough for the birth of further siblings not to pose a threat to it and when any offspring that may have appeared is sufficiently separated from it in age for competition with it to be a less serious matter. Indeed, once an existing child is approaching later childhood but has not yet reached puberty, it may find that its best tactic for securing parental investment is to identify with the parents and their role with regard to any younger siblings. We could certainly expect conflict with the parents over the latency-age child's attitude to very much younger siblings to be much less marked than would be the case if the child were much younger itself. For example, suppose a parent wants an older child to give up some food for a much younger one. As we know, the parent is selected to favor this wherever the benefit to the younger exceeds the cost to the elder. If the elder child is nine or ten years old, the contribution of the food to its own growth may well be less than half what it would be to its much younger – and much smaller – sibling. Since, all other things being equal, the elder child will be selected to favor such a sacrifice when the benefit to its younger sibling is more than twice the cost to itself, it is quite likely that it will agree more often with its parents than would have been the case if the age and size gap were smaller (see above, pp. 190–1).

Where girls are concerned, identification with, and mimicry of, the mother's role in child-rearing does not have to be interpreted as the outcome of passive socialization. On the contrary, because a girl's ultimate reproductive success is directly related to her ability to raise children of her own or to help relatives rear their offspring, it follows that natural selection has probably taken a hand in facilitating such identifications. Indeed, the Freudian finding that little girls, frustrated in their desire for a penis seek unconscious substitute gratification in a wish for a baby of their own makes good evolutionary sense if we translate "penis" into "preferential parental investment in males." It makes even better sense if we notice that mothers who favor their sons are often found to do so because they unconsciously see sons as particularly gratifying substitutes for this wish. If males who have been the subject of preferential parental investment normally have greater than average reproductive success as compared with other males and considerably more than females, a woman who was disappointed in not receiving such preference herself because she was female rather than male could indeed gratify her wish vicariously in her son. If her son's subsequent reproductive success was enhanced as a result, her behavior would effectively have been naturally selected. Indeed, a circle of causation would have been closed which could then go on for ever: with little girls envying males the preferential investment made in them, only to make it themselves in their own sons when the time came for them to be parents.

Yet oedipal behavior in little girls suggests that fathers are also important sources of parental investment. We have already seen that in the case of the Ache hunter-gatherers a father who is one of the better hunters enhances his offsprings' chances of survival and that loss of a father does the reverse (see above, p. 67). Fathers were also shown to be an important factor in the survival and reproductive success of their children in the study of seventeenth- to nineteenth-century Ostfriesland (see above, pp. 67–8). An analysis which concentrated on father–daughter interactions in a rural Caribbean village revealed that the frequency of such interactions peaked when daughters were aged eleven to fifteen years and that girls with resident fathers had more stable mating relationships and were mated to more prosperous males than those without resident fathers.[5] If we turn to the case of Australian aborigines, who almost certainly provide a reliable guide to primal hunter-gatherer conditions because of their isolation until recent times, we find that all such societies were polygynous and that a young woman's marriage opportunities were strongly influenced by her father's social contacts. Fathers – the most prolific of whom, of course, were successful polygynists themselves – tended to give their daughters to other such men who were friends and allies and to use them to cement alliances, return favors, and generally advance their own interests.[6] The result was that a young woman's chances of marrying a successful and well-established man were critically dependent on the standing of her own father and the extent of his social contacts and influence.

Perhaps this explains why studies show that girls brought up without fathers in early childhood experience fewer orgasms when they are married and why inappropriate or inadequate fathering seems to be a major factor in the development of lesbianism.[7] If we are correct in seeing lesbianism as essentially a second-best reproductive strategy in which two women team up to raise their joint progeny when neither can secure a male themselves (see above, pp. 183–4), we might conclude that the absence of a father could be linked to such outcomes through the factor of his parental investment. Presumably a father's characteristic parental investment would have promoted his daughter's chances of securing an adequate father for her children in primal conditions, and his absence or inadequacy may have indicated the converse, rather as the modern studies quoted above suggest it still does. Even in our own societies, in which life is allegedly more emancipated from primal, biological, and evolutionary constraints, there is a wealth of evidence indicating that a woman's marital opportunities as far as the social standing and wealth of her prospective husband are concerned are vitally affected by the status and resources of her own father.

Of course, much the same is also true of sons. If mothers are the crucial providers of parental investment in early childhood, as one would expect them to be in the case of a mammal with a lengthy infancy, then fathers become critical later, thanks to the characteristic sex-role specialization which makes them the chief providers of wealth and income in most circumstances. This in itself probably explains much about why Freud found that by some apparently innate, genetically determined means, sons repressed their oedipal antagonism towards their fathers as childhood reached its end. If what Freud called the Oedipus complex in boys is indeed mainly a psychological adaptation designed to solicit preferential parental investment at a time when the mother is the key agent of investment, then what he regarded as the "dissolution" or "resolution" of that complex may simply be a comparable adaptation to the fact that the father is the critical agent in later childhood and that cooperation with him, rather than antagonism towards him, is the best policy if his investment is to be secured.

Here, Freud reports that in children of both sexes, but in males in particular, the change in relation to the father comes about via the mechanism of identification, which we have already seen is probably the prime human psychological mechanism for producing cooperative behavior in general and facilitating kin altruism in particular (see above, pp. 108–17). But where fathers are concerned, there is a problem which is not encountered with mothers. This is the perennial uncertainty of paternity which we examined earlier in a different context (see above, pp. 211–12). Experiments with newborn children show that while they cannot identify their mothers by taste and smell at birth, they can do so within a week.[8] A wealth of evidence suggests that throughout the animal world individuals identify their kin by similar means. But human offspring do not get the same chance to taste and smell their fathers that they do their mammalian, breast-feeding mothers.

But who is the father, and how is he identified? Here, significantly, the effect of identification by smell works the. other way round, with Australian aborigine fathers "putting their smell" on the newborn baby by first placing their hands under their own armpits and then rubbing them over the baby. (Such practices are not peculiar to human beings: male lions mark their offspring with their scent, and those of a previous resident in the pride are likely to be killed by a newcomer because they are not his, thereby making the marking of those that are his critical for their survival.) Even in our own culture, studies show that people remark more on the resemblance between newborn babies and their fathers than they do on the resemblance with their mothers.

One way in which paternity can be determined, at least in terms of probability, is by the means suggested in my earlier discussion of altruism and identification: so-called phenotypic matching. This is the comparison of another with oneself and the assumption that the more the other resembles oneself, the more closely one is likely to be related to them. Successful comparison with oneself is fundamental to identification with someone, and perhaps this is why Freud found that identification was such a critical factor in the relation of children to their fathers, particularly in the case of boys. Looked at from this point of view, his findings regarding oedipal behavior in boys seem to boil down to paternal mimicry in their relationship with both their mothers and their fathers, albeit in different ways. Where the mother is concerned, the mimicry produces an antagonistic attitude to the father as a rival male resembling the father's sexual situation regarding other men. Where the father is concerned, it produces one of mimicry by identification with the father, as if the son were saying, "Look, invest in me, I am just like you!"

Oedipal effects in adult life

The outcome discussed above would correspond to only one of the possibilities suggested by the findings of Freud. The other is represented by the so-called negative resolution of the Oedipus complex: one in which the boy identifies more with his mother than with his father and which is found to be implicated in many cases of homosexuality in males. Psycho-analytic observations often indicate that a common reason for such an outcome is that the father is absent, inadequate, or for some other reason fails to provide a successful basis for his son's identification with him. Nor are Freudians alone in finding this. A surprisingly large number of studies by mainstream, academic psychologists have come to exactly the same conclusion. A comprehensive summary of the dozens of separate studies in question concludes that the degree of the son's masculinity is frequently found to be related to the father's perceived role within the family, with men who tend to play a passive, feminine role or who are dominated by their wives tending to have less masculine sons. Such studies also show that an inadequate identification with a strong, masculine father is a prime factor in the development of homosexuality, reactive hypermasculinity, and various kinds of psychological and social problems in sons.[9]

Insofar as a strong identification with the mother is associated with such problems in the case of boys, we have already noticed in passing that Robert Stoller's accounts of so-called transsexuals reveal a similar picture: one in which the mother is everything to the son and the father virtually nothing (see above, p. 228). Transsexuals, who are evidently overwhelmed by parental investment on the part of the parent of the opposite sex and do not form any very significant relationship with the same-sex parent, may be explicable as an extreme case of "helper in the nest" recruitment. In other species a situation is sometimes found in which the over-investing parent seeks to make the offspring dependent on it to the extent that the offspring gives up any desire to have a reproductive life of its own. Although paradoxical at first sight, such behavior can pay a parent if the offspring who is induced by these means to become nonreproductive can be used as a "helper in the nest" to raise the parent's other progeny. Perhaps the striking beauty of their sons which mothers of transsexuals report reflects their implicit judgment that these are boys who are already partly feminized. Perhaps the psychological and/or socio-economic stress which such mothers are often found to experience makes them unconsciously conclude that their sons are unlikely to enjoy much reproductive success as adult men and so try to feminize them further, making them effectively into helpmate daughters because they can never be reproductive sons. If such a view were to prove correct, transsexuals would be not merely non-oedipal, as pointed out earlier, but would represent a more or less completely reversed situation: one in which a parent manipulated the behavioral sex of its offspring in its own, parental self-interest, rather than the offspring manipulating parental investment in its own sexual self-interest, as may be the case with oedipal behavior.

As far as homosexuals in general are concerned, it is possible that the absence of identification with an adequate father may be important in two different, but related aspects. In the first place, it may mean that a boy does not receive the paternal investment which he requires to succeed in competition with other men for women, so that he becomes a homosexual for fundamentally the same reason that a daughter might: the absence of a supportive father. However, a second reason may be that, lacking a father who has already proved that he possesses "the right stuff" for male reproductive success, a son may implicitly conclude that he himself is also defective in this respect and that he is unlikely to have inherited genes for it from his father. There is certainly one research finding which suggests that homosexual men are significantly lighter in body weight and weaker in muscular strength than heterosexual men.[10] This reduced degree of sexual dimorphism, although evident in the homosexuals themselves, may in part be heritable and one of the factors involved in determining the estimation which a boy unconsciously makes at the culmination of the oedipal period about his prospects for future reproductive success. This line of reasoning suggests that, transsexuals apart, we should regard homosexuals in particular and perhaps all male sexual "perverts" in general as cryptic males, intent on secondary, "deviant" sexual strategies because they lack a satisfactory basis for confidence in their own reproductive success thanks to an inadequate or unsatisfactory identification with a father (see above, pp. 149–56).

As in the case of the link between weak or absent fathers and homosexuality in sons, nonpsychoanalytic reasearch has also occasionally produced findings which would support this interpretation. A study in which male experimental subjects were led to believe that they were unsuccessful in attracting women found that the men's responses to shoes, underwear, and other "fetishes" associated with women increased, while studies of practicing fetishists show them to be sexually inexperienced and likely to suffer various serious disabilities such as skin and personality disorders, epilepsy, anxiety, and depression. Again, as figure 7.1 suggests, male sexual deviants of various kinds show a tendency towards shyness and introversion, and the fact that only training in improving social skills seems to have much effect on paedophile men supports the view that they are attracted to children because they find them less daunting than adults as sex-objects.[11]

Nevertheless, sexual deviations of the kind I am portraying as instances of human cryptic sexuality need not be wholly based on inadequate relationships with fathers. One of the most apparently biologically unacceptable findings of psycho-analysis is that so-called oedipal transferences are regularly found in the unconscious, which appears to indicate that adult sex-objects are often chosen on the basis of some resemblance to the mother in the case of men or the father in that of women. Psychoanalysts have assumed, unavoidably, that such attractions are to the actual mother, for the simple reason that in Western, ostensibly monogamous cultures, the father's wife and the mother will usually be one and the

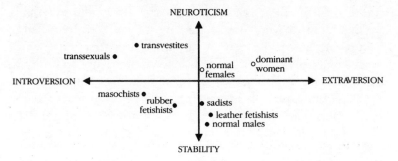

Figure 7 1 Sexually variant and normal groups in relation to scales measuring extraversion and neuroticism.
(Redrawn with kind permission from G. D. Wilson, "The Sociobiological Basis of Sexual Dysfunction," in *Sex Therapy in Britain*, eds M. Cole and W. Dryden (Open University Press, Milton Keynes, 1988), p. 55.)

same. However, if human beings are basically adapted for polygyny, then they must be basically adapted for a situation in which only one of the father's wives is the actual mother of any particular male and his other wives are not. Studies show that wives apart from the mother are prime targets for the sexual advances of sons in some cultures, and in most polygynous cultures older women, often of the same generation as the mother, are likely to be the most promising sexual targets for younger, unmarried men.[12]

This is because polygyny produces a significant age difference between husband and wife, thanks to the fact that most men who are going to have several wives cannot acquire or afford them until they themselves are well into their thirties, forties, or fifties. Their wives, however, tend to be much younger. In fact, husbands tend to be somewhat older than wives in any mating system, including our own, monogamous one; but studies of Australian aborigines demonstrate typical age differences between husbands and wives of approximately eighteen years. In one statistical analysis, husbands averaged forty-two years of age, but wives twenty-four. An inevitable consequence of these age disparities between husbands and wives was that husbands tended to die first, releasing widows who would invariably remarry. However, they tended in the main to be recycled to younger, less prominent men, often as a first wife, while powerful polygynists granted their young daughters only to their equals and associates in age and status. The result was that a young man in his twenties might often marry a first wife who was old enough to be his mother and might even be his mother-in-law if one of her daughters had already married his father.

But, quite apart from problems with official sexual partners such as these, consider the plight of a young, unmarried man where other partners are concerned. In a polygynous mating system, most young girls will already be married or promised to older, powerful polygynists: the very persons from whom a young man is himself ultimately likely to get a wife. Poaching the young wives of such men is hardly sensible, especially if one is found out. Furthermore, a young man is likely to come up against the resistance of the young lady herself. She, at the beginning of her reproductive life, has maximum reproductive value to a future or existing husband. She needs to think carefully about who she becomes mated to and needs to be wary about duplicity, because an existing husband who finds that he has been cuckolded may well abandon her and her offspring or, at the very least, discriminate against her and her children. Again, an unmarried young woman who gets a reputation for promiscuity may find it difficult to secure a husband who is prepared to invest in her offspring if there is always a chance that they may not be his. Nor are these expectations purely theoretical; the study of Ache hunter-gatherers from which I have quoted before found exactly this.[13]

However, the older wives in the population may be a different matter. They may be most of the way through their reproductive lives and, in any case, may be secure in their social position in a way in which a young wife often is not. Beginning to age and probably finding that their husbands prefer their younger co-wives, such women may find the covert attentions of younger, unmarried men worth considering and may respond accordingly. Indeed, these considerations may well explain the finding that young women arouse more reluctantly and orgasm less frequently and intensely than older ones. It may also explain why Freud remarked on a "considerable increase" in libido in women of menopausal age and why Kinsey and subsequent researchers have found that masturbation in women – evidently an expression of personal sexual need – follows a trajectory exactly contrary to that in males by increasing steadily up to age forty, rather than declining steadily from age eighteen. Far from being mismatched, as they are normally assumed to be, the sexes may be adapted to correspond to one another in a more oedipal way than is normally assumed. Younger women may be adapted to be "coy" and selective and to be mated to older men, while older women may be tuned to respond to younger men, and vice versa. The rapid arousal and quicker ejaculation of young men may not merely mirror the less coy and reluctant sexual physiology of older women, but may be directly paralleled in the behavior of other young male mammals such as mountain sheep, who mount females hurriedly and ejaculate almost instantaneously before being unceremoniously butted off by the resident harem-holder. Premature ejaculation in particular, far from being pathological, may only be an extreme form of a completely normal adaption in younger men, and oedipal transferences in general may turn out to be pre-eminently explicable from a biological, evolutionary point of view if this line of reasoning is correct.

Finally, what of the no less important oedipal transferences found in women? Such tendencies in men relate mainly to secondary, "alternative" sexual preferences, since, clearly, it would always be in a young man's best biological interests to mate a young woman rather than an older one. In men it seems that oedipal love-objects represent just the first, most normal examples of cryptic sexuality in a range which runs from there to bizarre, totally inanimate examples in the case of fetishism and take in a man's own sex (homosexuality) and own self (narcissism) on the way. In women the situation cannot be the same because, as we have already seen, cryptic sexuality will seldom pay a female, thanks to her greater concern with investment in offspring rather than in mating effort.

However, oedipal transferences could still be adaptive if we note that in a polygynous mating system such as almost certainly typified our evolutionary ancestors most daughters will be born to a few, successful polygynists. Furthermore, those that are born to them will usually be among the best placed when it comes to their own mating opportunities, because, as we have also seen, wealth, status, and general success correlate strongly with reproductive success in a polygynous society. Admittedly, such daughters may not have much choice in marriage partners if marriages are arranged for them, as they evidently often were in the case of many Australian aboriginal societies; but even were this not so, a young girl's best reproductive interests might be served by marrying an older, proven, successful polygynist, one who had already shown that he had "the right stuff," both genetically and otherwise. Since her father would in all probability be one of these, a sexual preference which made her prefer men who reminded her of her own father might prove adaptive.

Perhaps this explains why studies of the mating preferences of young women in modern societies do reveal some evidence of the influence of oedipal, paternal transferences on their choice of love-object. A study of people born to mixed-race marriages showed a tendency for both sexes to marry into the ethnic group of the parent of the opposite sex, and a study of Italian census data revealed a correlation between father's and husband's age.[14] Another recent study of 314 British young women showed weakly significant correlations between father's and boyfriend's eye color, as well as a tendency for girls to reproduce the age and dominance relationships of their parents in their own relationships with men. Although the correlations were weak, the authors of the study nevertheless point out that, given the high number of possible attributes of her father which a girl might consciously or otherwise seek to reproduce in her sexual partner, it is not surprising that only small effects were found. Multiple correlations over a great many characteristics might well reveal much stronger effects.[15] All in all, it seems that, when placed in the context of modern evolutionary theory, oedipal conflicts, identifications, and transferences are not as implausible as they might otherwise have seemed.[16]

Conclusion:
The Nature of Culture

Culture as a problem of scale

Evolution by natural selection is a slow process. The reason is simple: natural selection selects for reproductive success, and the tempo of that process must be set by the rate of reproduction of the organism in question. Although this may be only a matter of minutes or hours in the case of some bacteria and only days or weeks in that of some of the smaller multicellular organisms, most large plants and animals require years or even decades to reproduce. In the case of human beings, the conventional figure of thirty years for a generation suggests that selection for reproductive success is tied to a clock whose "ticks," if we may call them that, occur at the rate of approximately three per century. Furthermore, the fact that multicellular organisms did not appear until simpler, unicellular ones had existed on earth for what is believed to have been at least a billion years suggests that although the evolutionary clock may have ticked much faster in the past than it does today in the case of human beings, the time required to produce anything capable of slowing it down appreciably was a very long one indeed – so long that the total duration of life on earth is only approximately ten times less than the age of the universe itself.

As far as we know today, the universe came into being sometime between ten and twenty billion years ago. (In the convenient exponential method of notation of such large figures, ten billion – 10,000,000,000 – can be written 10^{10}. Here the superscript figure 10 represents the ten zeros which we would otherwise have to write after the initial 1 if we were to write out the number in full decimal notation.) Although the probable age of the universe, (10^{10} to 2×10^{10} years), seems a very long period of time by comparison with the probable total period that life has existed on earth, it is in fact only approximately an order of magnitude – that is, a difference of one in the superscript – more: a few billion (10^9) years as opposed to a few tens of billions (10^{10}) of years.

But by any standard these are large numbers. The numbers remain large as we progress down the evolutionary time scale from the beginnings of life on earth towards the emergence of our own species. If life as a whole existed for the order of 10^9 years, then multicellular organisms, as opposed to single cells, have existed only for some hundreds of millions, or 10^8 years – another order of magnitude less. The mammalian class of animals to which we belong represents a further order of magnitude less: 10^7, or, to be more precise, some sixty-odd million years (6×10^7). The genus *Homo* is believed to have existed for a mere one or two million, or 10^6 years; while our species, *Homo sapiens*, can number a mere few tens of thousands: 10^4 years, or two more steps down in orders of magnitude.

Cultural evolution, by contrast, is a relatively recent affair. The most ancient cultures of the world existed for a mere few thousand – or, in exponential notation, a mere 10^3 years, another order of magnitude less. Indeed, the historian Oswald Spengler pointed out that, in historical times at least, cultures or civilizations often showed an uncanny preference for a lifetime of approximately 1,100 years. Both Roman Empires certainly qualify here if we take the original, Western Roman Empire to have begun with the foundation of the city in 753 BC and to have ended with its sack by the Goths in AD 410. Some 1,100-odd years later. If we note that the Eastern one was founded by Constantine in the city of his name in AD 330 and finally fell to the Turks in 1453, we have another, almost exact period of 1,100 years. (Indeed, the third, Holy Roman Empire might qualify too if we date it from Charlemagne's coronation in AD 800 to the end of the last central European empire, the Austro-Hungarian, in 1918.)

But exact historical periods are not at issue here; what concerns us is the fact that if evolutionary history spans orders of magnitude ranging from 10^9 years for life as a whole to 10^6–10^4 years for our particular genus and species, then cultural evolution spans periods of time at least an order of magnitude less and, if more detailed historical events are included, two to three orders of magnitude less: tens and hundreds, as opposed to thousands, of years.

In the light of this fact, it is tempting to conclude that evolution has no relevance and that, as is often erroneously asserted, human beings – or, at the very least, human cultures – have ceased to evolve in the sense in which biologists speak of other organisms evolving. Of course, it is easy to show that such statements – at least about human beings as such – are meaningless and mistaken. In order to cease to evolve by natural selection, organisms would have to violate the two necessary conditions which Darwin postulated for evolution. In the first place they would all have to be genetically identical – which human beings manifestly are not – and in the second place there would have to be no differences of any kind in the reproductive success of individual human beings. This again is something which no sane person would claim, because, in practical terms, it would mean that every single human being would have to have the same number of offspring, who themselves had the same number of offspring, *ad infinitum.* Looked at in these terms, it is clearly quite wrong to claim that human beings have ceased to evolve by natural selection, because it is obvious that both genetic variation and differential reproductive success are characteristic of our species. Admittedly, once we restrict our attention to very short time periods, the necessarily long-term effects of evolution become difficult or impossible to see; yet that would be true of any evolving species if one restricted one's view in a comparable kind of way.

But with cultural evolution we are in a more difficult position. This is because cultures, at least if understood as distinct, historical entities, have existed only relatively recently in evolutionary time and because their own lifetimes, although long by the standards of individual human lives, are nevertheless short by evolutionary standards. Again, cultures can clearly be seen to respond to individual human beings and to their initiatives and to be affected by the personal interests and aspirations of their members – something which again seems to suggest that long-term, evolutionary perspectives cannot be relevant to them. Even if it is manifestly wrong to claim that human beings as organisms have ceased to evolve by natural selection, it nevertheless seems dubious to claim that human cultures can be seen in the light of Darwinian evolution, given their relatively brief and recent existence.

If culture appears to be out of scale with nature in terms of time and, indeed, to be something which is some orders of magnitude less, then, looked at from the point of view of spatial magnitudes, it appears to relate to something far larger. Archaeologists and historians of culture take artifacts, such as potsherds, weapons and tools, building sites and middens, to be the objects which are evidence of culture in our species' past. The term "cultural evolution" is usually taken to mean evolution – or, at the very least, gradual change – in objects such as these and, in the case of the oldest known cultures, refers to the gradual changes observable in the stone implements which represent their technology. But these objects are many orders of magnitude larger than the genes which biologists take to be the essential elements on which biological, as opposed to cultural, evolution works.

Physically, genes are very small and stand in relation to the spatial dimensions of cultural objects much as cultural history does to evolutionary history in terms of time. In the latter respect cultural time spans orders of magnitude at least six times smaller than evolutionary time: 10^3 years as opposed to 10^9, or thousands as opposed to billions. If we take it that cultural artifacts exist on centimeter scales and observe that genes are measured in millionths of a centimeter, we have a similar discrepancy: about six orders of magnitude. In other words, it would seem that whichever way we look at it, in terms of either time or space, culture is quite out of proportion with evolution, by a staggering six orders of magnitude, or something in the region of a millionfold! With such a vast discrepancy in quantitative terms, it is hardly surprising that many have concluded that qualitatively too natural evolution and cultural history are incommensurate and incompatible, two separate realities which can never meet.

This seems all the more credible once one realizes that, quite apart from any problem relating to scale in space or time, there is a fundamental discrepancy between cultural and biological evolution in relation to the unit of selection involved. Indeed, strictly speaking, there can be no such thing as *cultural* evolution by natural selection. This is because, as we have already seen, selection acts on individuals, not groups. Since "cultures" are normally thought of as constituted by very large groups of people, it follows that, in this strict sense, cultures cannot be described as "evolving" without committing the error of assuming that natural selection can act on groups as such. Evidently, then, along with apparently irreconcilable discrepancies in terms of temporal and spatial scales, there is a third problem of scale involved: one involving the unit of selection. If this is the individual gene in the case of evolution by natural selection, then the unit in the case of cultural evolution would appear to be groups of individuals numbering from tens to billions. Yet if group selection is incompatible with evolution by natural selection at the level of the gene, as we have indeed seen it to be, then cultural evolution by natural selection would appear to be impossible.

But however that may be, it is nevertheless worth observing that enormous problems of scale exist elsewhere in science and suggest another conclusion. For instance, modern physics rests on two separate scientific paradigms: quantum mechanics and general relativity, which have not until recently been compatible. In large part this is also a problem related to scale: quantum mechanics applies to the very smallest scales, the subatomic, general relativity to the very largest, the universe as a whole. To date, no general theoretical unification has worked, but this has not prevented physicists from trying to bring it about. Clearly, if physical science is to be complete and consistent, it ought to stand on a single basis, not find itself uncomfortably divided between two, apparently irreconcilable ways of looking at things.

Culture and evolution would seem to represent a similar problem of scale, with evolution ostensibly tied to the spatial dimensions of the gene and to the time dimension of evolutionary history, while culture is committed to the very different scales represented by human history and activity. It would seem that in this respect behavioral science faces a problem comparable to that of physics and needs to find some way in which two, ostensibly disproportionate realities could be related to one another and, ideally, understood by a single theory. If such an insight could be found, life on the largest scale, that represented by Darwinian evolution, might in reality not be completely unrelated to the much more intimate scale represented by human culture.

Three cultures of cooperation

If we adhere to a genuinely Darwinian approach, the problem of cultural evolution becomes one of explaining how natural selection at the level of the individual gene could relate to culture, given that we have already ruled out group selection of entire cultural groups. But such a problem is already familiar to us: we encountered it earlier as "the problem of altruism" and saw that, essentially, it reduces to having to confront the difficulty of explaining how selection at the level of the individual could favor the evolution of cooperative behavior. Indeed, a moment's reflection will show that, to a large extent at least, what we mean by "human cultures" are large cultural groups which we identify as such *because their members cooperate preferentially with one another.* At the lowest and most obvious level this may be expressed by no more than simply speaking the same language; but at a higher level it may embrace sharing the same beliefs, values, and aspirations. Yet however expressed and at whatever level of generality, such common, unifying cultural factors could be seen as reflecting the fundamental requirements of social cooperation expressed by the triumph of TIT FOR TAT in Axelrod's tournaments: *cooperate with other cooperators, but defect against defection.* Indeed, such a formulation would reveal not merely the unifying, cohesive force of culture in human affairs, but also its no less significant divisive potentialities expressed in ethnic conflict, religious antagonism, and inter-state wars.

If our evolutionary theory of cooperation is correct and complete, we could characterize human cultures as ultimately based on three – and only three – fundamental forms of cooperation and perhaps see some of the inevitable conflicts to which they give rise as originating not merely in the discrimination of cultural cooperators from noncooperators, but also in the very form of cooperation itself. For example, traditional cultures might be seen as based essentially on kin altruism and, in their origins at least, literally so if the cultural group was indeed small and intimate enough for most of its members to be related by some overall structure of kinship. Here the hereditary principle of recruitment to particular offices such as chieftainships would reflect a social structure fundamentally based on kin altruism and genetic relatedness: one in which the "cultural" and the "kin" group were essentially the same. Modern cultures based on free markets might be seen as founded principally on reciprocal altruism:

societies in which cooperation is based not so much on kinship, as on the exchange of goods and services between individuals whose social identity is in part determined by their economic role. Finally, societies which specifically repudiate both free markets and traditional, kin-based organization – socialist ones – would seem to be based on the third, induced form of altruism. In these cases cooperation is induced by bureaucratic rules and political principles which would attempt to coordinate the society by means of some central plan or authority. Thus, whereas individuals may fill their social role thanks to kinship considerations in a traditional society and by virtue of a labor market in one based on reciprocal altruism, they would be directed to it by some rule or authority in a socialist one. Essentially, kin-based societies can be seen as families, reciprocity-based ones as markets, and those based on induced altruism as bureaucracies.

Of course, these categorizations could not possibly be exclusive, and it would be absurd to imagine that kin altruism of any kind did not exist side by side with reciprocal cooperation in a market society anymore than it would be foolish to imagine that in societies based on cooperation induced by rules and regulations considerations of kinship or reciprocity played no part at all. On the contrary, we have to see the three fundamental forms of altruism concerned in these three types of cultures as merely the central, preponderant forms, and certainly not exclusive or completely predominant over the others. It seems that whatever culture is in question, kin altruism will tend to show itself in family matters, reciprocal altruism in economic interactions, and induced altruism in legal and political affairs. Nevertheless, it does not seem impossible that some cultural conflicts in the modern world between market, socialist, and traditional societies indeed reflect fundamental differences in the forms of cooperation on which they are essentially based.

Indeed, within modern Western cultures it would be tempting to see these three fundamental forms of cooperation as underlying not merely three types of social life, but three views of human nature which go with them. We might begin by distinguishing between what we might term the *optimistic* view of human nature and society and distinguish it from the opposed and opposing *pessimistic* one. Let us take the optimistic pole of this continuum first.

This view, associated with the names of Jean-Jacques Rousseau (1712–78) and Karl Marx (1818–83), to name but two of the most notable, holds that human beings are born basically cooperative but that, if in later life they act selfishly or uncooperatively, they do so because their natural cooperativeness has been corrupted by such things as the existence of private property, class, or ethnic groups or because they have been forced into selfish and antisocial behavior by the selfish and antisocial behavior of others. According to this view of human nature and social existence, the fundamental altruism and sociability of human beings would re-emerge if people could get back to the original state of natural cooperation or forward to a better, future society without class, private property, ethnic prejudice, or whatever other corrupting influences are at work. Correspondingly, this view holds that if children were allowed to grow up free from social pressures to the contrary, their natural cooperativeness would be retained, and they would mature as better people as a result.

The view of the pessimists is almost the exact opposite of this. According to thinkers of this persuasion, represented by the English philosopher Thomas Hobbes (1588–1679) or by the influential French sociologist Émile Durkheim (1857–1917), human beings are basically antisocial, egoistic, and selfish by nature. If they ever act otherwise, it is only because they are prevailed upon by their fellows to do so. Without some kind of social constraint or control, society would degenerate into a war of all against all – anarchy, in other words – and 'revert to a natural state which Hobbes graphically described as "solitary, poor, nasty, brutish, and short." In this, pessimistic view of the possibilities of human cooperation, children are regarded as the next best things to wild animals, who must be tamed and controlled if they are ever to learn to act in any way other than as selfish, aggressive, and antisocial brutes. According to this view, human beings are not so much corrupted by culture, as civilized by it. Without some kind of external constraint represented by social or governmental control, any kind of cooperation would be next to impossible.

In terms of the earlier discussion of the evolution of cooperation, we might say that the optimists believe that human beings are natural cooperators who inevitably end up playing SUCKER to others who exploit them for selfish gain. In the opinion of the pessimists, human beings are basically noncooperators whose natural social strategy is DEFECTOR. The remedy, the optimists believe, is defection against the defectors who exploit them: bloody revolution in the most extreme case, nonviolent protest or withdrawal of labor in the least. If the optimists are inclined to see any form of authority as corrupting and something to be defected against, the pessimists, by contrast, see most forms of authority as sacred and representative of civilized cooperation, a refuge from natural anarchy. For them any defection against practically any established order is an invitation to chaos and so must be resisted wherever possible.

In this way the optimists acquire a reputation for revolution, the pessimists one for reaction. To the extent that the pessimists teach acceptance of existing forms of cooperation as the preferred alternative to defection, they are seen as conservative, whereas the optimists are seen as radicals, because they impugn all forms of existing cooperation as flawed by defection. Paradoxically, whereas the optimists begin by assuming that human beings are naturally predisposed to unconditional cooperation (the SUCKER strategy in iterated Prisoner's Dilemma) but then conclude that the fact of defection against them in real life entitles them to adopt an attitude of radical defection themselves, the pessimists begin with the belief that all human beings would like to play

DEFECTOR but then advocate unconditional cooperation with established authority – that is, play SUCKER. The result is that the pessimists tend to be traditionalists and to stress the need for common identification with traditional values, which they see as exemplified in the kin-based societies of the past. For them, kin altruism seems to be the ideal form of cooperation. For the optimists, however, the fact that human beings cannot in reality be induced to act as pure altruists means that they must be constrained by ideal standards to do so, and so induced altruism in the form of state regulation of every aspect of life becomes the inevitable outcome and perhaps explains why every utopia intended to liberate the masses always ends by enslaving them.

For the optimists, culture is mere "ideology": something which exists to justify and maintain an inequitable and corrupt status quo. Not merely economic and political, but cultural revolution is required if human beings are to be truly liberated. For the pessimists, by contrast, culture is a form of social consensus without which civilized existence would be impossible and anarchy would result. Just as the optimists see culture as "alienating" individuals by inducing a false consciousness of social existence, so the pessimists see its absence as making them "anomic" by depriving them of socially approved values, standards, and expectations.

But between these two extreme views of human nature and social life lies a third, which we may call by comparison with them the *realistic* view. This holds that human beings are neither pure cooperators nor defectors, but, as we saw earlier when discussing the whole question of altruism and human nature, able both to cooperate and to defect (see above, pp. 109–16). For the realists, the ideal social strategy is not SUCKER or DEFECTOR, but TIT FOR TAT, and the best society is one based on reciprocity and free exchange, not bureaucratic regulation or traditional privilege. According to this view, culture neither alienates by its existence nor produces an anomic condition by its absence. Nor is culture something opposed to nature, as both optimists and pessimists believe in their different ways. If individuals have both good and bad, cooperating and defecting, tendencies within them from birth, one can no longer hold the view that culture is a bastion of reason and restraint against the chaos and anarchy of nature, as the pessimists tend to believe, or that culture is the alienating factor preventing the emergence of pure human altruism, as the optimists appear to hope. On the contrary, the realistic view is that what we call "culture" is as much a part of nature as anything else and that no sharp distinction can be drawn between the two.

According to this way of looking at things, cultural cooperation is essentially no different from any other kind of cooperation and involves no new unit of selection or unbridgeable gap in terms of temporal or spatial scale. Axelrod's analysis of iterated Prisoner's Dilemma showed that, contrary to the expectations of traditional social theory represented by the pessimistic and optimistic extremes as I am calling them, cooperation can emerge spontaneously out of the self-interested actions of individuals. Just as insect societies can comprise millions or billions of individuals but still be understood as having evolved by natural selection at the level of the individual gene, so human societies of similar size can be understood as based on principles of cooperation which apply at the individual – indeed, even at the genetic – level. This approach to the problem suggests that individual cooperative behavior can be "scaled up" to practically any size, so to speak, and that if cooperation can exist between individuals who encounter one another face to face, it can also exist between great masses who may never meet personally but who interact indirectly via social institutions such as markets, kinship networks, or bureaucratic institutions. Looked at from this point of view, culture seems not so much something opposed to nature or imposed upon it, but rather its supreme expression.

Culture, conflict, and parental investment

Although natural selection cannot act directly on cultural groups as such, it is self-evident that culture is related to reproductive success at the individual level. Even if we interpret culture in the restricted sense of *agriculture*, it is obvious that an agricultural economy can sustain vastly more individuals than could a hunting and gathering one. Indeed, it would not be too crude a generalization to say that, as far as the rough order of magnitude of the total human population is concerned, hunting and gathering cultures sustained on the order of ten million (10^7) human beings; agriculture produced a population of hundreds of millions (10^8); and industrialization, thousands of millions (10^9). Evidently, culture does promote the reproductive success of millions of individual human beings.

Indeed, the observation that the total number of human beings has been slowly increasing more or less continuously for some thousands of years, rapidly increasing for some centuries, and explosively increasing for a few decades gives the impression that population growth is an incremental process linked to cultural advances which seem to have followed a parallel curve of exponential growth. This has suggested to some the concept of gene–culture "co-evolution": the idea that cultural and genetic evolution are linked in some significant manner. This term is perfectly acceptable in a loose sense; but if we are to avoid falling back into the Social Darwinist errors of the past to which I briefly alluded in the introductory chapter, we must be completely clear about what we mean by the term "evolution" when we apply it to culture and should not assume that it means exactly the same thing as it does when applied to actual organisms (see above, pp. 27–31).

This is important because, almost always, what people have in mind when they talk of cultural evolution is not classical Darwinian evolution by natural selection for individual reproductive success, but Spencerian "survival of the fittest," simple to complex, "primitive" to "advanced" evolution of entire cultural groups. The problem here, as we saw at the very beginning, is that, despite considerable social pressure to the contrary expressed in his use of double negatives, Darwin concluded that "After long reflection, I cannot avoid the conviction that no innate tendency to progressive development exists."[1] While sociologists, historians, and other students of human cultures have every right to conceive of types of cultural evolution which do include such a progressive development, they have no right to imagine that their concepts of cultural evolution are the same as Darwin's concept of evolution by natural selection. For this reason, we must be circumspect in using the term "co-evolution" and should not allow ourselves to fall into the natural – but serious – error of imagining that cultural and natural evolution are essentially the same thing.

One reason why such mistakes have been made in the past may be the consequence of thinking of culture in the wrong terms. As long as culture was conceived as something which related to a group as such, it tended to be seen as something greater than the sum of its individual parts. Indeed, the sociologist-in-chief of the pessimists, as I called them earlier (see above, pp. 260–1), Émile Durkheim, conceived of a "collective consciousness" above and beyond individual consciousness, which, because "it has a collective origin . . . defies critical and rational examination."[2] For the optimists, on the other hand, and for their sociologist-by-appointment Karl Marx, culture was an ideological conspiracy of the ruling class – again an intrinsically collective concept.

Yet the moment we come to think about it, we can see that everything we call "culture" and understand to be something apart from "nature" in the sense that it does not constitute a part of our genetically determined heritage of behavior must in fact be some kind of parental investment. Excepting what it adds itself, the "culture" of every generation had to be passed on to it by preceding generations and, if it were to be relevant to Darwinian evolution by natural selection, would have had to promote the reproductive success of its possessors. Such considerations would have to apply to material culture as much as to anything less tangible, of course, and there is every reason to think that it does indeed do so. If we take the very earliest cultures known to us, the material objects left by Stone Age peoples, we can readily see that every one of those stone, bone, and wooden tools was made because it was worth something to someone. If we also note that most of the objects concerned were directly or indirectly used in hunting and food-processing, we can see that such material cultures must have dramatically enhanced the overall reproductive success of their possessors and that the skills and techniques involved must have been passed on to them at some cost in instruction and example by their forebears.

Admittedly, there is much to culture – so-called primitive cultures not excepted – which is not so obviously utilitarian. Even extinct Stone Age cultures show evidence of this in the female figurines which were made with techniques otherwise used for tools. Émile Durkheim's widely influential work *The Elementary Forms of the Religious Life* argued that the elaborate ritual culture of Stone Age peoples such as the Australian aborigines was in effect a worship of the collective consciousness, which, insofar as it created individual consciousness, as Durkheim believed it did, could be seen as the social equivalent of God: an ultimate reality inexplicable because ultimately self-explicable. But we do not necessarily have to think of Australian aborigine culture in this way. If we look more closely, we see that central to much aboriginal adult religious culture are so-called *initiation rites*. According to the sociological, Durkheimian way of seeing these things, such rites indicate and dramatize changes in social status: they are something which Society does to the individual for its own good reasons. But the moment we notice that such initiations are predominantly male affairs in all Australian aboriginal societies and that a young man expects a wife to be given to him by the man who initiates him, we begin to glimpse an altogether more individualistic meaning and one, furthermore, intimately touching on male reproductive success. It begins to look as if it is not so much a question of Society defining a boy as a man by means of initiation as one of a young man undergoing an ordeal at the hands of his prospective father-in-law in order to prove his claim to one of the latter's daughters.

It seems unlikely that young men would voluntarily undergo beatings, fastings, scarification, burnings, head-buttings, and hair- and nail-pulling – not to mention tooth-extraction and very often circumcision – purely for the benefit of Society. But since they also win a young man acceptance by older men who have daughters to give away in marriage, their benefit to the individual's ultimate reproductive success almost certainly does outweigh their very considerable cost. In other words, such cultural activities as initiation need not necessarily be interpreted in terms of what they do for Society as a whole, but can be seen to have more individualistic aspects as well, some of which touch directly on the issue of individual reproductive success.

Another aspect of culture which would previously have been ignored by group selectionist theories would be the whole question of sex in general and of women's interest in culture in particular. This is important because up to now there has been a tacit assumption that culture is a mainly masculine activity and that it is women, not men, who are more concerned with immediate, "biological" concerns such as child care. Basic tenets of parental investment theory which we examined earlier show that almost universally, and especially in the case of the highly sex-role-specialized mammals, it is the female who is most concerned with parental investment, rather than the male, who tends to be preoccupied with mating success. Of course, the latter can and probably does have its cultural manifestations. Drawing a striking parallel between bowerbirds and human males, Glenn Wilson remarks:

Perhaps the creativity of the human male, seen in such things as the Taj Mahal, Disneyland, Wagner's Ring Cycle and Einstein's theory of relativity, is equivalent in some way to the courtship-motivated industry of the male bower-bird. Certainly megalomania is a characteristically male trait, and accomplishment is one of the attributes that women find most attractive in men.[3]

Nevertheless, Wilson's point is that male cultural achievements may appeal to women as an aspect of female choice, rather than as a factor in direct inter-male conflict. Indeed, if we recall my earlier speculations about the possibility that our species owes its large brain and paedomorphic form to female choice of the first male hunters, then we can see that even cultural achievement directly linked to male violence via hunting, such as stone technologies, may indirectly have been the outcome of female choice (see above, pp. 179–81). Again, the fact that having been initiated is usually an essential qualification for any young man expecting to have sexual success with a woman in an aboriginal society suggests that women too value these tests of manhood and insist on unimpeachable evidence – such as circumcision – of a man having undergone it.

But however that may be, some forms of cultural achievement almost certainly do relate directly to female reproductive interests and their greater relative concern with parental investment as such. It seems almost certain that the universally found division of labor in primal hunting and gathering societies meant that, while men hunted, women collected vegetable matter, and that in so doing, some of them took the first, critical steps towards domestication of plants and so set the scene for true agriculture. Again, observations among the Australian aborigines suggest that it was women who were perhaps suffering painful lactation and emotional stress after the loss of a child who domesticated animals such as dogs by rescuing puppies from the hunters and putting them to the breast. Domestication of plants and animals would have vastly increased the food resources of early human agricultural cultures, and the innovations concerned would have had a dramatic effect on female reproductive success if we recall my earlier observations about the critical relationship between fat and fertility (see above, pp. 160–3). However, they would not have affected male reproductive success in the same direct and immediate way. To gain any personal advantage to his reproductive success, a man would have had to acquire female horticulturalists as wives and realize his gain indirectly through them. The fact that this remains the predominant family structure in sub-Saharan Africa to this day suggests that, at least until the coming of plough agriculture with its more direct input of male labor, agriculture was a cultural innovation which was mainly the work of women, much as the theory of parental investment would predict.[4]

Another respect in which parental investment theory would contrast strongly with the traditional approach to culture as related to Society rather than to individuals would be the question of conflict. As we saw earlier, the theory of parental investment predicts conflict between parents and offspring over the issue of altruism. We saw that parents are selected to want at least twice as much self-sacrifice (or half as much selfishness) directed towards kin than offspring will be selected to favor (see above, pp. 191–3). Insofar as culture in general can be seen as parental molding of offspring behavior, it follows that parents will be expected both to value culture more and to wish offspring to be at least twice as constrained by it where judgments about their own behavior towards relatives is concerned. As we also saw, offspring can be expected to value culture less and to be more critical of it, especially where it coincides with parental self-interest in inducing altruism in them beyond what they themselves would wish. Little wonder, then, that every generation decries the morals and lack of culture of its successor!

If we revert to my earlier characterization of optimistic and pessimistic social theories along with their characteristic views of human nature, it is interesting to note that these two, opposed attitudes tend to see the parent–child relation in the opposite way to that in which they regard individuals. Pessimists, believing that human beings must be constrained and civilized by outside forces, see the family as a key institution in bringing this about. Overt parental discipline or more subtle processes of "socialization" tend to be seen as necessary in saving the child from its egoism, boundless aspirations, and inherently antisocial nature. The family is seen rather like a microcosm of Thomas Hobbes's view of the state: a benevolent tyranny exercised by the parents in the name of order and civilization against the wild, untamed will of the child. Insofar as such an ideology correlates with a traditional, kin-based culture, we can see that it agrees beautifully with the prediction immediately above. Pessimism about human nature in general, and about the nature of the child in particular, justifies parental discipline and attempts to induce greater self-sacrifice and less selfishness than the refractory offspring itself would favor.

But as far as the optimists regarding human nature are concerned, the opposite is the case. According to this way of looking at things, the family is an "alienating," "exploiting" environment in which children, born into the world as naturally good, cooperative, and humane, are corrupted, demeaned, and dehumanized. Here the family is seen rather as Jean-Jacques Rousseau saw the human race: with children born as noble savages, only to be transformed into slaves by the chains of parental authority, love, and dependency. From this perspective, what seems to be important is liberation from the family and an overcoming of its negative, antisocial, and self-perpetuating tendencies. Yet the fact that the child is meant to be naturally good, cooperative, and altruistic means that parents can be every bit as authoritarian in their own, more subtle way as are the pessimists. The practical outcome will probably be that such parents will use other methods, such as withdrawal of love, rather than overt discipline, to achieve essentially the same result as the pessimists: the inducement of much more altruism, or much less selfishness, in the child than the child itself would wish. In other words, it matters little ultimately if one tells a child that it is intrinsically good or innately evil if the practical effect is that what is "good" or "evil" is dictated by the parents. All in all, it seems that whatever the parental ideology and however the child is regarded, parent–offspring conflict is an inevitable part of culture.

The gene–culture interface

The problem of explaining the links between culture and evolution ultimately boils down to a consideration of what, borrowing a useful term from computer technology, we might call the "gene–culture interface." In computing an *interface* is the meeting point of two systems, analogous, for example, to the surface of a liquid, which is the interface between it and the air above it, or to an animal's sense organs, which are at the interface between the organism and its surroundings. For the purposes of this discussion, I propose to use a third example, one much closer to the original usage: what we may term *the machine–user interface* found in the computer which I have used to write this book, the Apple Macintosh.

Here, an analogy suggests itself between the genetic code in which genes are written and the electronic code in which this book was stored on computer disks. The genetic code, like this book, is essentially encoded information; but, like the digital code in which my book was entered in the computer system, it is recorded in a form many orders of magnitude smaller than the tiniest book and in a medium very different from English words. The letter *h*, for example, is rendered 01001000 in the computer code, with each 0 and 1 represented by electromagnetic charges. As we saw at the beginning, the genetic code is actually written in three-base units composed of the four chemical bases which form the "rungs" on the polymer "ladder" of DNA (see above, pp. 11–12). So difficult is this code to read directly that it was not until the early 1950s that its nature was divined, and even today our detailed knowledge of it is extremely sketchy and highly incomplete. We may be able to read out the sequence of bases which code for many proteins, but we are still far from understanding how genes relate to behavior in general and to culture in particular.

However – and to revert to my computer analogy – although the information with which my computer works is totally inaccessible to me in a direct way, I am able to access it conveniently in an indirect manner. I do so via the user interface, which itself comprises two principal parts: the interface *hardware* and the interface *software*. The hardware comprises the keyboard on which I type, the "mouse" which I use to drive a cursor, and the screen on which I view it. The keyboard enables me to enter data and commands; the mouse is an aid to manipulating data and the computer; and the screen allows me to know what data are entered and what is being done with it. In order to interpret what is going on, I rely on the interface software, which in the Apple Mac is particularly easy to interpret. This is because the software interface between my senses and the computer's systems is represented graphically as things I can see (and sometimes hear).

For example, suppose I want to open the data files in which the contents of this book are recorded. Direct manipulation of the disk, analogous to the reader's direct manipulation of the printed book, is out of the question. Instead, I insert the disk in the machine's disk drive and let it read it for me. I communicate my intentions by moving the cursor on an imaginary desk top represented by the computer screen, complete with trash can and other *icons*, which represent folders and individual documents lying on it. All this makes sense to me as a human being because I live in a world of desks, folders, documents, and trash cans. However, the computer knows – and needs to know – nothing of these things. According to its way of doing things, each action of mine is interpreted as a digital code which sends microscopic electrical signals through its circuits.

The point of this analogy is that if an interface exists between two completely different systems like my brain and the computer, we can understand their interaction in terms of what goes on at the interface, because this is the critical point at which information passes from one to the other. Such information transfers are correlated, but, as we have just seen, not necessarily exactly so. Perhaps genes, behavior in general, and culture in particular interact in a similar kind of way, given that there is an enormous disparity in size and content between DNA and human cultures and behaviors. Perhaps if we could find the gene–culture interface, the problem of how genes relate to culture could at least be seen in its proper context. Indeed, we might find that there were some intriguing parallels between the computer–user interface and the gene–behavior one.

Indeed, if we adopt a parallel approach to the computer case, we can immediately see that what we might call the "hardware interface" between genes and human behavior is constituted by the brain, central nervous system, and the senses. Perhaps if we understood the brain well enough, we could reconstruct its workings, just as an engineer could in principle reconstruct the working of a computer merely by examining its component parts in sufficient detail to see how they would work if it were turned on. However, our knowledge of the brain and its workings is far too limited for us to be even remotely able to do this where genes and behavior are concerned. A more promising line might be the software interface. Here the analogy must be with the human mind and with psychology, as opposed to the brain and its physiology. Genes, mind, and culture (to quote the title of a well-known book) seem to go together, and presumably it is in the mind that the critical software interface – human psychology – is to be found.

Of course, software has to come from outside the computer, and so we might regard cultural learning as its human, psychological equivalent. Just as computers can use different software languages, so human minds can use different verbal languages, and we might see culture as wholly the outcome of such "programming." This would correspond to the belief that the human mind is indifferent to what it learns and that cultures are free to inscribe there what they will. However, we saw in our earlier discussion of free will and biological determination that it is most unlikely that natural selection would leave human behavior totally re-programmable in any respect, particularly in those respects which might reduce, rather than enhance, reproductive success (see above, pp. 94–9).

Indeed, even in computing there are limits to programming in the sense that any program run on a computer must be compatible both with its hardware and with its built-in operating principles. One cannot just install any software on any hardware. In practice, computers need what is sometimes called "firmware." This is software which is permanently installed in the machine, usually in a so-called Read Only Memory (or ROM for short). Without such pre-existing instructions a computer could not accept software pro-gramming, for example, because it would not "know" how to read the disks on which the software instructions came. The ROM also contains the firmware for "booting": the means by which the computer turns itself on and sets up its operating system, ready to receive instructions.

Almost certainly, human beings are the same in the sense that the genetic code is indeed a "read only" memory in that it cannot be changed by the user but must be handed on intact (mutations apart) from generation to generation. Without some innate, preparatory organization comparable to "boot-ing," human beings would not be able to respond to environmental cues or to get their psychological process running in a way which would enable them to make sense of the world. It is by no means far-fetched to suppose that genes ultimately dictate which parts of the brain will process visual information, for example, as opposed to sound. Again, the finding that certain areas of the brain are critical to linguistic ability suggests that the genetic ROM lays down the basic operating principles on which linguistic software in the form of actual languages will run. Indeed, as I suggested earlier, it seems quite possible that the compulsive sucking which Freud called "oral behavior" is an example of such an innate, preprogrammed response presumably ultimately encoded in the human ROM (see above, pp. 215–18). If this is so, then numerous other findings of depth psychology relating to apparently irrational, compulsive behaviors may be similar, such as penis envy. Indeed, the penis may be a fundamental icon if the arguments I advanced earlier about children's needs to evaluate sex independent of parental "programming" is correct (see above, pp. 233–4).

However, just because genes and behavior may be correlated in some way does not mean that they have to be rigidly, or even simply, linked. What means one thing to me may mean something quite different to my genes. For example, my conscious memory is limited, and in the virtual reality of my mind some things may be lost altogether. Indeed, common experience of life shows that I can forget a name for a while but recall it again later. This suggests that, just as data which are deleted or lost by the user of a computer may still be recorded somewhere in its systems, so information temporarily lost to consciousness can still be registered somewhere else in the mind. Indeed, we saw earlier that today there are good evolutionary reasons for thinking that being able to become unconscious of some things pays in the hard currency of reproductive success (see above, pp. 99–107).

Considerations such as these suggest that genes need not be rigidly and directly linked to human behavior in every instance, as simple biological determinism may suppose; but neither need they be totally unrelated, as simple cultural determinism would claim. An altogether more sensible conclusion seems to be that genes and behavior are correlated, rather as computer systems and the human beings who manipulate them are correlated. A computer operating system and the mind of the person who uses it may proceed in different ways. I may dispose of a file by symbolically dragging its icon to the trash can on my imaginary computer screen desk top, but my Apple Mac merely registers the address at which it was stored as vacant and does not overwrite the information in it until it needs to use that address again. Nevertheless, although computer and user operate quite differently in respect of deleting the information in a file, the outcome is the same for both: the file is deleted. User and computer interact via an interface which "translates" the wishes of the former into the actions of the latter. Again, user and machine are operating on totally different temporal and spatial scales, with the human user seeing symbols on the screen which are many orders of magnitude larger than their corresponding electronic signals and working to a time scale many orders of magnitude slower than the speeds at which the electronic components switch. Nevertheless, the disparity is mediated by the interface, where user and machine time and space come to a convenient accommodation.

In the case of genes and much human behavior it seems sensible to conclude that the mind is the interface through which the need of an individual's genes to survive and replicate is translated into actions which (in primal conditions and all other things being equal) would tend to safeguard and reproduce them. Here, a number of evolutionary biologists have recently suggested that Freud's model of the mind may be helpful. According to Freud's view, the mind could be thought of as divided into three independent psychological agencies: the id, the ego, and the superego. Freud conceived the *id* to be a totally unconscious, chaotic region of the psyche where primal, biological drives and repressed thoughts and wishes struggle for expression. Reflexes, automatic bodily processes, and much of the unconscious were under its control and subject to the demands of the pleasure principle, whose sole concern was gratification of the organism's biological needs. The *ego* was a largely unconscious but also partly conscious agency charged with responsibility for voluntary actions, conscious thought, and monitoring of the senses through which it was in contact with external reality. Ideally it obeyed the reality principle dictated by the objective, outside world. Finally, the *superego*, also largely unconcious, was a specialized subdivision of the ego modeled on parental figures by means of identification and internalization. It tended to obey cultural and moral principles and to provide the ego with its sense of values and aesthetics (along with a sense of reality derived from the superior functioning of the reality principle in the parents during the individual's infancy).

It is tempting to see Freud's ego as the critical interface between the id and actual behavior, with the id being the embodiment of the genetic ROM and its associated evolutionary firmware. This would make the ego an *Executive and Governing Organization* (EGO for short) charged with responding to the *Inclusive-reproductive-success-maximizing Demands* (ID for short) of the organism. The superego would represent cultural software acquired by identification and other forms of internalization and could be seen as a *Supernumerary Executive and Governing Organization* (SuperEGO for short). The EGO would be subject to internal stress if it failed to meet the reproductive-success-maximizing demands of the ID or the cultural demands of the SuperEGO in its dealings with reality. If it succeeded in gratifying the ID, it would experience pleasure (see above, pp. 97–9); whereas gratifications of the SuperEGO would be felt as moral or aesthetic triumphs, with guilt and shame being the means by which the SuperEGO might make its displeasure felt. According to this view, human beings would be neither wholly subject to genetic determinism represented ultimately by the ID nor wholly subservient to culture or parental conditioning represented by the SuperEGO. On the contrary, the EGO would be a sovereign agency, subject to the demands of both genetic and cultural factors but with a considerable degree of self-determination also. Human psychology would be dynamic, not enslaved to culture or conditioning, and the EGO would, ideally at least, be master in its own house: required to hear the demands of its ID or SuperEGO but not always obliged to meet them exactly as those agencies might themselves wish.

Wherever the EGO had a choice to act, the inclusive-reproductive-success-maximizing demands of the ID would have to express themselves via this agency and with its cooperation, rather than in spite of it (as they may do, for example, where reflex actions are concerned). This means that the EGO, ideally at least, would not be a slave to the immediate and peremptory demands of the unconscious. Putting the EGO center stage, as the Freudian model does, preserves the freedom and dignity of the individual in the face of cultural demands and collective values just as much as it does in the face of biological demands and genetic imperatives. The EGO may feel social pressures from its SuperEGO to behave in certain ways, but it does not necessarily have to obey them, anymore than it necessarily has to capitulate to the demands of the ID. On the contrary, the EGO's independence guarantees that human behavior will never be as simple or as automatic as both biological and cultural determinism might demand.

But this is an ideal picture. In reality the EGO will experience much of its interaction with the ID and the SuperEGO as entailing stress, ranging from mild ambivalence to severe internal conflict. Indeed, the EGO might be seen principally as a stress-management agency, concerned with trying to mediate not merely conflicts between inner demands and outer reality but between various inner demands themselves. Like computer software charged with the management of complex, semi-autonomous systems such as space probes or nuclear power plants, we would expect the EGO to be programmed to drop into "safe modes" of varying depth if internal conflicts or outside threats reach critical thresholds. In this respect it is worth recalling that, at least since the 1920s, psychoanalysis has understood the EGO principally in terms of its relation to the many mechanisms of defense open to it. Much in psychology that seems "beyond the pleasure principle," to quote the title of one of Freud's last and most forward-looking books, seems to involve various kinds of internally dictated "safe-mode" defenses which, like their software parallels, often function to inhibit, shut down, or limit the operation of other systems and functions, often giving rise to what are sometimes perceived to be psychopathic symptoms (such as postnatal depression or anorexia; see above, pp. 166–7 and 162–3). Indeed, many classic psychopathic syndromes have always been seen by psychoanalysis as symptoms produced by such internal conflicts, and the addition of an evolutionary dimension to such a view might well bring many benefits, albeit that it would take us far beyond the discussion here.[5]

Another benefit of adopting the Freudian model of the mind for purposes of evolutionary explanation of human behavior and culture is that it would facilitate the unification of three fields of study which have hitherto tended to go their own separate ways, to the evident detriment of behavioral science overall. The ID as defined here is evidently the institution of the personality which is most immediately affected by evolution and whose time scale could be measured in thousands, hundreds of thousands, or even millions of years (10^3–10^6 years). As the psychological agency charged with expressing the demands of the genetic ROM, its rate of change would evidently be set by changes at the most elemental evolutionary level of all: the mutation rate of the individual gene. The ID, then, would be the psychological embodiment of basic, evolutionary biology. The SuperEGO, by contrast, would represent cultural continuity, and its proper time scale would be measured in tens and hundreds, but seldom much more than thousands of years (10–10^3 years). It would be the psychological agency which represented cultural "software," rather than evolutionary "firmware," and would entail the social, rather than the biological, sciences in its exploration. Finally, the EGO would represent psychological adaptation to time scales as short as a second or less but never longer than a century (10^{-6}–10^2 years). Its proper study would be psychology, but a psychology which, because of this tripartite ID-EGO-SuperEGO model, would be firmly integrated both with evolutionary and with social science. Indeed, since all three institutions of the personality would ultimately have to be seen as the products of evolutionary adaptation, both psychology and the social sciences would be based on evolutionary theory, and both would ultimately have to be seen as branches of a more general biological science, just as biology is itself only a part of the broader physical sciences. Today such a fundamental unification of behavioral science may seem even more distant than the much-discussed grand unification now being so earnestly pursued in physics. However, if the arguments advanced here are anything to go by, it might actually be much more readily to hand. If this book has brought that outcome any nearer, it will have achieved all its author could have wished for it.

Notes

Notes to the Introduction

1 L. Badash, "The Age-of-the-Earth-Debate," *Scientific American*, 261, 2 (Aug. 1989), pp. 78–83.
2 R. Trivers, *Social Evolution* (Benjamin/Cummings, Menlo Park, California, 1985), p. 304.
3 R. V. Short, "Sexual Selection: The Meeting Point of Endocrinology and Sociobiology," in *Endocrinology 1980*, ed. I. A. Cumming et al. (Australian Academy of Science, Canberra, 1980), p. 54.
4 E. O. Wilson, *Sociobiology: The New Synthesis* (Belknap Press, Cambridge, Massachusetts, 1975), p. 3.
5 C. Darwin, *The Descent of Man, and Selection in Relation to Sex*, vol. 1 (J. Murray, London, 1871), p. 257.
6 C. Darwin, *The Origin of Species*, ed. J. W. Burrow (Penguin, Harmondsworth, 1968), p. 348.

Notes to chapter 1

1 R. Axelrod, *The Evolution of Cooperation* (Basic Books, New York, 1984), p. 40.
2 Ibid., p. 137.
3 Ibid., p. 75.
4 Ibid., pp. 85 and 79.
5 Written answers to parliamentary questions, *Hansard*, 13 Feb. 1990, cols 123–4 (HMSO, London, 1990).
6 Axelrod, *Evolution of Cooperation*, p. 65.
7 Ibid., p. 68.

Notes to chapter 2

1 M. Daly and M. Wilson, *Homicide* (Aldine de Gruyter, New York, 1988), pp. 17–35.
2 Ibid., pp. 87–8.
3 K. Hill and H. Kaplan, "Tradeoffs in Male and Female Reproductive Strategies among the Ache," in *Human Reproductive Behavior*, ed. L. Betzig, M. Borgerhoff Mulder, and P. Turke (Cambridge University Press, Cambridge, 1988), p. 302.
4 E. Voland, "Differential Infant and Child Mortality in Evolutionary Perspective: Data from late 17th to 19th Century Ostfriesland," in *Human Reproductive Behavior*, ed. Betzig et al., pp. 253–61.
5 R. Trivers, *Social Evolution* (Benjamin/Cummings, Menlo Park, California, 1985), p. 119.
6 S. J. O'Brien et al., "The Cheetah in Genetic Peril," *Scientific American*, 254, 5 (May 1986), pp. 68–76.
7 G. S. Wilkinson, "Food Sharing in Vampire Bats," *Scientific American*, 262, 2 (Feb. 1990), pp. 64–70.
8 Hill and Kaplan, "Tradeoffs among the Ache," p. 302.
9 C. Boesch, "First Hunters of the Forest," *New Scientist*, 19 May 1990, pp. 38–41.
10 Trivers, *Social Evolution*, pp. 49–52; C. Badcock, *The Problem of Altruism* (Blackwell, Oxford, 1986), pp. 120–51.

Notes to chapter 3

1 R. Trivers, "Sociobiology and Politics," in *Sociobiology and Human Politics*, ed. E. White (Lexington Books, Lexington, Massachusetts, 1981), p. 35.
2 For a more detailed account, see C. Badcock, *The Problem of Altruism: Freudian-Darwinian Solutions* (Blackwell, Oxford and Cambridge, Massachusetts, 1986), pp. 37–47.
3 For a full account, with examples, see C. Badcock, *Essential Freud* (Blackwell, Oxford and Cambridge, Massachusetts, 1988), pp. 12–21.
4 Trivers, "Sociobiology and Politics," p. 35.
5 S. Freud, "Fragment of an Analysis of a Case of Hysteria,"

Standard Edition of the Complete Psychological Works of Sigmund Freud (Hogarth Press, London, 1953–71), vol. 7, pp. 77–8.

6 P. Ekman, *Telling Lies: Clues to Deceit in the Marketplace, Politics and Marriage* (W. W. Norton, New York, 1985).

7 Badcock, *Problem of Altruism*, pp. 134–5.

8 A. Freud, *The Ego and the Mechanisms of Defence* (Hogarth Press, London, 1966), p. 126.

9 Ibid., pp. 110, 111, and 112.

10 M. Daly and M. Wilson, "Homicide and Cultural Evolution," *Ethology and Sociobiology*, 10, 1–3 (Jan. 1989), p. 102.

11 Ibid., p. 108.

12 Trivers, "Sociobiology and Politics," p. 17.

13 R. D. Alexander, *The Biology of Moral Systems* (Aldine de Gruyter, New York, 1987).

14 Ibid., p. 142; my emphasis.

15 Quoted in Badcock, *Problem of Altruism*, p. 143.

Notes to chapter 4

1 J. L. Gould and C. G. Gould, *Sexual Selection* (Scientific American Library, New York, 1989), pp. 147 and 158–9.

2 W. Shapiro, *Miwuyt Marriage* (University of Philadelphia Press, Philadelphia, 1981), pp. 76–7.

3 For a fuller discussion using the same example, see C. Badcock, *Oedipus in Evolution* (Blackwell, Oxford and Cambridge, Massachusetts, 1990), pp. 47–61.

4 J. H. and S. J. Crook, "Tibetan Polyandry" in *Human Reproductive Behavior*, ed. L. Betzig, M. Borgerhoff Mulder, and P. Turke (Cambridge University Press, Cambridge, 1988), pp. 97–114.

5 A. P. Møller, "Female Choice Selects for Male Sexual Tail Ornaments in the Monogamous Swallow," *Nature*, 332 (1988), pp. 640–1.

6 L. Betzig, *Despotism and Differential Reproduction: A Darwinian View of History* (Aldine de Gruyter, New York, 1986), p. 26.

7 N. Chagnon, "Life Histories, Blood Revenge and Warfare in a Tribal Population," *Science*, 239 (26 Feb. 1988), pp. 985–90.

8 M. Daly and M. Wilson *Homicide* (Aldine de Gruyter, New York, 1988), pp. 146 and 161; original emphasis.

9 M. Borgerhoff Mulder, "Kipsigis Bridewealth Payments," in *Human Reproductive Behavior*, ed. Betzig et al., pp. 65–82.
10 R. V. Short, "Sexual Selection: The Meeting Point of Endocrinology and Sociobiology," in *Endocrinology 1980*, ed. I. A. Cumming et al. (Australian Academy of Science, Canberra, 1980), p. 50.
11 R. Trivers, *Social Evolution* (Benjamin/Cummings, Menlo Park, California, 1985), p. 267.

Notes to chapter 5

1 R. E. Frisch, "Fatness and Fertility," *Scientific American*, 258, 3 (Mar. 1988), pp. 70–7.
2 K. Hill and H. Kaplan, "Tradeoffs in Male and Female Reproductive Strategies among the Ache," in *Human Reproductive Behavior*, ed. L. Betzig, M. Borgerhoff Mulder, and P. Turke (Cambridge University Press, Cambridge, 1988), pp. 294–6.
3 Frisch, "Fatness and Fertility."
4 E. and R. Voland, "Evolutionary Biology and Psychiatry: The Case of Anorexia Nervosa," *Ethology and Sociobiology*, 10 (1989), pp. 223–40. For some speculations relating it to human evolution and the Alexander–Noonan theory, see C. Badcock, *Oedipus in Evolution* (Blackwell, Oxford and Cambridge, Massachusetts, 1990), pp. 158, 184–6.
5 W. P. Bernds and D. Barash, "Early Termination of Parental Investment in Mammals, Including Humans," in *Evolutionary Biology and Human Social Behavior*, ed. N. Chagnon and W. Irons (Duxbury, North Scituate, Massachusetts, 1979), pp. 487–506.
6 Ibid., p. 499.
7 J. Horgan, "Science and the Citizen," *Scientific American*, 262, 4 (Apr. 1990), pp. 8–9.
8 S. M. Essock-Vitale and M. T. McGuire, "What 70 Million Years Hath Wrought: Sexual Histories and Reproductive Success of a Random Sample of American Women," in *Human Reproductive Behavior*, ed. Betzig et al., pp. 221–35.
9 W. D. Hamilton and M. Zuk, "Heritable True Fitness and Bright Birds: A Role for Parasites," *Science*, 218, pp. 384–7.

10 B. M. Beehler, "The Birds of Paradise," *Scientific American*, 261, 6 (Dec. 1989), pp. 66–73.

11 B. S. Low, "Pathogen Stress and Polygyny in Humans," in *Human Reproductive Behavior*, ed. Betzig et al., pp. 115–27.

12 Ibid., p. 120.

13 G. Borgia, "Sexual Selection in Bowerbirds," *Scientific American*, 254, 6 (June 1986), pp. 70–9.

14 R. D. Alexander and K. M. Noonan, "Concealment of Ovulation, Paternal Care, and Human Evolution," in *Evolutionary Biology*, ed. Chagnon and Irons, p. 447.

15 T. Burke et al., "Parental Care and Mating Behavior of Polyandrous Dunnocks," *Nature*, 338 (16 Mar. 1989), pp. 249–51.

16 Hill and Kaplan, "Tradeoffs among the Ache," pp. 277–89.

17 P. W. Turke, "Concealed Ovulation, Menstrual Synchrony, and Paternal Investment," in *Biosocial Perspectives on the Family*, ed. E. E. Filsinger (Sage Publications, Newburdy Park, California, 1987), p. 125.

18 J. M. Diamond, "Goslings of Gay Geese," *Nature*, 340 (13 July 1989), p. 101.

19 For a more detailed account of this version of the Alexander–Noonan theory, see Badcock, *Oedipus in Evolution*, pp. 151–86.

Notes to chapter 6

1 R. Trivers, "Sociobiology and Politics," in *Sociobiology and Human Politics*, ed. E. White (Lexington Books, Lexington, Massachusetts, 1981), p. 32.

2 T. H. Clutton-Brock, "Reproductive Success in Red Deer," *Scientific American*, 252, 2 (Feb. 1985), pp. 68–74.

3 M. Dickemann, "Female Infanticide, Reproductive Strategies, and Social Stratification: A Preliminary Model," in *Evolutionary Biology and Human Social Behavior*, ed. N. Chagnon and W. Irons (Duxbury, North Scituate, Massachusetts, 1979), pp. 321–67.

4 A. Ramanamma and U. Bambawale, "The Mania for Sons: An Analysis of Social Values in South Asia," *Sociology and Medicine*, 14B, pp. 107–10.

5 Dickemann, "Female Infanticide," pp. 341 and 350.

6 E. Voland, "Differential Infant and Child Mortality in Evolutionary Perspective: Data from late 17th to 19th Century Ostfriesland," in *Human Reproductive Behavior*, ed. L. Betzig, M. Borgerhoff Mulder, and P. Turke (Cambridge University Press, Cambridge, 1988), pp. 253–61.

7 E. Voland, "Human Sex-Ratio Manipulation: Data from a German Parish," *Journal of Human Evolution*, 13 (1984), pp. 99–107.

8 J. L. Boone III, "Parental Investment, Social Subordination, and Population Processes among the 15th and 16th Century Portuguese Nobility," in *Human Reproductive Behavior*, ed. Betzig et al., pp. 201–19.

9 B. Malinowski, *Sex and Repression in Savage Society* (Meridian Books, New York, 1955), p. 24.

10 E. van den Berghe, "Piracy as an Alternative Reproductive Tactic for Males," *Nature*, 334 (1988), pp. 697–8.

11 J. Kurland, "Paternity, Mother's Brother and Human Sociality," in *Evolutionary Biology*, ed. Chagnon and Irons, p. 154.

12 S. Thapa, R. V. Short, and M. Potts, "Breast Feeding, Birth Spacing and their Effects on Child Survival," *Nature*, 335 (1988), pp. 670–82.

Notes to chapter 7

1 R. J. Stoller, *Presentations of Gender* (Yale University Press, New Haven, 1986), p. 33.

2 S. Freud, "Female Sexuality," in *Standard Edition of the Complete Psychological Works of Sigmund Freud* (Hogarth Press, London, 1953–71), vol. 21, p. 234.

3 For an account of Freudian findings on these matters, see C. Badcock, *Essential Freud* (Blackwell, Oxford and Cambridge, Massachusetts, 1988).

4 Badcock, *Essential Freud*, pp. 12–21, 168–9.

5 M. V. Flinn, "Parent–Offspring Interactions in a Caribbean Village: Daughter Guarding," in *Human Reproductive Behavior*, ed. L. Betzig, M. Borgerhoff Mulder, and P. Turke (Cambridge University Press, Cambridge, 1988), pp. 189–200.

6 C. W. M. Hart and A. R. Pilling, *The Tiwi of North Australia* (Holt, Rinehart and Winston, New York, 1961), p. 15.

7 M. Lamb (ed.), *The Role of the Father in Child Development*, (2nd edn, Wiley, New York, 1981), pp. 28 and 346–7.

8 J. A. McFarlane, *The Psychology of Childbirth* (London, Open Books, 1977), pp. 84–6.

9 Lamb (ed.), *Role of the Father*, p. 27.

10 R. Evans, "Physical and Biochemical Characteristics of Homosexual Men," *Journal of Consulting and Clinical Psychology*, 39 (1972), pp. 140–7.

11 G. D. Wilson, "The Sociobiological Basis of Sexual Dysfunction," in *Sex Therapy in Britain*, ed. M. Cole and W. Dryden (Open University Press, Milton Keynes, 1988), pp. 49–68.

12 M. E. Spiro, *Oedipus in the Trobriands* (University of Chicago Press, Chicago, 1982), pp. 103–4.

13 K. Hill and H. Kaplan, "Tradeoffs in Male and Female Reproductive Strategies among the Ache," in *Human Reproductive Behavior*, ed. L. Betzig, M. Borgerhoff Mulder, and P. Turke (Cambridge University Press, Cambridge, 1988), pp. 298–9.

14 D. Jedlicka, "A Test of the Psychoanalytic Theory of Mate Selection," *Journal of Social Psychology*, 112 (1980), p. 295; G. Zei, P. Astolfi, and S. D. Jayakar, "Correlation between Father's Age and Husband's Age: A Case of Imprinting?" *Journal of Biosocial Science*, 13 (1981), p. 409. I am indebted to Dr G. D. Wilson for bringing these references to my attention.

15 G. D. Wilson and P. T. Barrett, "Parental Characteristics and Partner Choice: Some Evidence for Oedipal Imprinting," *Journal of Biosocial Science*, 19 (1987), pp. 157–61.

16 For a further discussion, see C. Badcock, *Oedipus in Evolution* (Blackwell, Oxford and Cambridge, Massachusetts, 1990).

Notes to the Conclusion

1 Darwin to Alpheus Hyatt, quoted by S. J. Gould, *Wonderful Life* (Century Hutchinson, London, 1990), p. 257.

2 C. Badcock, *Lévi-Strauss* (Hutchinson, London, 1975), p. 27; quoting E. Durkheim and M. Mauss, *Primitive Classification* (Cohen and West, London, 1963), p. 86.

3 G. D. Wilson, "The Sociobiological Basis of Sexual Dysfunction," in *Sex Therapy in Britain*, ed. M. Cole and W. Dryden (Open University Press, Milton Keynes, 1988), p. 53.

4 R. J. Lesthaeghe, *Reproduction and Social Organization in Sub-Saharan Africa* (University of California Press, Berkeley, 1989).

5 For a further discussion see B. Wenegrat, *Sociobiological Psychiatry* (D. C. Heath, Lexington, Massachusetts, 1990), and C. Badcock, *Oedipus in Evolution* (Blackwell, Oxford and Cambridge, Massachusetts, 1990), pp. 4–14 and 187–210.

Glossary of Technical Terms

altruism: a behavior whereby one organism promotes the reproductive success of another at its own expense

anorexia nervosa: a psychological syndrome based on the evolutionary link between fatness and fertility, featuring aversion to eating, almost always in young women

bridewealth: a payment made by a man for a wife, usually to the bride's family

chromosome: an extended piece of DNA encoding many genes and coiled up as one unit in the nucleus of a cell

clone: a genetically identical copy of an organism

cryptic estrus: concealment of any sign of impending ovulation in a sexually cyclic female

cryptic sexuality: disguised or hidden appearance or behavior relating to sex

degree of relatedness (*r*): the proportion of genes which two related individuals share by common descent

diploid: the possession of two complete sets of chromosomes, one inherited from each parent

DNA: an acronym for *deoxyribonucleic acid*, the organic polymer in which genetic information is encoded in nearly all known organisms

dominant: in genetics, a gene is dominant if it is preferentially expressed in relation to a corresponding *recessive* one on the paired chromosome

dowry: a payment which the bride or her family makes to her husband on marriage

dynamic unconscious: the concept of the unconscious as the result of active exclusion of psychological material from direct conscious access

ego: a term used by Freud to describe the partly conscious, largely unconscious agency of the personality charged with responsibility for voluntary thought and action

EGO: an acronym modeled on Freud's *ego* standing for Executive and Governing Organization, understood as an agency ultimately responding to evolutionary demands

estrus: a point in the sexual cycle of a female when ovulation occurs

evolution: according to Darwin, a process of gradual change resulting from some organisms leaving more descendants than others as a consequence of natural selection

exogamy: a social norm requiring individuals to marry outside their natal group

female: where sex cells vary in size, the female always has the larger

female choice: a tendency for females to prefer some males as reproductive partners to others

fitness: in strict Darwinian terms, the ultimate reproductive success of an organism in some indefinite, future generation

gene: a sequence of DNA coding for one particular protein

genome, genotype: the total complement of genetic information in an organism

group selection: the idea that natural selection can act on entire groups of organisms

haplo-diploid: a genetic system in which some individuals are haploid and some are diploid, for example the social insects, where males are haploid and females diploid

haploid: the possession of only one set of chromosomes

hypergyny: marriage of a woman into a group of superior status

id: Freud's term for the unconscious part of the personality constituted by repressed elements and primal drives

ID: an acronym based on Freud's *id* standing for Inclusive-reproductive-success-maximizing Demands and describing the unconscious as an evolved mechanism

identification: a psychological mechanism by means of which one individual comes to believe that they resemble, or share something in common with, some other individual or attribute

identification with the aggressor: a psychological mechanism by means of which an individual identifies with another who is dominating, attacking, or endangering that individual

inclusive fitness, inclusive reproductive success: the reproductive success of identical genes carried in organisms related by common descent

induced altruism: a form of altruism brought about by coercion, deceit, or error and not accountable as a case of kin or reciprocal altruism

interface: the point of contact between two different systems

kin altruism: a behavior by means of which identical copies by common descent of a gene for altruism may be favored by sacrifices of the same gene in close relatives of the beneficiary of the altruistic act

libido: Freud's term for a generalized, sexual energy

lordosis: the characteristic posture for mating adopted by many female vertebrates when mounted by a male

male: where sexes can be distinguished, the male is always characterized by the smaller, more mobile sex cell

matriliny: descent or inheritance through the female, as opposed to the male, line

menarche: the point at which menstruation in particular, and sexual cycling in general, occurs in a woman

mitochondria: specialized subunits of the cell involved in metabolism

monogamy: a mating system in which one male is normally mated to one female, either for a season or for longer

natural selection: the influence which purely natural factors have on the differential reproductive success of organisms

nice: in Prisoner's Dilemma a strategy is *nice* if it begins with a cooperation

oral behavior: compulsive sucking independent of hunger

paedomorphosis: a tendency for an organism to resemble the young of its ancestors

parental investment: any benefit to the reproductive success of an offspring at a cost to the remainder of the parent's reproductive success

phenotype: the totality of an organism's body and behavior

phenotypical matching: comparison of genetic similarity by the indirect means of comparing how genes express themselves in an organism's appearance and behavior

pleasure principle: according to Freud, the prime motivation of the unconscious concerned with gratifying the organism's needs irrespective of reality or others

polyandry: a mating system in which one female is mated to a number of males

polygamy: a mating system in which a number of females are mated to a number of males

polygyny: a mating system in which one male is mated to a number of females

projection: a psychological mechanism whereby an individual perceives the contents of their own unconscious in another individual or the outside world

reality principle: according to Freud, the ego's awareness of reality which conflicts with the workings of the pleasure principle in the id

recessive: a gene which is not expressed if paired with a dominant one on the corresponding chromosome

reciprocal altruism: an altruistic act whose benefit is reciprocated

reciprocity: the equalization of benefit in a two-party interaction

regression: an action or appearance which makes an organism seem younger than it really is

repression: the active exclusion of thoughts, wishes, and feelings from consciousness

reproductive success: the total number of an organism's descendants

ribosome: a subunit of the cell responsible for transcribing the genetic code into proteins

robust: in Prisoner's Dilemma a strategy is robust if it cannot easily be exploited by other strategies

ROM: an acronym for Read Only Memory; that is, a data store from which information can be read, but in which no new information can be entered

sexual dimorphism: a regular difference in appearance between the sexes which is typical of the sex in question

sexual selection: natural selection for traits which bear closely on sex

steatopygia: an enlargement of the hips and buttocks characteristic of women in some African ethnic groups

superego: according to Freud, a part of the ego constituted by internalization of, and identification with, parental figures, values, and aspirations

SuperEGO: an acronym based on Freud's *superego* standing for Supernumerary Executive and Governing Organization, understood as an evolved agency incorporating culture

topographic: the differentiation of consciousness into various levels and parts, such as conscious and unconscious

unconscious: that which is inaccessible to conscious, voluntary recall

zero-sum game: a game in which points gained by one side are lost by the other

Suggestions for Further Reading

On Darwin, no one has written better than Darwin himself, and readers might in the first instance be recommended to try any one of the various editions of *The Origin of Species* which are available (but should avoid the later editions published in Darwin's own lifetime for reasons explained in the Preface). *The Descent of Man* makes a logical sequel, dealing as it does with material more directly concerned with this book, but readers must be prepared for lengthy discussions of sexual selection in many other species. One of the best general books on Darwin which takes sociobiology seriously is Michael Ruse's *Darwinism Defended* (Benjamin/Cummings, Menlo Park, California, 1982). The classic modern refutation of the many misunderstandings and misrepresentations of Darwin's theory of evolution by natural selection is Richard Dawkins's *The Blind Watchmaker* (Penguin, Harmondsworth, 1988).

As I pointed out in my preface, Robert Trivers's *Social Evolution* (Benjamin/Cummings, Menlo Park, California, 1985) is in many ways the best general introduction to what I called "Darwin version 3.3" and at the time of writing remains the most authoritative and complete general summary of recent evolutionary insights into behavior. A surprisingly complete and succinct summary of Robert Trivers's personal contributions to the field can be found in his essay "Sociobiology and Politics," in a collection edited by Elliot White entitled *Sociobiology and Human Politics* (Lexington Books, Lexington, Masschusetts, 1981).

Another excellent, if slightly older, general introduction is the second edition of David Barash's *Sociobiology and Behavior* (Hodder and Stoughton, London, 1982). This is particularly good in its sensitive treatment of human material, although much more of a textbook than his earlier *The Whisperings Within: Evolution and the Origin of Human Behavior* (Elsevier, New York, 1979), which remains one of the most readable, as well as one of the most interesting, books on the subject. Another textbook is Martin Daly and Margo Wilson's *Sex, Evolution and Behavior* (PWS, Boston, 1983), which, as its title suggests, concentrates on the evolutionary understanding of sexual behavior. A more recent publication, and one more tailored to the general reader than Daly and Wilson's book, is James L. Gould and Carol Grant Gould's beautifully illustrated and produced book *Sexual Selection* (Scientific American Library, New York, 1989). Based on *Scientific American*–style illustrations and intended for the same kind of reader, this book vindicates my earlier observation about the link between sexual selection and sheer beauty in the natural world.

Moving on to more detailed matters, Robert Axelrod's *The Evolution of Cooperation* (Basic Books, New York, 1984) has become a classic and is a must for anyone who wishes fully to understand modern social theory. Daly and Wilson's other book, *Homicide* (Aldine de Gruyter, New York, 1988), contains much beside detailed data on violent crime, and – despite grievously misrepresenting some of my own earlier work – can be highly recommended as an antidote to traditional social science treatment of the subject.

Much of the material summarized here is drawn from Laura Betzig, Monique Borgerhoff Mulder, and Paul Turke's co-edited book of readings *Human Reproductive Behavior* (Cambridge University Press, Cambridge, 1988), which is a prime source of descriptive material for anyone interested in the subject. Another, somewhat older collection from which I have also drawn is Napoleon Chagnon and William Irons's *Evolutionary Biology and Human Social Behavior* (Duxbury, North Scituate, Massachusetts, 1979). Jan Wind's two-volume *Essays on Human Sociobiology* (Academic Press, London and New York, 1985–6) contains numerous excellent discussions of important issues. Laura Betzig's *Despotism and Differential Reproduction: A Darwinian View of History* (Aldine, New York, 1986) makes a powerful case for the relevance of Darwinism to an understanding of despotic regimes, as well as providing a sickening catalog of human cruelty, albeit one which merely scratches the surface of this vast subject. Finally, some readers may wish to follow up my own more detailed publications on altruism (*The Problem of Altruism*, 1986); on sexual theory and its links with psychoanalysis (*Oedipus in Evolution*, 1990); and on Freud and evolution generally (*Essential Freud*, 1988; second edition forthcoming 1991), all published by Basil Blackwell, Oxford, and Cambridge, Massachusetts.

Index

abortion, 163–6, 201, 203
acacia trees, 79
Ache, 67, 86–7, 161, 179, 248
aggression, 30, 113–15, 142–9
agriculture, 264, 268–9
Aichorn, August, 113
alarm calling, 26, 65
Alexander, Richard, 118, 122, 177,
    178, 179, 180, 182
altruism
    and culture, 258–63
    and identification, 108–16
    induced, 87–93, 100–1, 121–2,
        194–6, 259, 262
    kin, 64–9, 85, 90, 108, 110–11,
        112, 189, 190, 192–3, 214
    and morality, 117–22
    and parent–offspring conflict,
        190–7
    as a problem, 23–7, 29, 31, 57
    reciprocal, 79–87, 90–1,
        100–1, 105, 108, 112, 193–4,
        258–9
    see also cooperation
amnesia, 234–8
anorexia nervosa, 162–3
ants, 79, 91
arms races, 101
asexuality, 167–8
Australian aborigines, 133, 227,
    247–8, 250, 266–7, 268

avunculate, 207–15
Axelrod, Robert, 40–1, 48, 50, 57,
    59, 95, 263

beauty, 169–70
Betzig, Laura, 144
birds of paradise, 172
bluegill sunfish, 149–54
bowerbirds, 173–5
brain evolution, 186–7
breasts, 181
bright birds, 169–72

cheating, 101–3
cheetah, 77–8
child abuse, child mortality, see
    infanticide
childhood amnesia, 234–8
chimpanzee, 78, 87, 146–9, 156,
    176, 180, 181, 185–6
chromosomes, 10–12, 62–3, 69,
    73–4, 157–8
cleaners, 79–84, 87–8
co-evolution, 264–5
confidence of paternity, 177–8
conflict
    among males, 141–56
    and sex, 137–56 see also
        aggression; parent–offspring
        conflict; violence
consciousness, 99–107

cooperation, 32–60, 61, 77, 87, 108, 111, 258 *see also* altruism, reciprocal altruism

cooperative hunting, 77, 86–7, 154–5, 179, 186

copulation, 168–9

Crick, Francis, 11, 12

crying, 218–19

cryptic estrus, 176–81

cryptic sexuality, 149–56, 183

cuckoos, 89, 92–3

culture, 253–80

Darwin
"3.3", xi–xvi
affected by prudery, 124–5
and age of the earth, 2–4
and altruism, 27
on female choice, 168, 169, 189
and genetics, 5–12
on natural and sexual selection, 19–20
on sexual conflict, 144
view of evolution, 1–2, 22–3, 265

death, 16–17,

deception, 101–8, 116

deer, 130, 151, 199

DEFECTOR, 42, 45, 47, 57–60, 83, 114, 120, 261, 262

degree of relatedness (*r*), 66, 69–71, 73–6, 77–9, 189, 190, 192, 209, 212–15

Dickemann, Mildred, 202, 203

differential life expectancy, 14–16, 19

diploid inheritance, 10, 62–3, 69, 125–6

DNA, 11–12, 18, 126, 271–2

dominant genes, 9–10

DOWNING, 42

dowry, 203

Durkheim, Émile, 260, 265, 266–7

ego, EGO, 277–80

Electra complex, 228

elephant seals, 130, 141–3

environmental sex determination, 198–9 *see also* sex, ratios

estrus, 147, 176–81

evolution
and age of the earth, 2–4, 253
and altruism, 24–31
and behavior, 123–4
of cooperation, 60–93
of culture, 253–80
Darwin's formulation, 1–2
and fitness, 13–23
and genetics, 7–13
of man, 185–7
and Social Darwinism, 21–3, 27–30
timescale of, 252–4
as understood by Spencer, 28–9

exogamy, 203

false cleaners, 81–2, 87–8,

family, 270–1
four forms, 129–37
Freudian theory of, 208, 222–51
matrilineal, 207–10, 211–15
nuclear, 207–10
and parent–offspring conflict, 188–97
in social theory, 270–1
violence, 66–8, 197–207
see also helper in the nest; kin altruism, marriage; monogamy; polyandry; polygamy; polygyny

fat, 144, 160–3

female
breast feeding and infertility, 215–18
as cause of male conflict, 144–5
choice, 168–76, 185–7, 268
defined by size of sex cell, 125–6, 128

degree of relatedness in haplo-diploid species, 73–5
diploid in social insects, 73
earlier maturation in humans, 146
latency period, 239–41
and low variance of reproductive success, 129, 135, 136–7, 141, 146
masculine female, 152
and oedipal behavior, 229–34
oedipal transferences, 249–51
and parental investment, 128–9, 157–67
role in culture, 267–9
as selected by males, 145–6
and sex ratios, 197–207
sexual dimorphism, 143–4
fertility, 161–5
fitness, 13–23, 27–8, 64, 71, 138
    see also reproductive success
free rider theorem, 35, 36, 65, 118–22
free will, 94–9, 100
Freud, Anna, 109, 113, 114, 115, 228
Freud, Sigmund, 97, 104, 106, 208, 222–51, 276–80
FRIEDMAN, 42–3

gelada baboon, 149, 181, 183
gene–culture interface, 271–80
genes, 7–13, 61, 64, 71, 73–4, 77–8, 255–6, 271–2
genetics, 5–13, 62–3, 72–9, 126
genome, genotype, 11–12, 77–8, 109
gorilla, 146–9
gratitude, 117
group selection, xii, 210
    and cultural evolution, 256–7, 265,
    and female interests, 159–60
    and kin altruism, 72–3, 74–6

and morality, 118–19
and parent–offspring conflict, 188–9
and sex, 123, 124–5, 137
and Spencer, 17, 29–31
guilt, 117, 122
guppies, 156, 170

haplo-diploid inheritance, 73–5, 200
haploid inheritance, 10, 73
HARRINGTON, 45
Helmholtz, Hermann von, 4
helper in the nest, 244–5
hemophilia, 9–10
Hobbes, Thomas, 260, 270
homicide, 66–7, 114–15, 144–5
homosexuality, 152–6, 245–6, 250
human nature, 95–122, 260–3
hunter-gatherers, 179, 268 *see also* Australian aborigines
hymenoptera, *see* social insects
hypergyny, 203

id, ID, 276–80
identification, 109–16, 122, 239–40, 242–4
identification with the aggressor, 113–15
inclusive fitness, 71, 75–6 *see also* reproductive success
India, 202–3
indignation, 116
induced altruism, 87–93, 100–1, 121–2, 194–6, 259, 262
infanticide, 66–8, 202–7, 216–17
infidelity, 138–41
initiation rites, 266–7
intentions, 93, 117

JOSS, 43, 44, 48, 78

Kelvin, Lord, 3–4

kin altruism, 64–9, 85, 90, 108, 110–11, 112, 189, 190, 192–3, 214
kin selection, 72–9
Kipsigis, 145–6
!Kung San, 216

language, 104–5
latency period, 238–43
lesbianism, 153, 183–5, 241
libido, 223–4
live-and-let-live, 49–52
liver fluke, 91, 92–3
lordosis, 151, 169, 181

male
  bias in estimates of polygyny, 133–4
  cryptic, 149–56
  defined by size of sex cell, 125–8
  desertion, 140–1
  displays, 169–76, 267–8
  and female choice, 168–76
  feminine male, 152
  haploid in social insects, 73
  later maturation in humans, 146
  life expectancy, 13–16, 19
  paedomorphic, 151–2, 154
  parental investment, 210–15, 240–3
  and perversion, 155–6
  and sex ratios, 197–207
  testis size, 147–9
  variance of reproductive success, 128–32, 134, 229–31
Malinowski, Bronislaw, 208–9, 215
mammals, 134
marriage, 132–3 *see also* family
Marx, Karl, 260, 265
mating strategies/systems, 131–7, 148–9 *see also* monogamy; polyandry; polygamy; polygyny; promiscuity

mating success, 131–2, 150, 179–80
meat for matings, 179–81, 182–3
Mendel, Gregor, 6–7, 62
menopause, 163
menstruation, 161–2, 181–3
mimicry, 112,
mitochondria, 126
Miwuyt, 133
monogamy, 131, 133, 134–5, 172
morality, 117–22
mother's brother, 207–15
mutation, 5–7, 12, 30, 61

natural selection
  and altruism, 24–6, 27
  and bright birds, 171
  and culture, 256–7
  defined, 1–2, 62
  and fitness, 13, 16, 18–23
  and free will, 96
  and genetics, 5, 9
  and modern humans, 254–5
  rate of, 252
  and reproductive success, 62, 64, 65, 71
  and sex, 124–5, 171
  of sterility, 68–9
neck biting, 169
nepotism, 65,
Newcomb, Simon, 4
nice programs, 42, 47, 49
Nietzsche, 120
Noonan, Katharine, 177, 178, 179, 180, 182
nuclear family, 207–8

Oedipus complex, 208, 224–32, 242–51
optimistic view of human nature, 260–3, 269–71
oral behavior, 215–18, 222–4
orgasm, 177–9
Ostfriesland, 67–8, 204–5

paedomorphosis, 151–2, 154, 185–7
pain, 98–9
parental care, 25, 66–8, 70, 73, 270–1
parental investment
  as culture, 265–6, 269–71
  as defining sex, 126–9
  and female choice, 175–6
  and female reproductive interests, 158–67
  and human evolution, 184–7
  and lesbianism, 184
  of male, 210–15, 240–3
  in mammals, 134
  in monogamous marriages, 135
  and oedipal behavior, 224–31
  and offspring sex, 197–207, 229–31
  and parent–offspring conflict, 189–97
  and postnatal depression, 166–7
  and sexual perversion, 155–6
  and variance of reproductive success, 136–7
parent–child conflict
  and amnesia, 236–8
  and culture, 265, 269–71
  in latency, 239–40
  and oral behavior, 214–21, 224–5
  and parental taboos, 227
  and penis envy, 232–3
  theory of, 188–97
paternity, 177–8, 208–15, 242–3
pay-off matrix, 36–40, 50–1, 53–4, 57, 82–3
peacock wrasse, 210, 11
peacocks, 169, 170
penis envy, 233–4, 240
perversion, 155–6, 246–7, 249–50
pessimistic view of human nature, 260–3, 269–71
phenotypic matching, 109, 243

pleasure principle, 97–9, 223
polyandry, 131, 134, 135–6
polygamy, 131, 172
polygyny, 129–30
  extent of human, 131–4
  and female choice, 172–3
  and oedipal transferences, 247–51
  and sex ratio, 197
  and sexual dimorphism, 142, 146
  and sperm competition, 147–9
Portuguese nobility, 205–7
postnatal depression, 166–7
premature ejaculation, 249
primal scene, 226–7
Prisoner's Dilemma, 32–60, 82–3, 90–1, 139–40, 263
progress, 21–2, 27–9
projection, 109–11, 112, 115–17
promiscuity, 131, 149, 211–13
psychoanalysis, 104 *see also* Freud; unconscious
psychological sexes, 152

r (degree of genetic relatedness), 66, 69–71, 73–6, 77–9, 189, 190, 192, 209, 212–15
RANDOM, 41, 44, 95
Rapoport, Anatol, 44
recessive genes, 9–10
reciprocal altruism, *see* altruism
reciprocity, 36, 47–56, 79–87, 90–1, 100–1
regression, 219
repression, 104, 236–8
reproductive success
  and altruism, 25, 26, 30–1, 57–60, 62–6
  and bower-building, 174
  and free will, 95
  of individuals in culture, 267–9
  and libido theory, 223–4

reproductive success (*cont.*):
  of males as opposed to
    females, 129–30
  of mutations, 5, 6
  and natural selection, 1–2, 13,
    16–23
  and sex, 124
  and sex ratio, 197–207
  and sexual dimorphism, 143
  and sterility, 68–71, 75
retaliation, 48–50, 51, 56
ribosome, 11
Rousseau, Jean-Jacques, 260, 270

Saud, Abdul Aziz Ibn, 129–30
Schleswig-Holstein, 205
self-consciousness, 94, 99–108
self-interest, 109–10, 119–20
selfishness, 24, 25, 26, 31, 65–8,
    70–1, 76, 90–1, 92, 120
sex, 17
  chromosomes, 157–8
  cryptic sexuality, 149–56
  and disease, 170–2
  and evolutionary study of
    behavior, 123–5
  and female interests, 157–67
  four psychological sexes, 152
  and Freud, 222–4
  and group selection, 124–5,
    137–9
  hormones, 14, 15
  and life expectancy, 13–16, 19
  and parental investment, 126–9
  ratios, 197–207
  reasons for, 171
  sex cells, 10, 63, 76, 125–8
  sex-determining genes, 8, 158
sexual dimorphism, 142–4,
    146–9, 172, 185–6, 245
sexual perversion, 155–6, 246–7,
    249–50
sexual selection, 19–20, 124–5,
    172 *see also* female choice

sheep, 151–2, 156
social action, 90–1
Social Darwinism, 21–2, 24,
    27–30, 76, 264–5
social insects, 20–1, 26–7, 29, 65,
    68, 72–5, 79, 91
social order, 51–2
socialization, 51–2, 270–1
Spencer, Herbert, 13, 18, 21–2,
    27–30, 76
Spengler, Oswald, 253
sperm competition, 148–9, 150,
    154–5
spite, 90–1
steatopygia, 181
step-parents, 66–8
sterility, 68–71, 75–6
Stoller, Robert, 228, 244
SUCKER, 47, 49, 57–60, 78–9,
    103, 120, 261, 262
superego, SuperEGO, 277–80
super-organisms, 28–30

TAT FOR TIT, 47–9
taxation, 53–6
TESTER, 46–7
testis size, 147–9
TIT FOR TAT, 41, 43–52,
    57–60, 83, 112, 114, 262
TIT FOR TWO TATS, 43, 46
TRANQUILIZER, 47
transsexuals, 228, 244–5
transvestites, 149–54
Trivers, Robert, 76, 101, 103, 104,
    116, 154
Trobriand Islands, 207–9, 211–15
twinning, 161

uncertainty of paternity, 211–15,
    242–3
unconscious, 99–108 *see also* Freud

vampire bats, 84–6
vendetta, 48–9, 56

violence, 13–14, 15, 29–31, 142–9

Wallace, Alfred, 2
Watson, James, 11, 12
weaning conflict, 215–18
Wilson, Glenn, xv, 267–8
womb envy, 233–4

World War I, 49–52

X chromosome, 157–8

Y chromosome, 157–8
Yanomamö, 67, 145

zero-sum game, 52–6